THE HYPERNATURALS

VOLUME ONE

BOOM! STUDIOS

ROSS RICHIE Chief Executive Officer • MATT GAGNON Editor-in-Chief • FILIP SABLIK VP-Publishing & Marketing • LANCE KREITER VP-Licensing & Merchandising
PHIL BARBARO Director of Finance • BRYCE CARLSON Managing Editor • DAFNA PLEBAN Editor • SHANNON WATTERS Editor • ERIC HARBURN Editor • CHRIS ROSA Assistant Editor
STEPHANIE GONZAGA Graphic Designer • JASMINE AMIRI Operations Coordinator • DEVIN FUNCHES Marketing & Sales Assistant • BRIANNA HART Executive Assistant

THE HYPERNATURALS

WRITTEN BY
DAN ABNETT & ANDY LANNING

PROLOGUE
ART BY
TOM DERENICK
& BRAD WALKER
WITH INKS BY MARK IRWIN

CHAPTER ONE
ART BY
ANDRES GUINALDO
WITH INKS BY MARIANO TAIBO & MARK IRWIN
& BRAD WALKER

CHAPTER TWO
ART BY
TOM DERENICK
& BRAD WALKER
WITH INKS BY TOM DERENICK

CHAPTER THREE
ART BY
TOM DERENICK
& ANDRES GUINALDO
WITH INKS BY BIT

COLORS BY
STEPHEN DOWNER

LETTERS BY
ED DUKESHIRE

COVER BY
PHIL NOTO

EDITOR
DAFNA PLEBAN

MANAGING EDITOR
BRYCE CARLSON

TRADE DESIGN BY
MIKE LOPEZ

QUANTINUUM CONTENT DESIGNS BY
STEPHANIE GONZAGA

CREATED BY
ABNETT, LANNING & WALKER

PROLOGUE

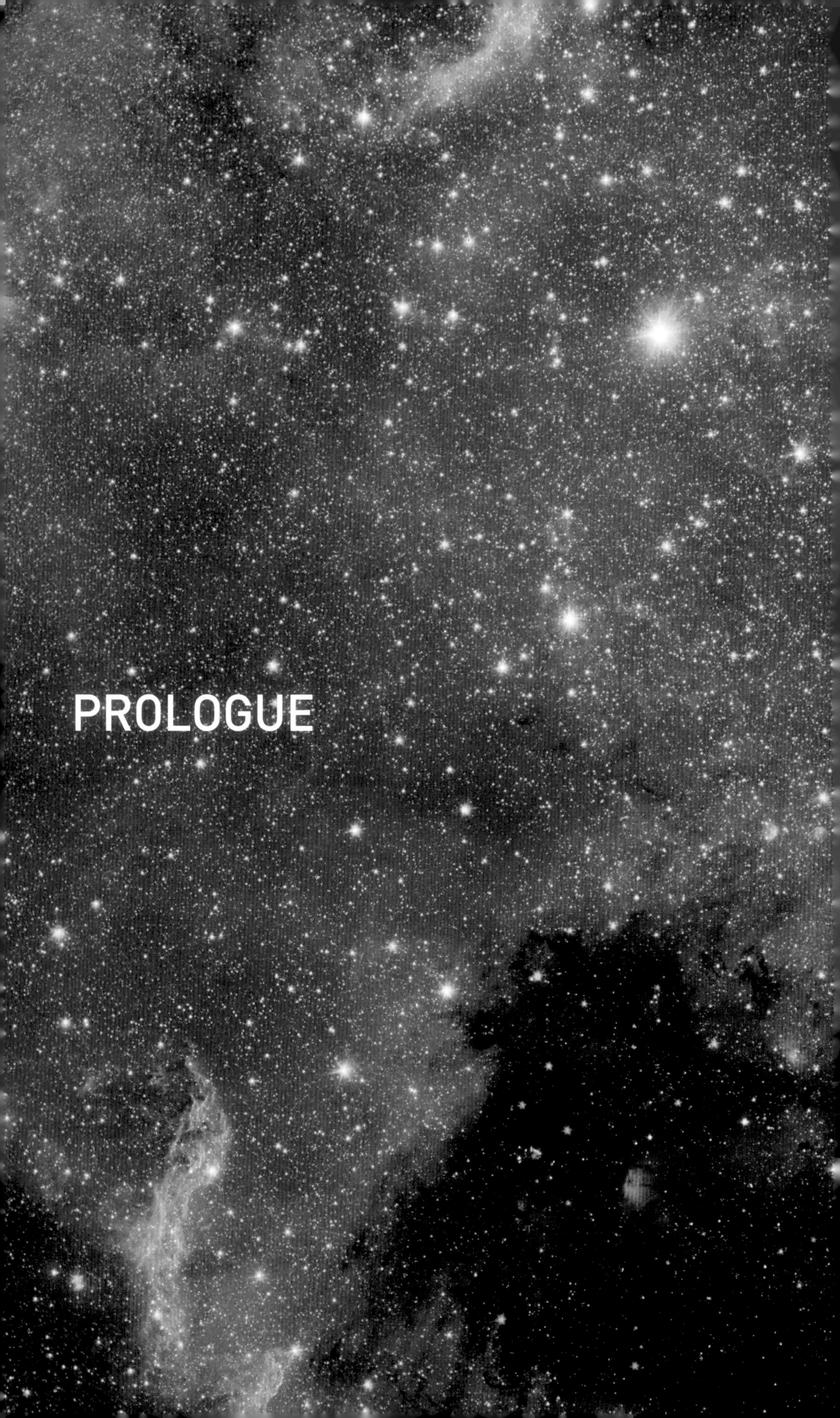

• You have selected Q-Data link.

- It is the 9th of January in the year **100 A.Q.**
  - Touch here to select an alternative to the **Anno Quantinuum** calendar system.
  - Touch here to load local weather reports for your **current cosmic location.**
  - Touch here to access **Q-Data newsflows** from planets near your current cosmic location.
  - Touch here for latest **Quantum Trip transit times.**

- Q-Data entry: The Quantinuum

- The Quantinuum is the name for the human galactic culture, and also for the **artificial intelligence** that controls its function.

- The Quantinuum was created 100 years ago at the start of the **Nanocene Era**. The Nanocene began when the Quantinuum AI achieved Singularity and refashioned human galactic culture. Succeeding the **Holocene Era**, the Nanocene is the next progression of human evolution and...

  (to read this entry in full, touch here)

- You have selected live feed newsflow.

- ...BREAKING NEWS...the Centennial Year Iteration of the Hypernaturals Team is assembling at the Hypernaturals Central Headquarters, San Diego, Earth for their first official mission...data concerning nature of emergency to follow...

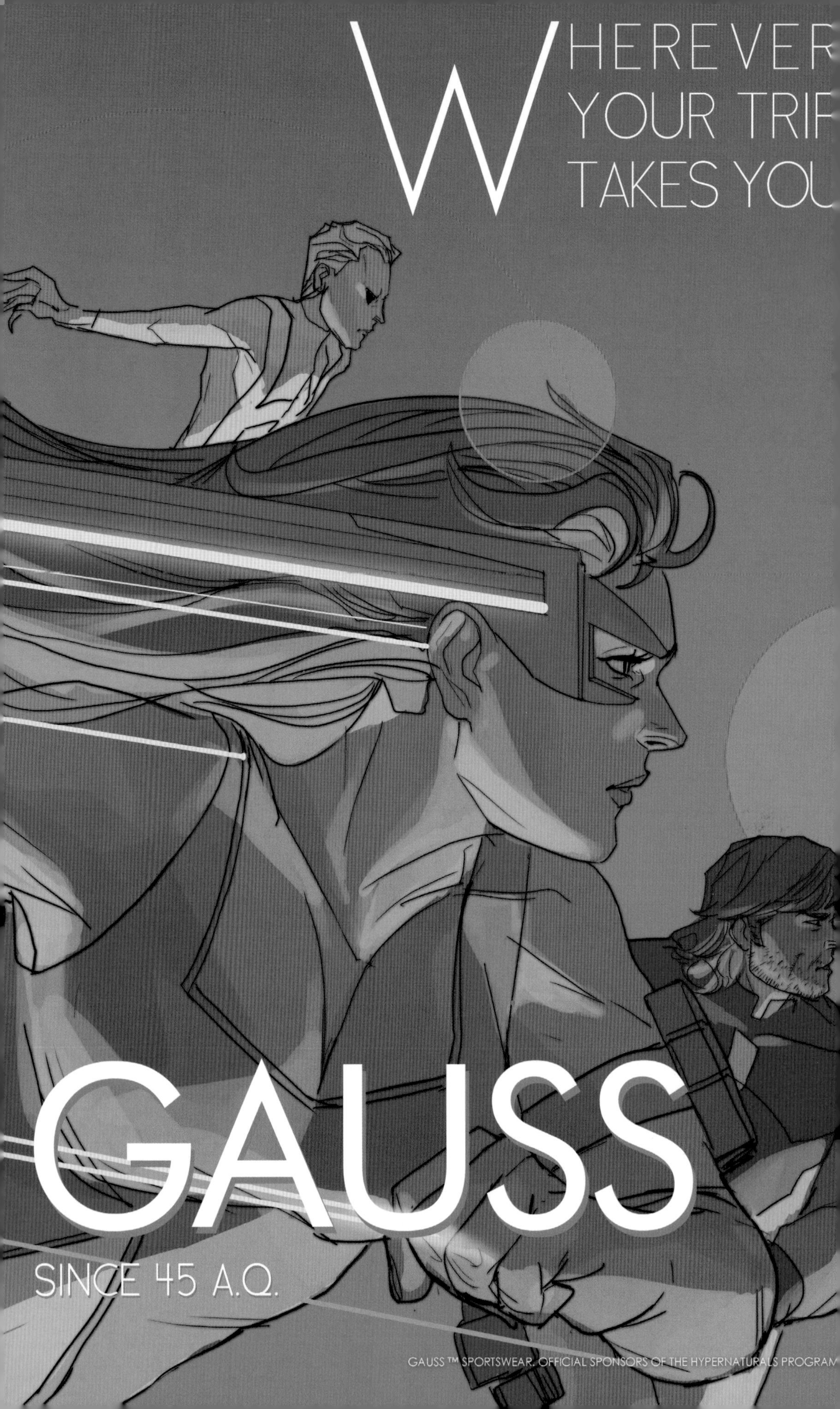
WHEREVER
YOUR TRIF
TAKES YOU
GAUSS
SINCE 45 A.Q.
GAUSS ™ SPORTSWEAR. OFFICIAL SPONSORS OF THE HYPERNATURALS PROGRAM

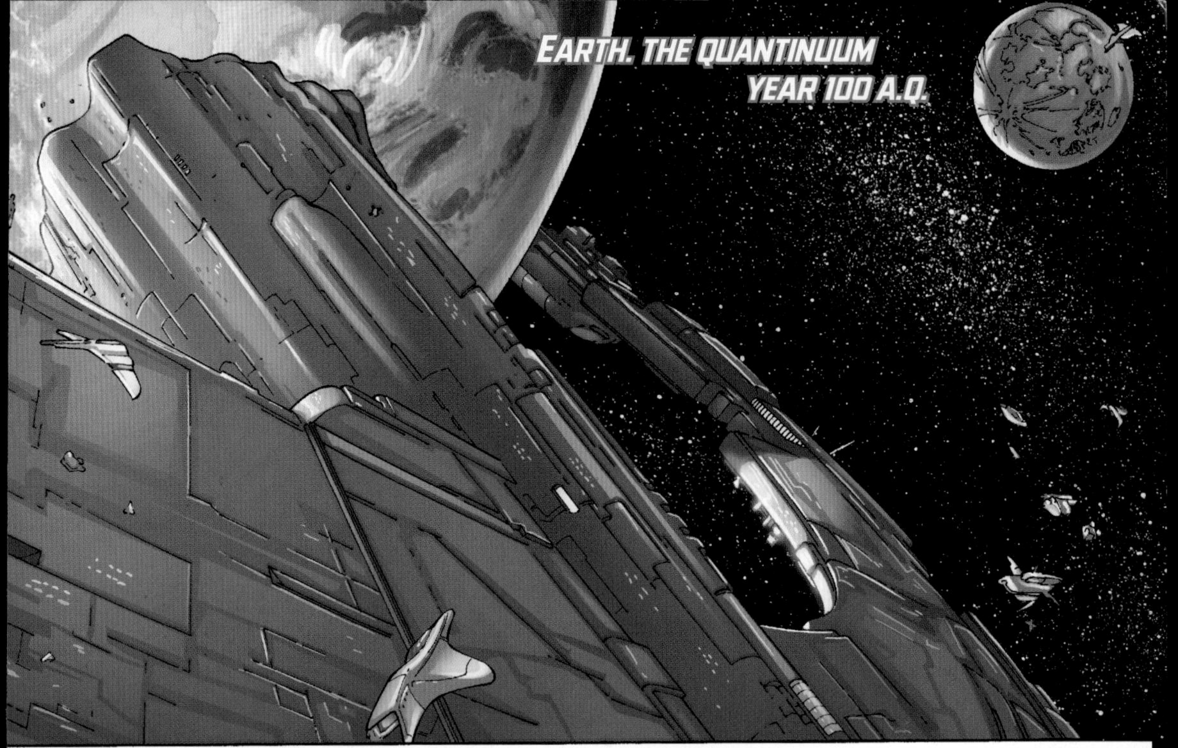
EARTH. THE QUANTINUUM
YEAR 100 A.Q.

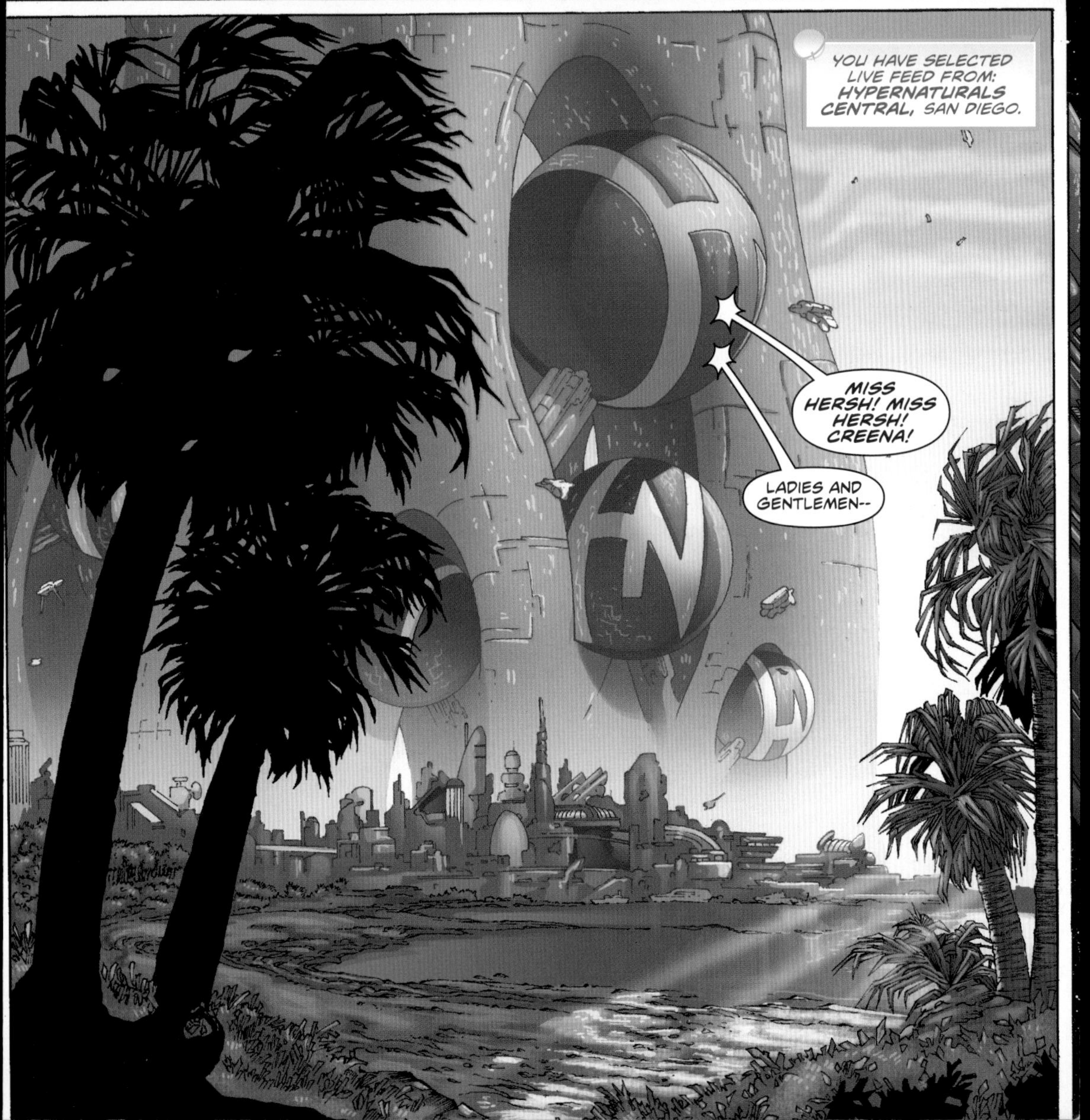
YOU HAVE SELECTED LIVE FEED FROM: HYPERNATURALS CENTRAL, SAN DIEGO.
MISS HERSH! MISS HERSH! CREENA!
LADIES AND GENTLEMEN--

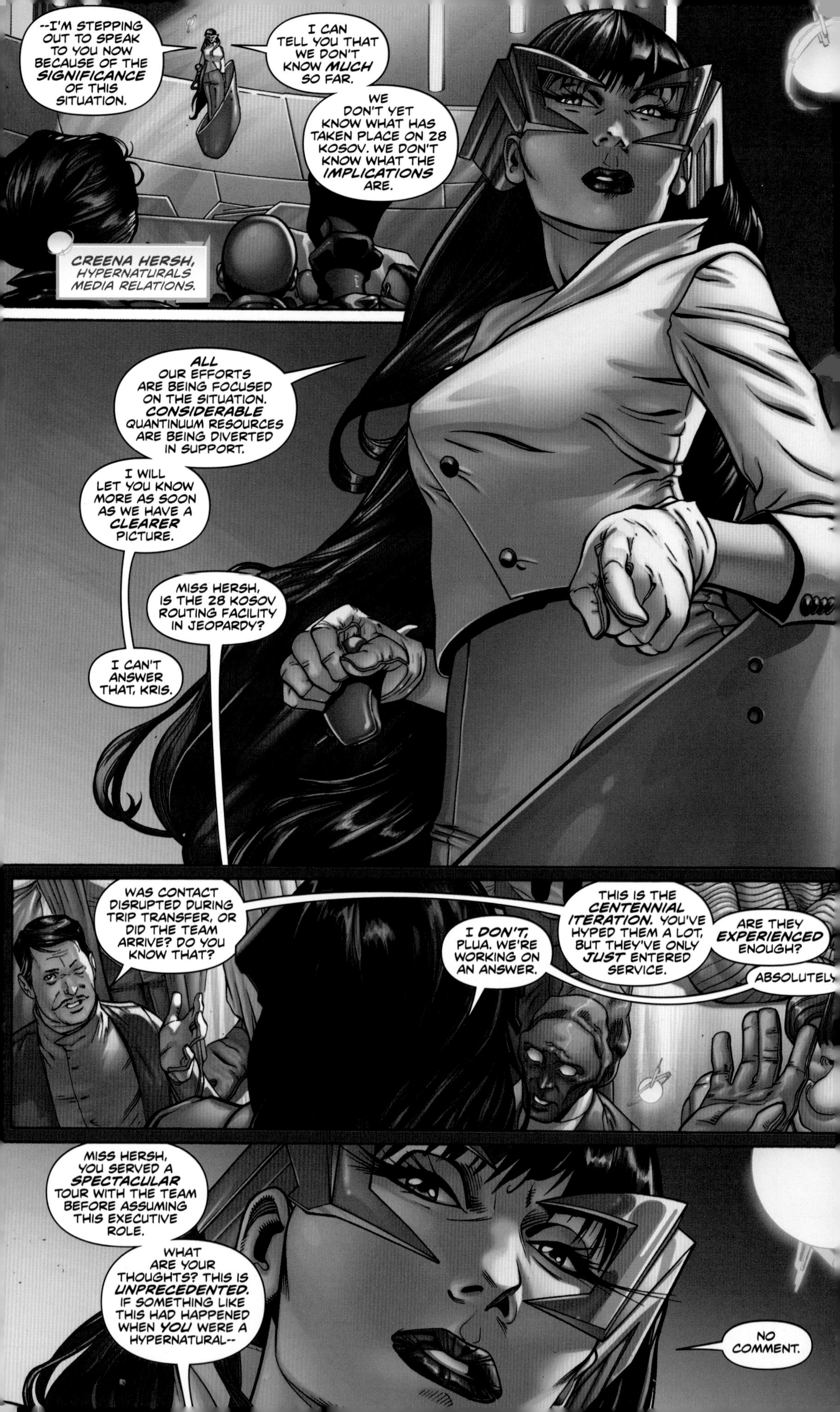
--I'M STEPPING OUT TO SPEAK TO YOU NOW BECAUSE OF THE SIGNIFICANCE OF THIS SITUATION.
I CAN TELL YOU THAT WE DON'T KNOW MUCH SO FAR.
WE DON'T YET KNOW WHAT HAS TAKEN PLACE ON 28 KOSOV. WE DON'T KNOW WHAT THE IMPLICATIONS ARE.
CREENA HERSH, HYPERNATURALS MEDIA RELATIONS.
ALL OUR EFFORTS ARE BEING FOCUSED ON THE SITUATION. CONSIDERABLE QUANTINUUM RESOURCES ARE BEING DIVERTED IN SUPPORT.
I WILL LET YOU KNOW MORE AS SOON AS WE HAVE A CLEARER PICTURE.
MISS HERSH, IS THE 28 KOSOV ROUTING FACILITY IN JEOPARDY?
I CAN'T ANSWER THAT, KRIS.
WAS CONTACT DISRUPTED DURING TRIP TRANSFER, OR DID THE TEAM ARRIVE? DO YOU KNOW THAT?
I DON'T, PLUA. WE'RE WORKING ON AN ANSWER.
THIS IS THE CENTENNIAL ITERATION. YOU'VE HYPED THEM A LOT, BUT THEY'VE ONLY JUST ENTERED SERVICE.
ARE THEY EXPERIENCED ENOUGH?
ABSOLUTELY
MISS HERSH, YOU SERVED A SPECTACULAR TOUR WITH THE TEAM BEFORE ASSUMING THIS EXECUTIVE ROLE.
WHAT ARE YOUR THOUGHTS? THIS IS UNPRECEDENTED. IF SOMETHING LIKE THIS HAD HAPPENED WHEN YOU WERE A HYPERNATURAL--
NO COMMENT.

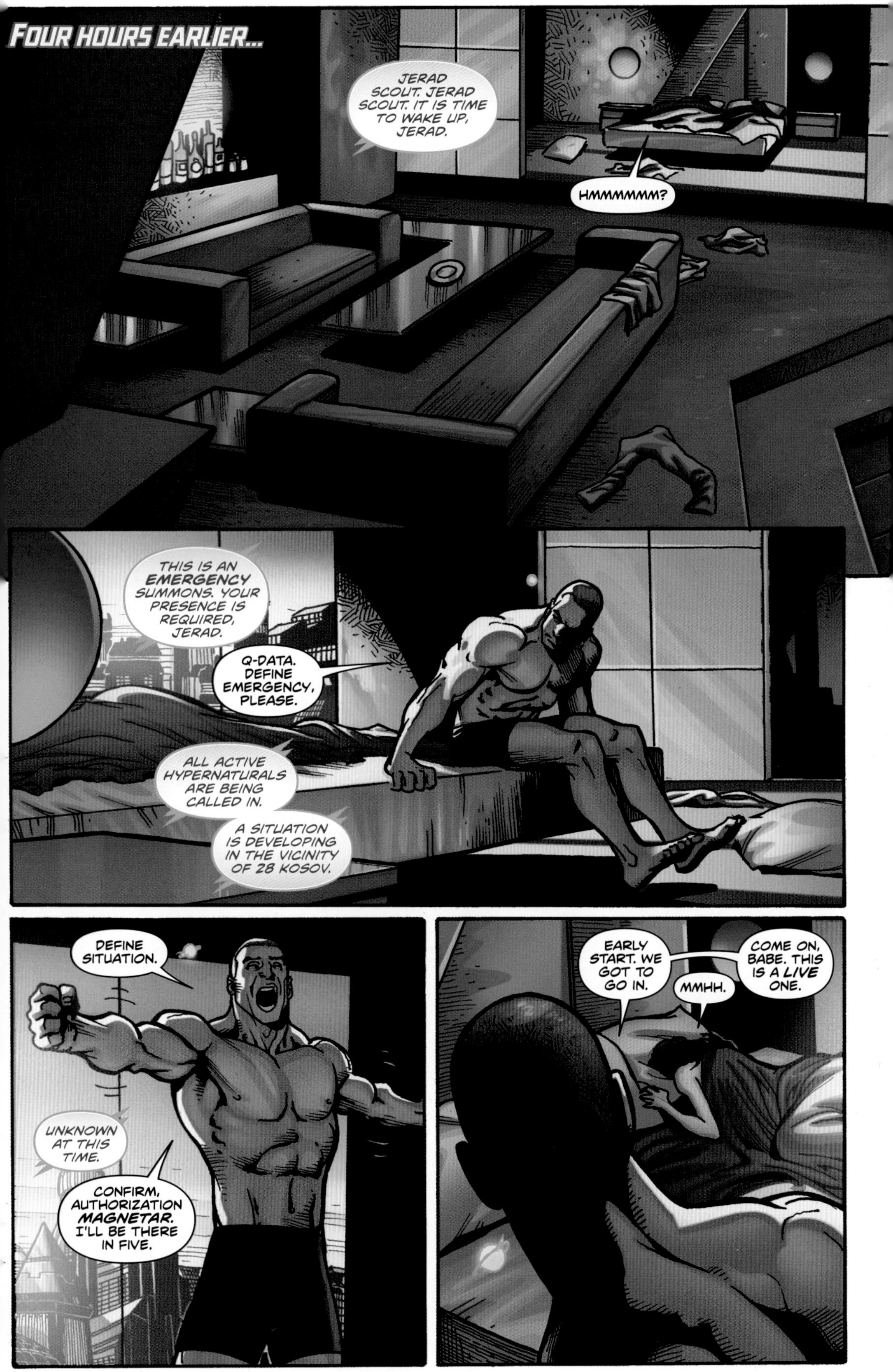
FOUR HOURS EARLIER...
JERAD SCOUT. JERAD SCOUT. IT IS TIME TO WAKE UP, JERAD.
HMMMMMM?
THIS IS AN EMERGENCY SUMMONS. YOUR PRESENCE IS REQUIRED, JERAD.
Q-DATA. DEFINE EMERGENCY, PLEASE.
ALL ACTIVE HYPERNATURALS ARE BEING CALLED IN.
A SITUATION IS DEVELOPING IN THE VICINITY OF 28 KOSOV.
DEFINE SITUATION.
UNKNOWN AT THIS TIME.
CONFIRM, AUTHORIZATION MAGNETAR. I'LL BE THERE IN FIVE.
EARLY START. WE GOT TO GO IN.
MMHH.
COME ON, BABE. THIS IS A LIVE ONE.

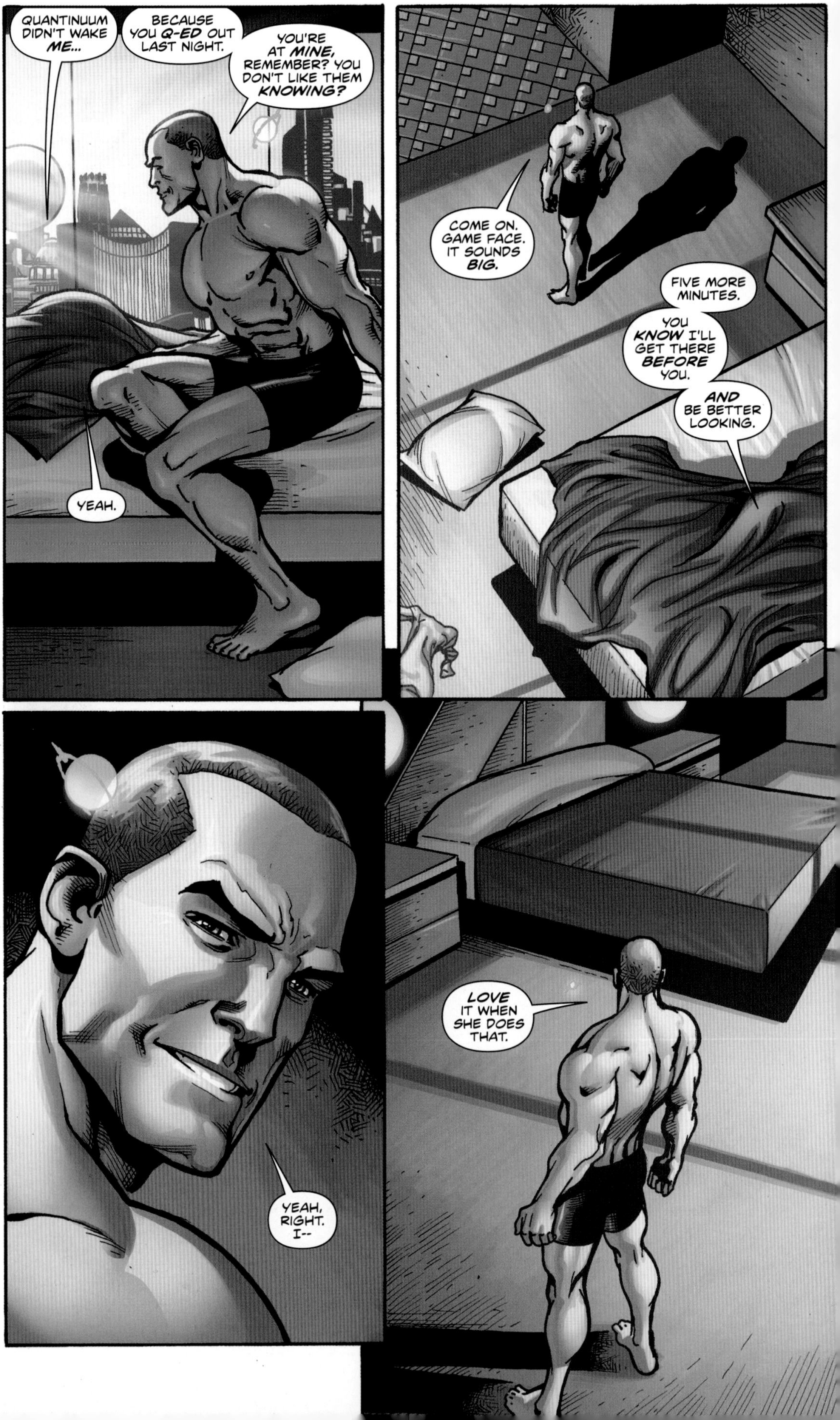
QUANTINUUM DIDN'T WAKE ME...
BECAUSE YOU Q-ED OUT LAST NIGHT.
YOU'RE AT MINE, REMEMBER? YOU DON'T LIKE THEM KNOWING?
YEAH.
COME ON. GAME FACE. IT SOUNDS BIG.
FIVE MORE MINUTES.
YOU KNOW I'LL GET THERE BEFORE YOU.
AND BE BETTER LOOKING.
YEAH, RIGHT. I--
LOVE IT WHEN SHE DOES THAT.

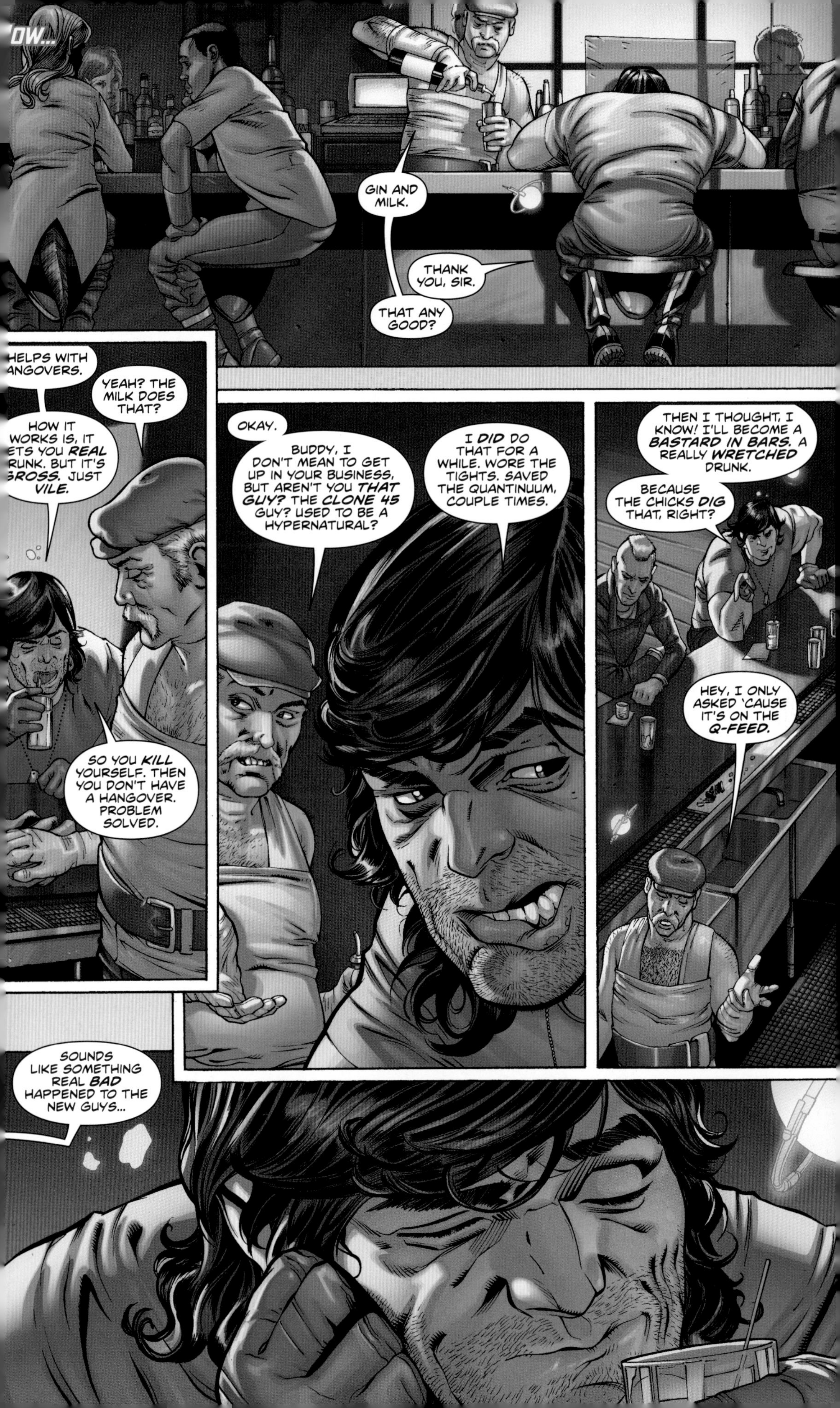

OW...
GIN AND MILK.
THANK YOU, SIR.
THAT ANY GOOD?
HELPS WITH ANGOVERS.
YEAH? THE MILK DOES THAT?
HOW IT WORKS IS, IT ETS YOU REAL RUNK. BUT IT'S GROSS. JUST VILE.
SO YOU KILL YOURSELF. THEN YOU DON'T HAVE A HANGOVER. PROBLEM SOLVED.
OKAY.
BUDDY, I DON'T MEAN TO GET UP IN YOUR BUSINESS, BUT AREN'T YOU THAT GUY? THE CLONE 45 GUY? USED TO BE A HYPERNATURAL?
I DID DO THAT FOR A WHILE. WORE THE TIGHTS. SAVED THE QUANTINUUM, COUPLE TIMES.
THEN I THOUGHT, I KNOW! I'LL BECOME A BASTARD IN BARS. A REALLY WRETCHED DRUNK.
BECAUSE THE CHICKS DIG THAT, RIGHT?
HEY, I ONLY ASKED 'CAUSE IT'S ON THE Q-FEED.
SOUNDS LIKE SOMETHING REAL BAD HAPPENED TO THE NEW GUYS...

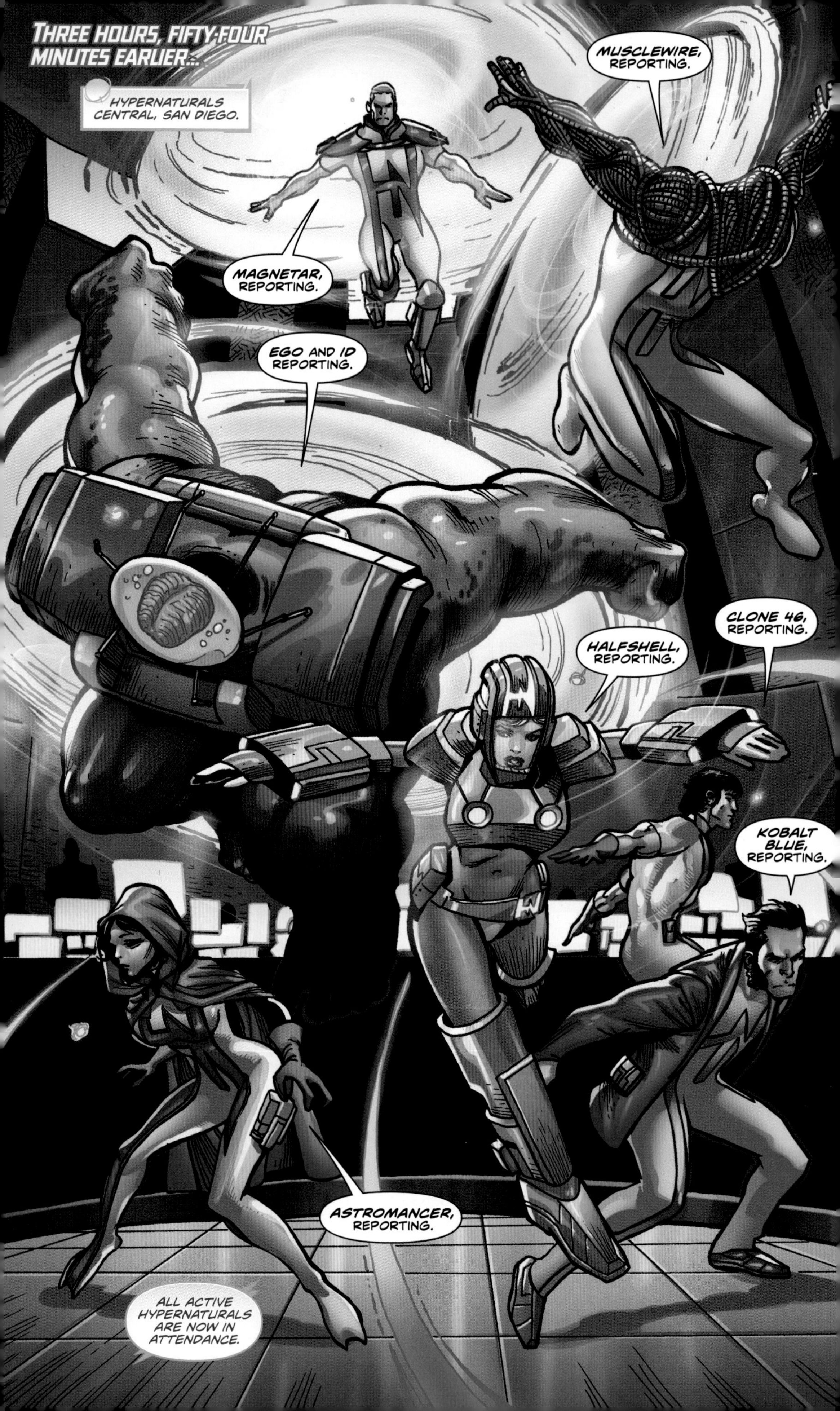
THREE HOURS, FIFTY-FOUR MINUTES EARLIER...
HYPERNATURALS CENTRAL, SAN DIEGO.
MUSCLEWIRE, REPORTING.
MAGNETAR, REPORTING.
EGO AND ID REPORTING.
CLONE 46, REPORTING.
HALFSHELL, REPORTING.
KOBALT BLUE, REPORTING.
ASTROMANCER, REPORTING.
ALL ACTIVE HYPERNATURALS ARE NOW IN ATTENDANCE.

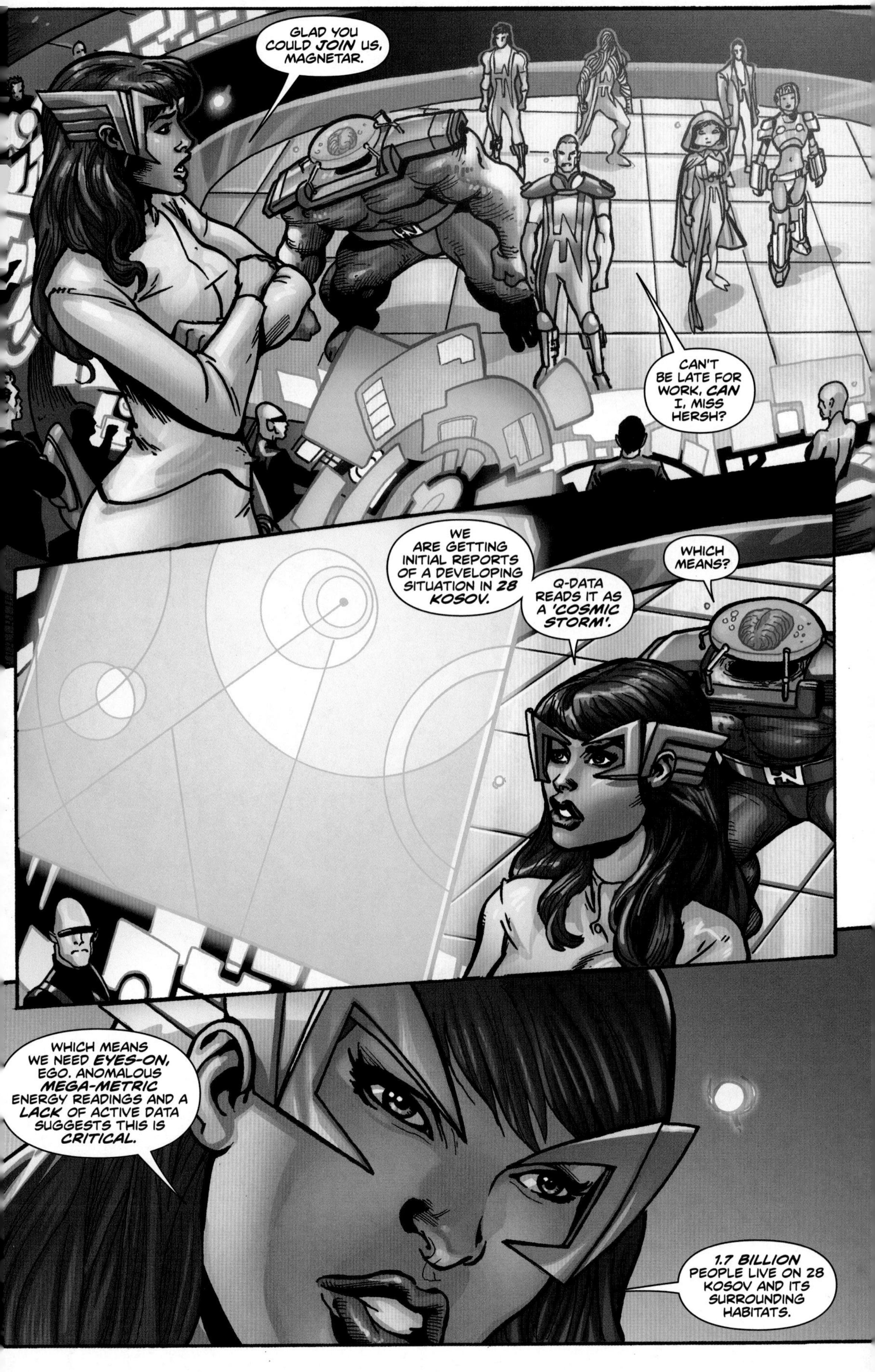
GLAD YOU COULD JOIN US, MAGNETAR.
CAN'T BE LATE FOR WORK, CAN I, MISS HERSH?
WE ARE GETTING INITIAL REPORTS OF A DEVELOPING SITUATION IN 28 KOSOV.
Q-DATA READS IT AS A 'COSMIC STORM'.
WHICH MEANS?
WHICH MEANS WE NEED EYES-ON, EGO. ANOMALOUS MEGA-METRIC ENERGY READINGS AND A LACK OF ACTIVE DATA SUGGESTS THIS IS CRITICAL.
1.7 BILLION PEOPLE LIVE ON 28 KOSOV AND ITS SURROUNDING HABITATS.

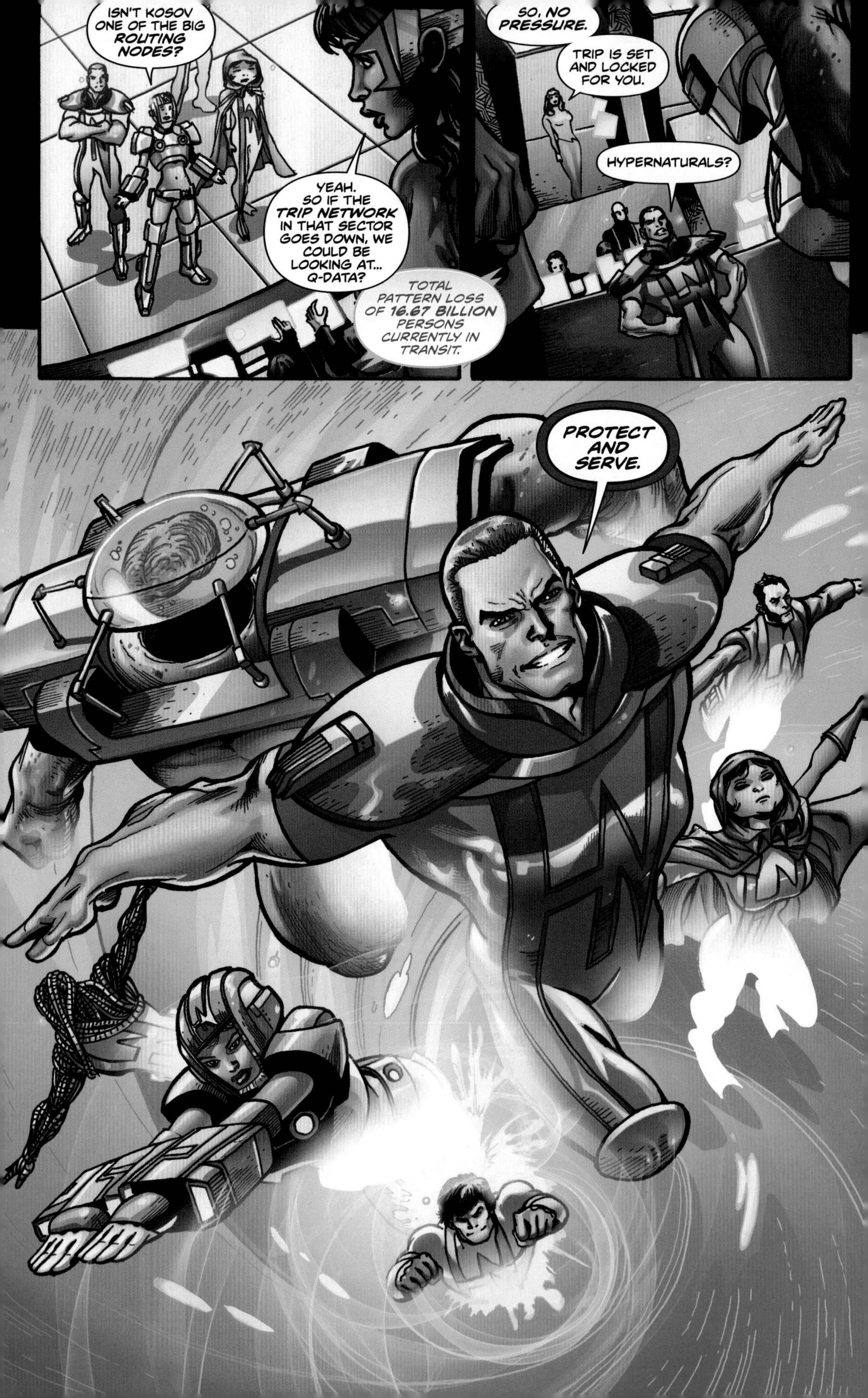
ISN'T KOSOV ONE OF THE BIG ROUTING NODES?
YEAH. SO IF THE TRIP NETWORK IN THAT SECTOR GOES DOWN, WE COULD BE LOOKING AT... Q-DATA?
TOTAL PATTERN LOSS OF 16.67 BILLION PERSONS CURRENTLY IN TRANSIT.
SO, NO PRESSURE.
TRIP IS SET AND LOCKED FOR YOU.
HYPERNATURALS?
PROTECT AND SERVE.

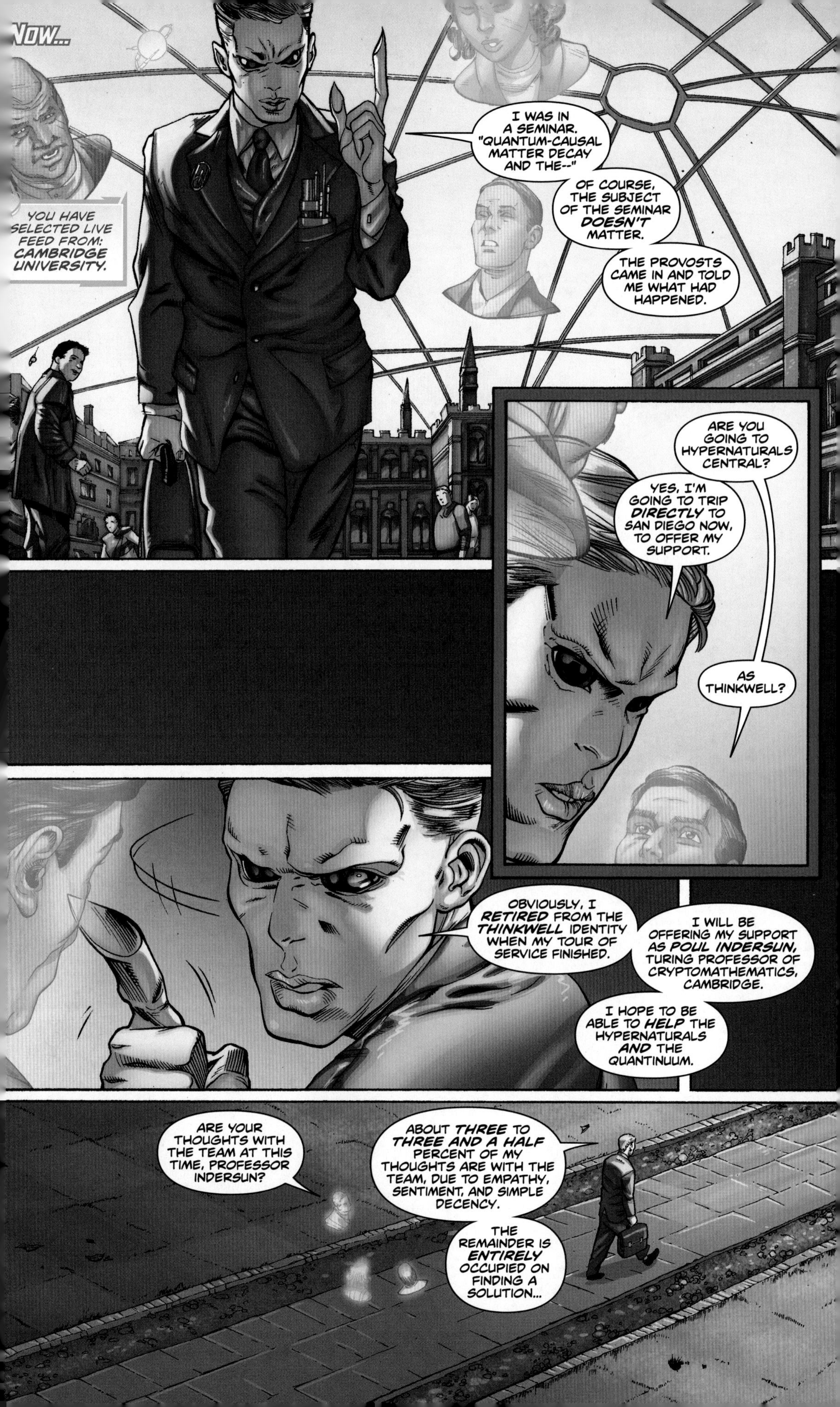
NOW...
YOU HAVE SELECTED LIVE FEED FROM: CAMBRIDGE UNIVERSITY.
I WAS IN A SEMINAR. "QUANTUM-CAUSAL MATTER DECAY AND THE--"
OF COURSE, THE SUBJECT OF THE SEMINAR DOESN'T MATTER.
THE PROVOSTS CAME IN AND TOLD ME WHAT HAD HAPPENED.
ARE YOU GOING TO HYPERNATURALS CENTRAL?
YES, I'M GOING TO TRIP DIRECTLY TO SAN DIEGO NOW, TO OFFER MY SUPPORT.
AS THINKWELL?
OBVIOUSLY, I RETIRED FROM THE THINKWELL IDENTITY WHEN MY TOUR OF SERVICE FINISHED.
I WILL BE OFFERING MY SUPPORT AS POUL INDERSUN, TURING PROFESSOR OF CRYPTOMATHEMATICS, CAMBRIDGE.
I HOPE TO BE ABLE TO HELP THE HYPERNATURALS AND THE QUANTINUUM.
ARE YOUR THOUGHTS WITH THE TEAM AT THIS TIME, PROFESSOR INDERSUN?
ABOUT THREE TO THREE AND A HALF PERCENT OF MY THOUGHTS ARE WITH THE TEAM, DUE TO EMPATHY, SENTIMENT, AND SIMPLE DECENCY.
THE REMAINDER IS ENTIRELY OCCUPIED ON FINDING A SOLUTION...

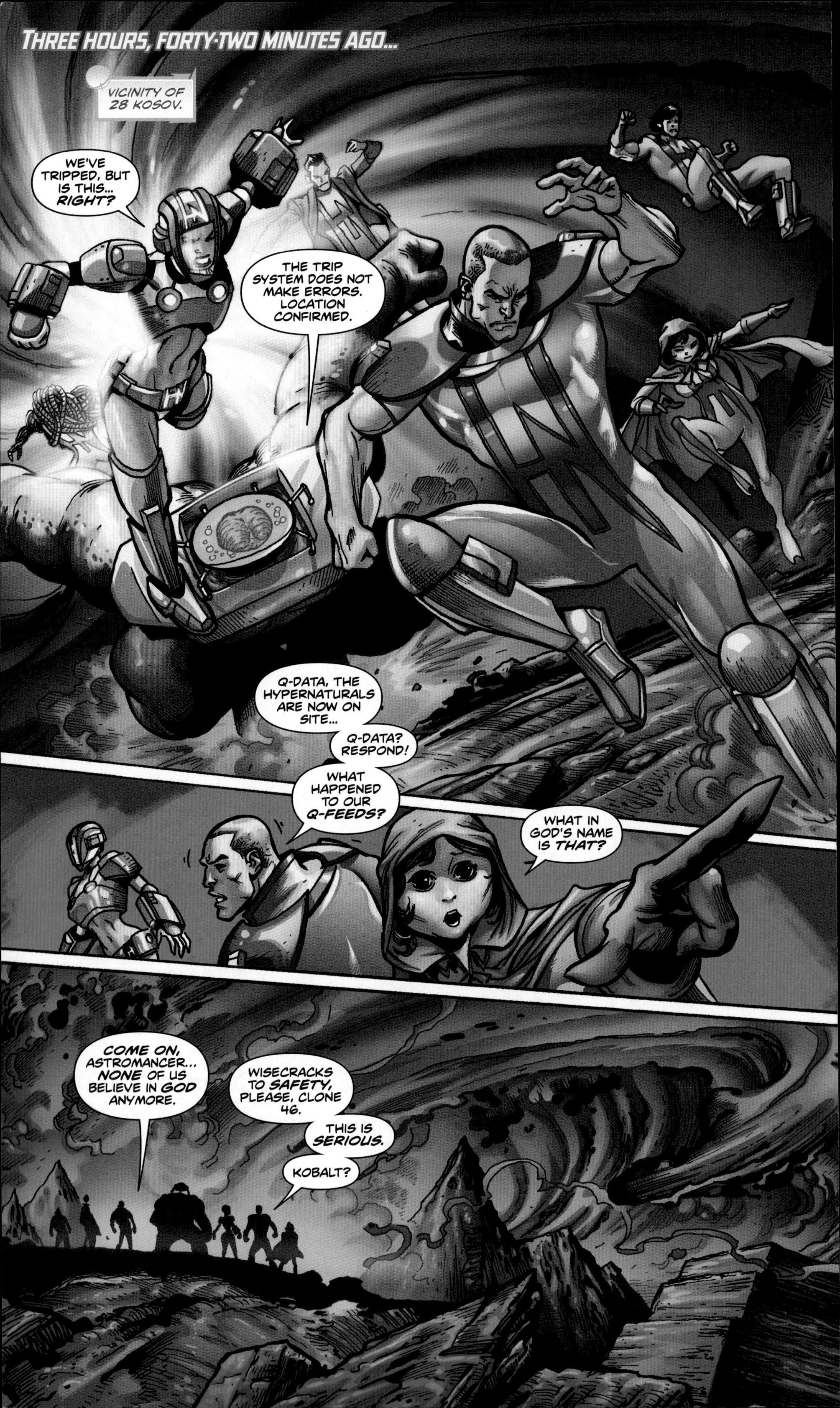

THREE HOURS, FORTY-TWO MINUTES AGO...
VICINITY OF 28 KOSOV.
WE'VE TRIPPED, BUT IS THIS... RIGHT?
THE TRIP SYSTEM DOES NOT MAKE ERRORS. LOCATION CONFIRMED.
Q-DATA, THE HYPERNATURALS ARE NOW ON SITE...
Q-DATA? RESPOND!
WHAT HAPPENED TO OUR Q-FEEDS?
WHAT IN GOD'S NAME IS THAT?
COME ON, ASTROMANCER... NONE OF US BELIEVE IN GOD ANYMORE.
WISECRACKS TO SAFETY, PLEASE, CLONE 46.
THIS IS SERIOUS.
KOBALT?

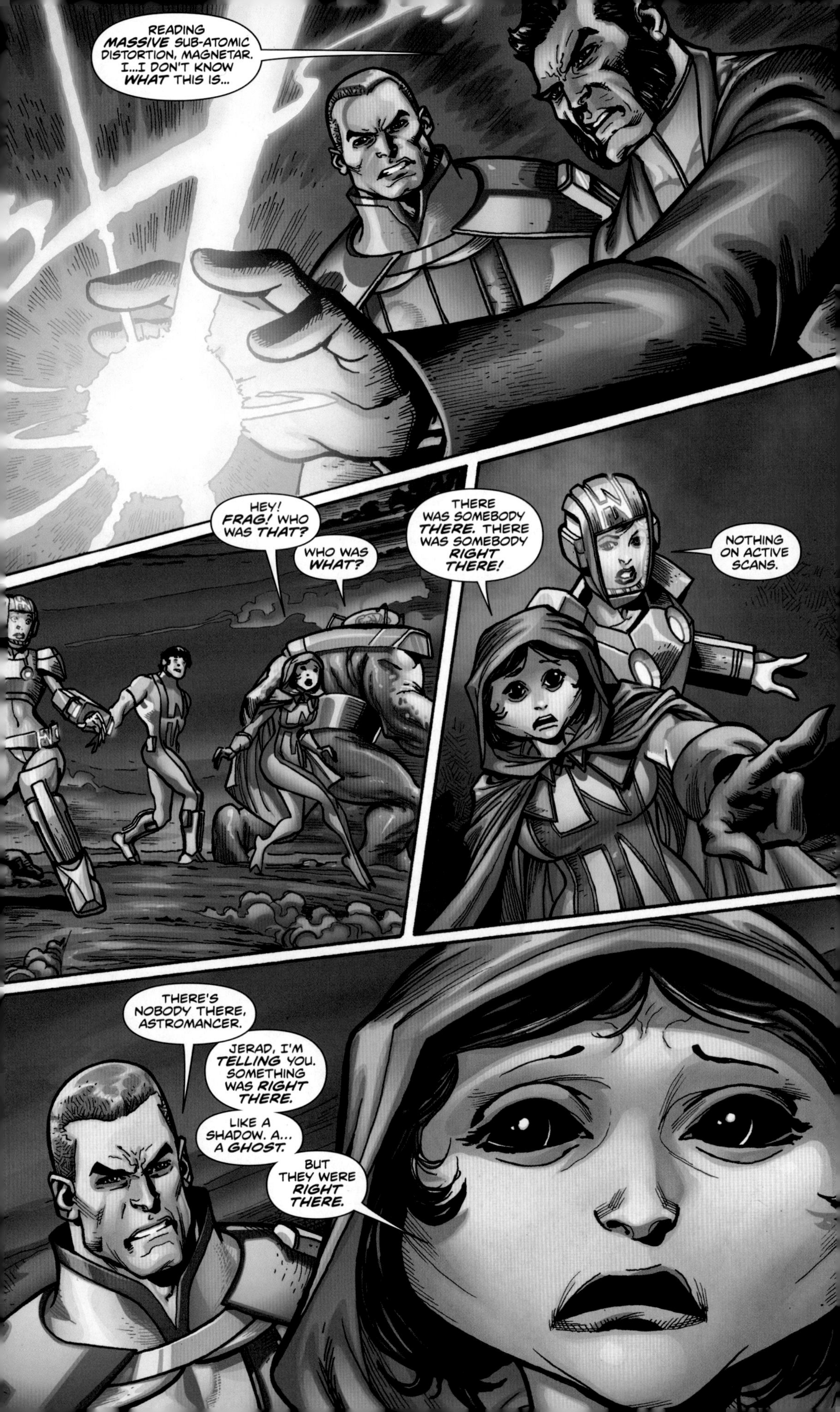
READING MASSIVE SUB-ATOMIC DISTORTION, MAGNETAR. I...I DON'T KNOW WHAT THIS IS...
HEY! FRAG! WHO WAS THAT?
WHO WAS WHAT?
THERE WAS SOMEBODY THERE. THERE WAS SOMEBODY RIGHT THERE!
NOTHING ON ACTIVE SCANS.
THERE'S NOBODY THERE, ASTROMANCER.
JERAD, I'M TELLING YOU. SOMETHING WAS RIGHT THERE.
LIKE A SHADOW. A... A GHOST.
BUT THEY WERE RIGHT THERE.

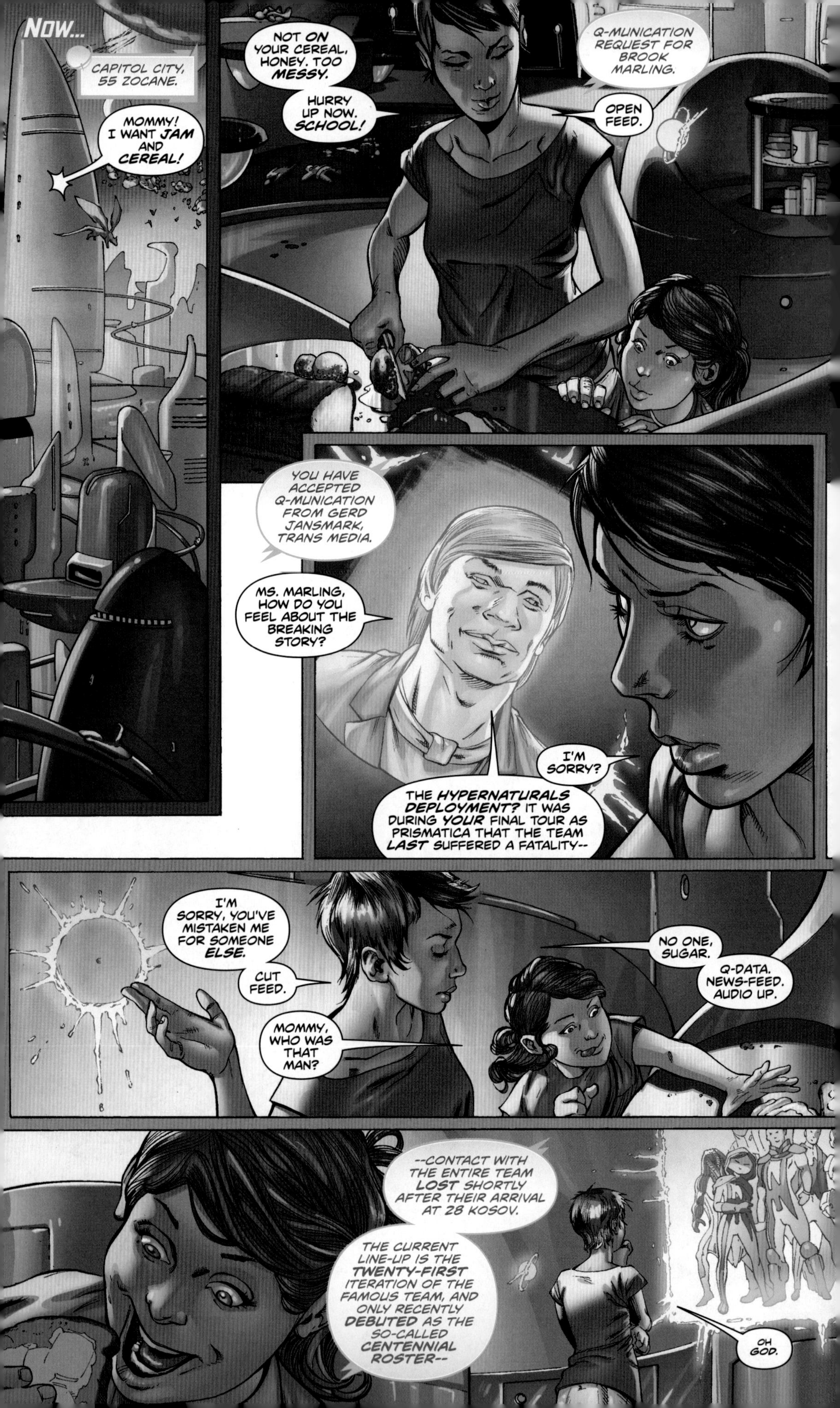

NOW...
CAPITOL CITY, 55 ZOCANE.
MOMMY! I WANT JAM AND CEREAL!
NOT ON YOUR CEREAL, HONEY. TOO MESSY.
HURRY UP NOW. SCHOOL!
Q-MUNICATION REQUEST FOR BROOK MARLING.
OPEN FEED.
YOU HAVE ACCEPTED Q-MUNICATION FROM GERD JANSMARK, TRANS MEDIA.
MS. MARLING, HOW DO YOU FEEL ABOUT THE BREAKING STORY?
I'M SORRY?
THE HYPERNATURALS DEPLOYMENT? IT WAS DURING YOUR FINAL TOUR AS PRISMATICA THAT THE TEAM LAST SUFFERED A FATALITY--
I'M SORRY, YOU'VE MISTAKEN ME FOR SOMEONE ELSE.
CUT FEED.
MOMMY, WHO WAS THAT MAN?
NO ONE, SUGAR.
Q-DATA. NEWS-FEED. AUDIO UP.
--CONTACT WITH THE ENTIRE TEAM LOST SHORTLY AFTER THEIR ARRIVAL AT 28 KOSOV.
THE CURRENT LINE-UP IS THE TWENTY-FIRST ITERATION OF THE FAMOUS TEAM, AND ONLY RECENTLY DEBUTED AS THE SO-CALLED CENTENNIAL ROSTER--
OH GOD.

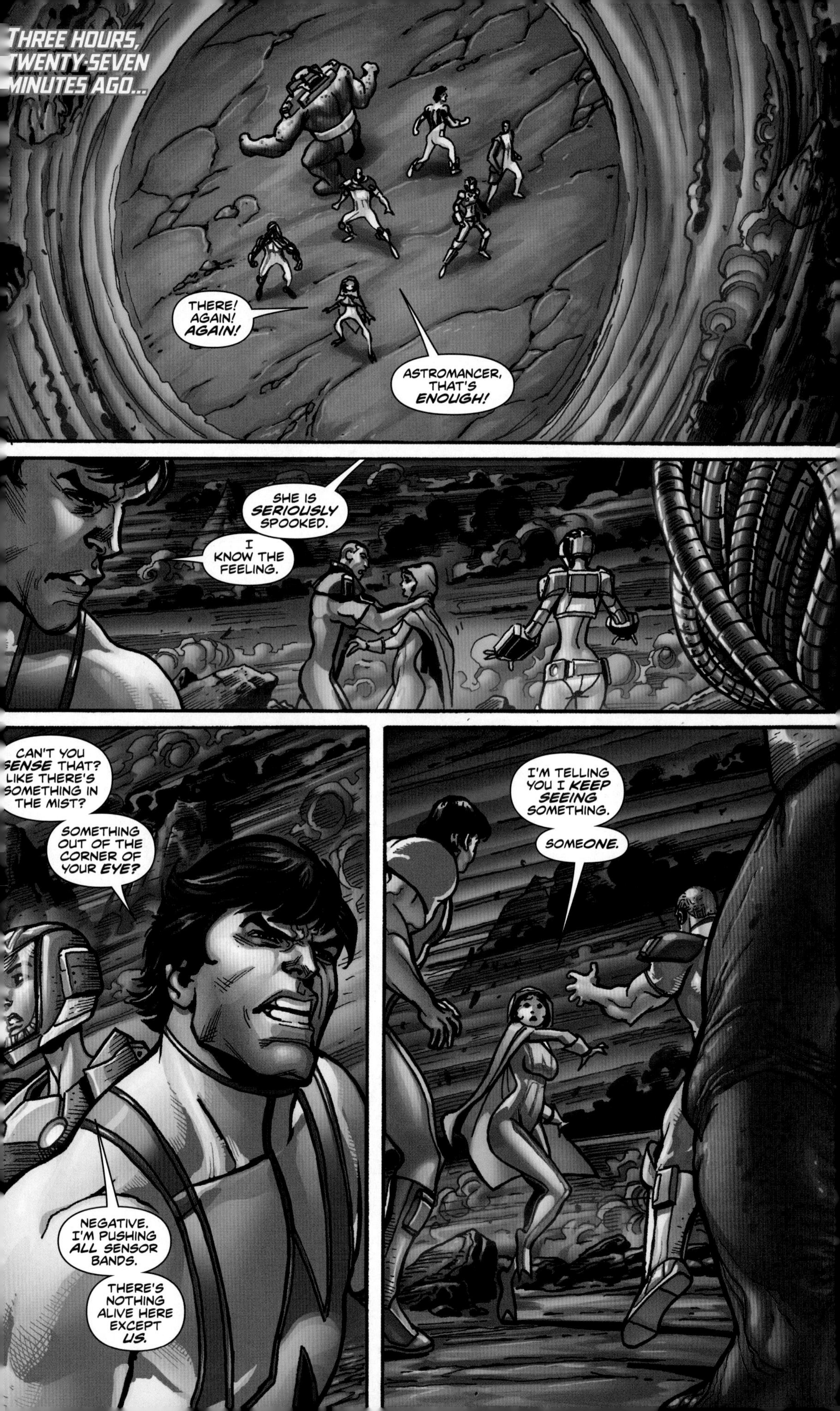
THREE HOURS, TWENTY-SEVEN MINUTES AGO...
THERE! AGAIN! AGAIN!
ASTROMANCER, THAT'S ENOUGH!
SHE IS SERIOUSLY SPOOKED.
I KNOW THE FEELING.
CAN'T YOU SENSE THAT? LIKE THERE'S SOMETHING IN THE MIST?
SOMETHING OUT OF THE CORNER OF YOUR EYE?
NEGATIVE. I'M PUSHING ALL SENSOR BANDS.
THERE'S NOTHING ALIVE HERE EXCEPT US.
I'M TELLING YOU I KEEP SEEING SOMETHING.
SOMEONE.

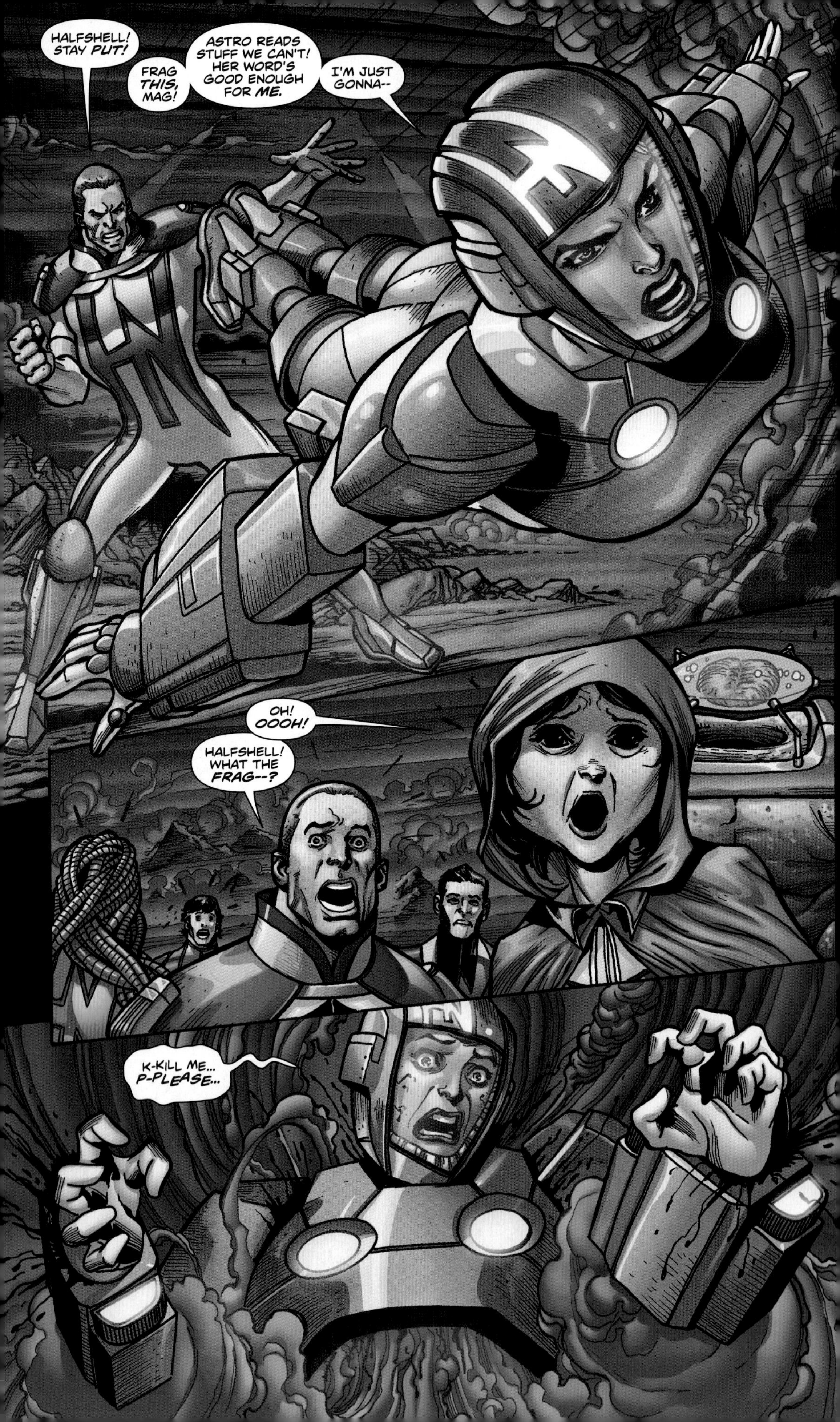
HALFSHELL! STAY PUT!
FRAG THIS, MAG!
ASTRO READS STUFF WE CAN'T! HER WORD'S GOOD ENOUGH FOR ME.
I'M JUST GONNA--
OH! OOOH!
HALFSHELL! WHAT THE FRAG--?
K-KILL ME... P-PLEASE...

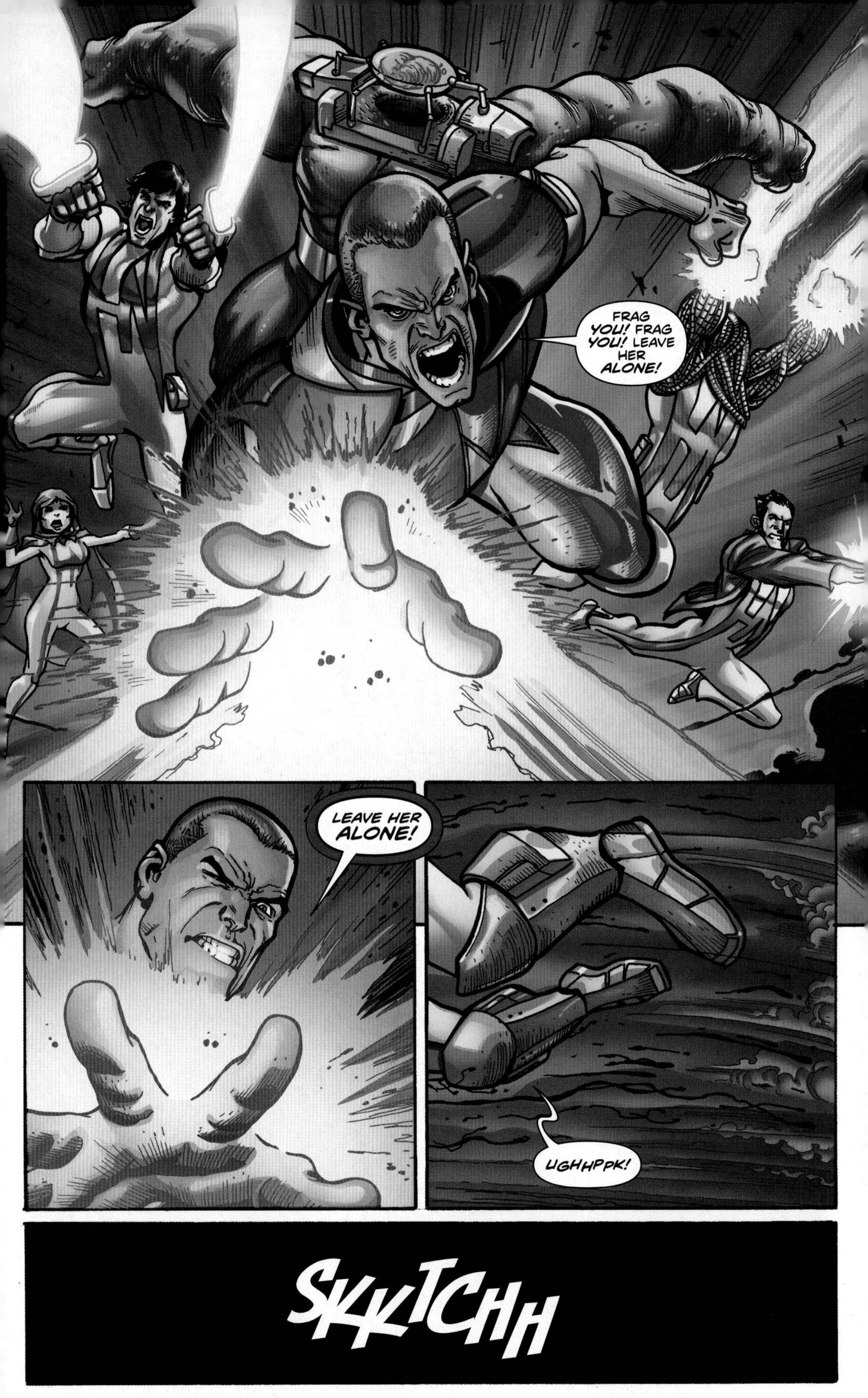
FRAG YOU! FRAG YOU! LEAVE HER ALONE!
LEAVE HER ALONE!
UGHHPPK!
SKKTCHH

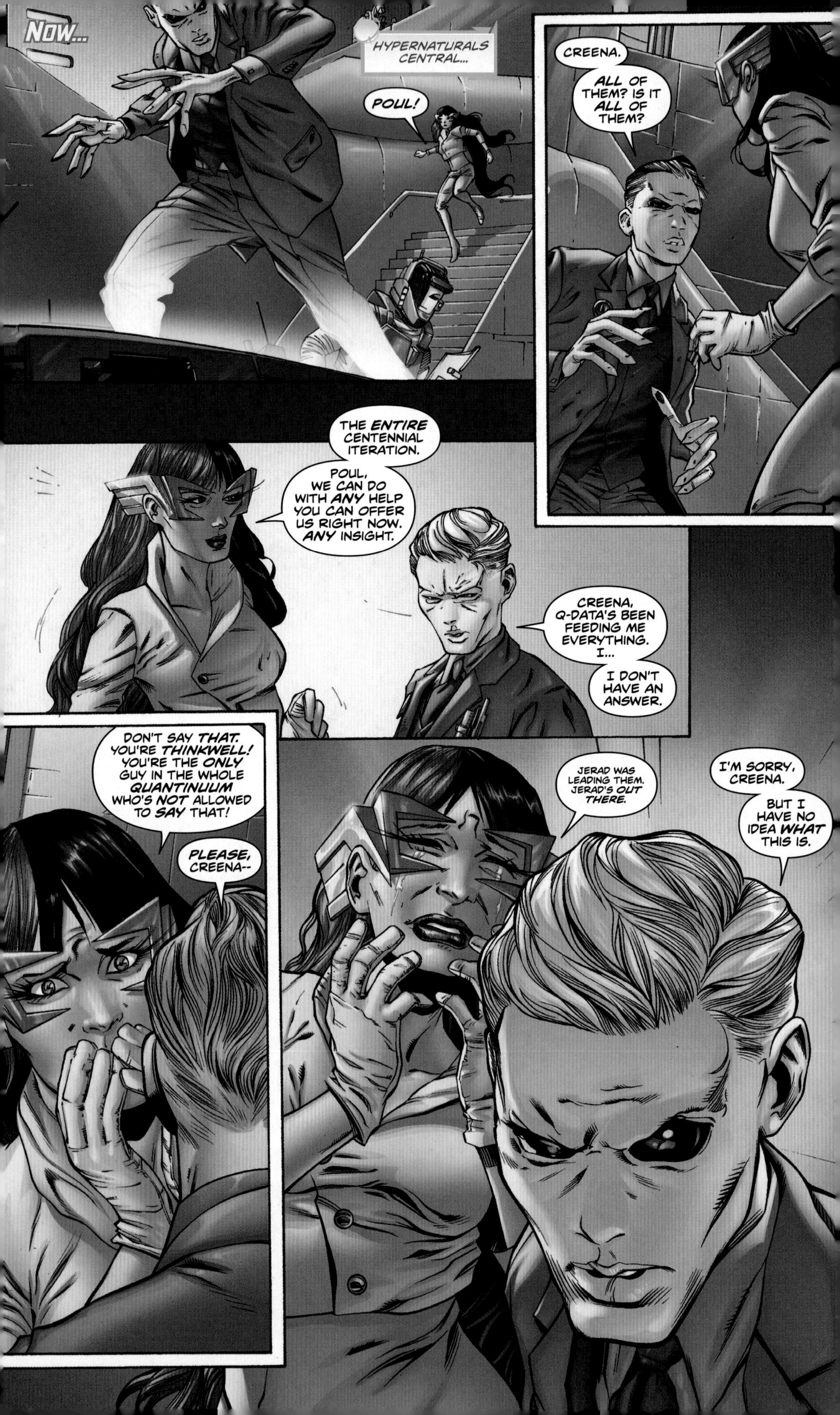

NOW...
HYPERNATURALS CENTRAL...
POUL!
CREENA.
ALL OF THEM? IS IT ALL OF THEM?
THE ENTIRE CENTENNIAL ITERATION.
POUL, WE CAN DO WITH ANY HELP YOU CAN OFFER US RIGHT NOW. ANY INSIGHT.
CREENA, Q-DATA'S BEEN FEEDING ME EVERYTHING. I...
I DON'T HAVE AN ANSWER.
DON'T SAY THAT. YOU'RE THINKWELL! YOU'RE THE ONLY GUY IN THE WHOLE QUANTINUUM WHO'S NOT ALLOWED TO SAY THAT!
PLEASE, CREENA--
JERAD WAS LEADING THEM. JERAD'S OUT THERE.
I'M SORRY, CREENA.
BUT I HAVE NO IDEA WHAT THIS IS.

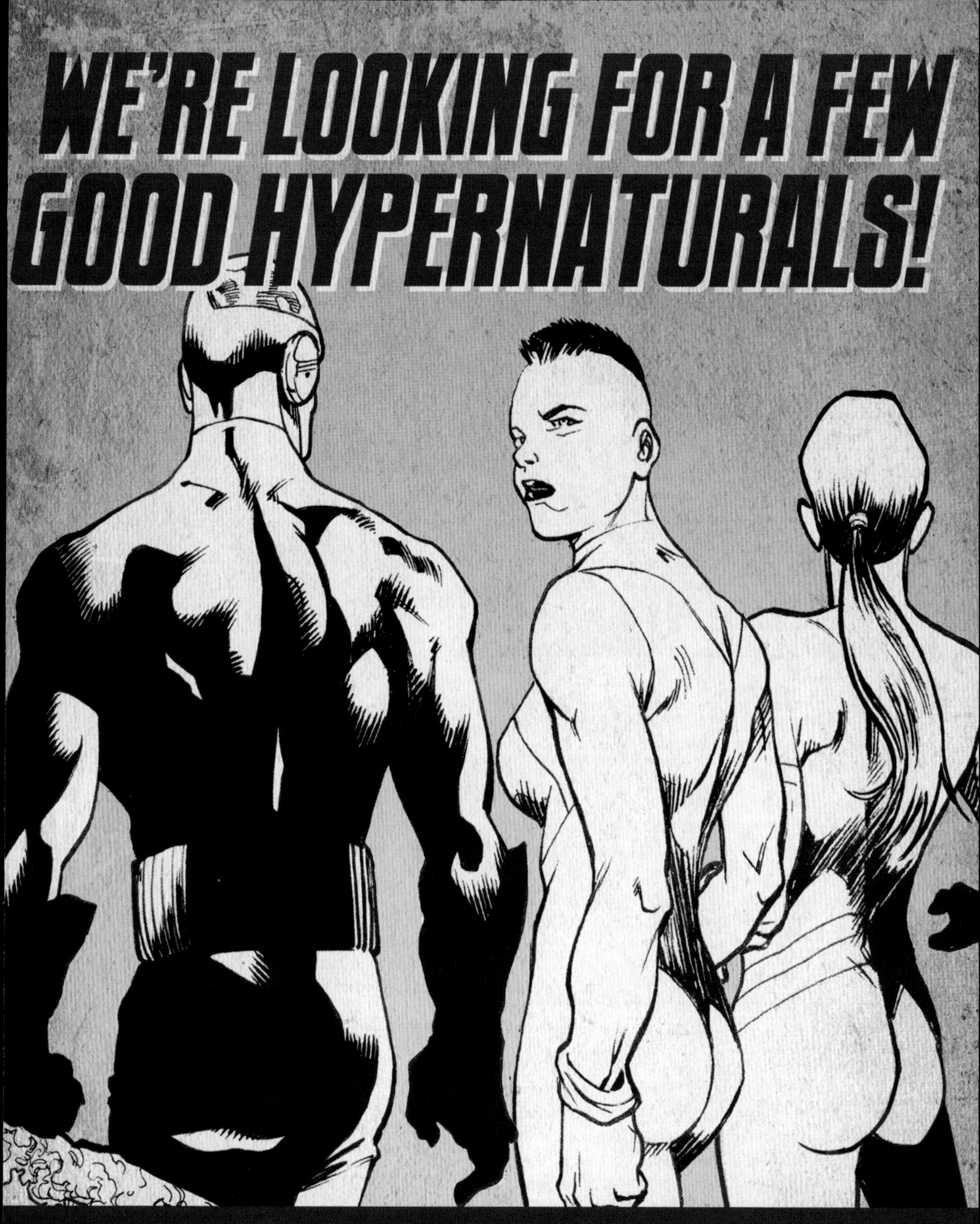
WE'RE LOOKING FOR A FEW
GOOD HYPERNATURALS!

For almost two decades, the Hypernaturals have protected the people of the Quantinuum from harm. These brave boys and girls are our first line of defense and our ultimate salvation.

But now greater dangers face us, including the threat of war. Do you have what it takes to stand up and be counted?

Do you have the right stuff to join the ranks of the few and the bold, alongside heroes like Clone 21?

Contact the Candidacy Program today and see if you can serve with the best of the best.

Born To Be Heroes

MAGNETIC ATTRACTION

Heartthrob. Hero. Role model. Jerad Scout — a.k.a. Magnetar — is the newly installed team leader of the Hypernaturals, fronting the group in its so-called *Centennial Iteration*. He talks about taking on the Hypernaturals' 100-year-old legacy, and what it means to be a leader when it's only your first term. *A Cosmopolis exclusive by Tyra Retane.*

T hey say you know when you've met a first-team Hypernatural because you have the overwhelming impression you've seen someone too beautiful to be true. Jerad Scout trips in late for our interview — a team portrait session at the San Diego HQ took longer than expected — and immediately apologizes with a smile so bright, main sequence stars would be jealous. "It's all been pretty intense," he confesses to me. "I spent five years in selection trials and try-outs to prove I was good enough to make the cut. I was up against thousands of candidates. And they were *high standard*, too. Seriously, every one of them was a Hypernatural, with attested Hypernatural gifts. The selection process was grueling. I can't believe I got through. I haven't had time to even *think* about the fact they made me leader."

He laughs, and it's clear that everyone in the bistro on 43 Xaros is looking at him. You just can't take your eyes off him. In showbiz, that's called *charisma*.

Cosmopolis: When did you first decide you were going to be a Hypernatural?

Jerad: You don't decide that. The selection committee decides who makes it. You just decide to try out. I was actually in college before I even knew I had hyper-gifts [*Magnetar is blessed with class nine magnetic manipulation powers*]. I was a history major. I was studying P.Q.E. history ("Pre-Quantinuum Era"), and rapidly realizing that no one was interested in the past anymore. If it happened before the Singularity, it doesn't count. The future is all that matters.

Cosmopolis: And the Hypernaturals protect that future?

Jerad: Completely. For a hundred years, hypernaturally gifted individuals have been chosen from the trillions of citizens in the Quantinuum to be the protectors of human culture. You wake up one day, like I did, and discover you have hyper-talents, you want to use them. I grew up watching the exploits of the eighteenth and nineteenth team iterations. Late eighties, early nineties. I never thought I'd make that grade.

Cosmopolis: Do you hope you'll serve the full three terms?

Jerad: One five-year term is enough to start with! I'll see how things go. There's a high burn-out rate because of the pressure. And I know there's been a lot of criticism in the press about the three-term service limit, but it's there for a reason.

Cosmopolis: You don't think all-time greats like Clone 40 or Warpstar, or even recent giants like Thinkwell or Clone 45, should have been allowed to serve beyond the fifteen-year cap?

MAGNETAR
ON HIS TEAMMATES:

HALFSHELL
"Cyber-enhanced tough. Nobody's fool. She beat out sixty girls for the privilege of wearing that armor. I'm proud to have her."

EGO & ID
"Brain and Brawn. It's hard not to think of them as one being. Ego's rep? Unwarranted. I've never found him anything less than friendly."

ASTROMANCER
"Cosmic sensitivity is a tough deal to live with. She copes with it brilliantly, and she's a vital asset."

MUSCLEWIRE
"We get on amazingly. He is the funniest guy. And that poly-alloy gift...sheer class."

CLONE 46
"Great, great honor to have one of the Clone Sequence on the team. I always think it isn't the Hypernaturals without a clone in the squad. Of course, '45 was one of the all-time greats, so Nute better bring his A-game."

KOBALT BLUE
"I was so pleased when they said we'd have a second-termer on the team, and when they said it was Blue, I was sold. Energy manipulation, plus the experience of prior service...he and I have been talking strategy a lot."

Jerad: Like I said, the limit's there for a reason.

Cosmopolis: The training's really intensive, then?

Jerad: Absolutely. Especially the leadership program.

Cosmopolis: No time for a social life?

Jerad: I try to wind down sometimes.

Cosmopolis: There's talk of a high-profile romance in your life.

Jerad: [laughs] No comment! Seriously, I don't have time for a serious relationship right now. Getting the Centennial Iteration ready for active duty is taking all my time. Besides, Magnetar, you can know everything about...*Jerad Scout*, he deserves a *little* bit of a private life, right?

Cosmopolis: Tell us about the Centennial line-up.

Jerad: We're starting the twenty-first five-year term this month, that's a hundred years of the Hypernaturals' service as a formal institution. It's a PR exercise, I know, but it's a huge responsibility. There's a legacy I'm painfully aware of. This is the team that stopped Bioerror. The team that saved 356 Barnard from the Replicator crisis. This is the team that put Sublime in iso, for Quant's sake! Big shoes. Big, *big* shoes.

Cosmopolis: After service, most Hypernaturals end up in high-profile roles. Seventeen planetary governors. Eight talk show hosts. Two presidents of the Quantinuum Council. There's sponsorship deals, endorsements...this is a ticket to the high life, though, right?

Jerad: [laughs] There are perks! But there's a lot of hard work to put in before we get to that kind of retirement.

Cosmopolis: What do you see as your main goals for (*continued overpage*)

CHAPTER ONE

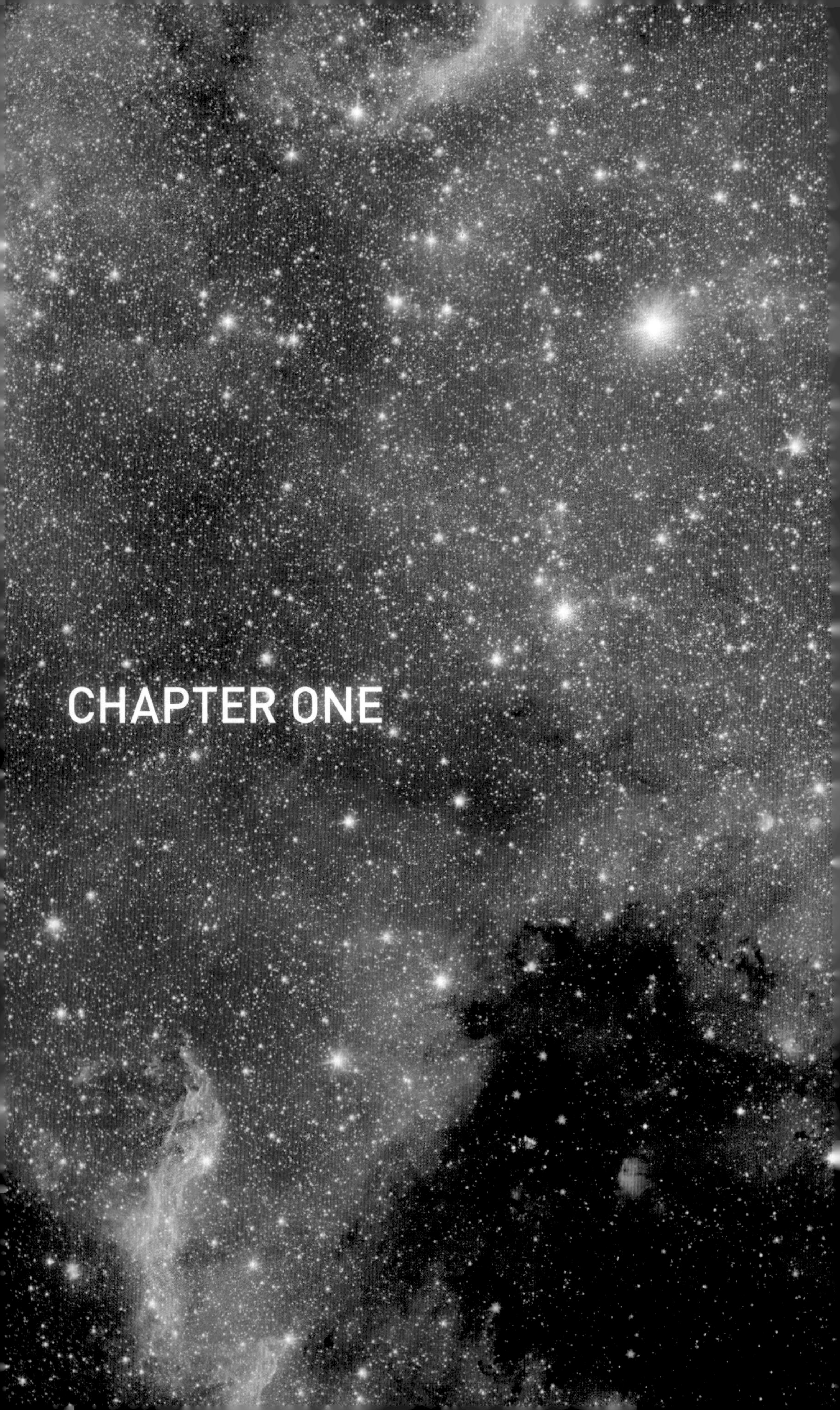

• You have selected Q-Data link.

• It is the 10th of January in the year **100 A.Q.**
  • Touch here to select an alternative to the **Anno Quantinuum** calendar system.
  • Touch here to load local weather reports for your **current cosmic location.**
  • Touch here to access **Q-Data newsflows** from planets near your current cosmic location.
  • Touch here for latest **Quantum Trip transit times.**

• Q-Data entry: The Quantinuum

• The Quantinuum is the name for the human galactic culture, and also for the **artificial intelligence** that controls its function.

• The Quantinuum was created 100 years ago at the start of the **Nanocene Era**. The Nanocene began when the Quantinuum AI achieved Singularity and refashioned human galactic culture. Succeeding the **Holocene Era**, the Nanocene is the next progression of human evolution and...

(to read this entry in full, touch here)

• You have selected live feed newsflow.

• **Harn Vamberg Nano** reports record half-year profits on the Q-index
• **Boston Gravs** take pennant in extra time
• **AI Law** star Lent Fraer trips to 33 Luxor to open nanossembly plant, denies romance with co-star Ilona Cray
• The Centennial Year Iteration of the **Hypernaturals** Team has assembled at the Hypernaturals Central Headquarters, San Diego, Earth for its first official mission

• The Hypernaturals are the Quantinuum's foremost champions. Famous across the entirety of human galactic culture, the team members are selected on the basis of their hypernatural powers and their strength of character, and serve for five-year terms. In honor of the start of the twenty-first term, the line-up of the team's so-called "Centennial Year Iteration" has recently been announced amid huge publicity and—

...BREAKING NEWS... unconfirmed sources report the entire Hypernatural Team has vanished on its inaugural mission to 28 Kosov...precise nature of the 28 Kosov emergency remains unclear...awaiting official statement from Hypernaturals Central, San Diego...

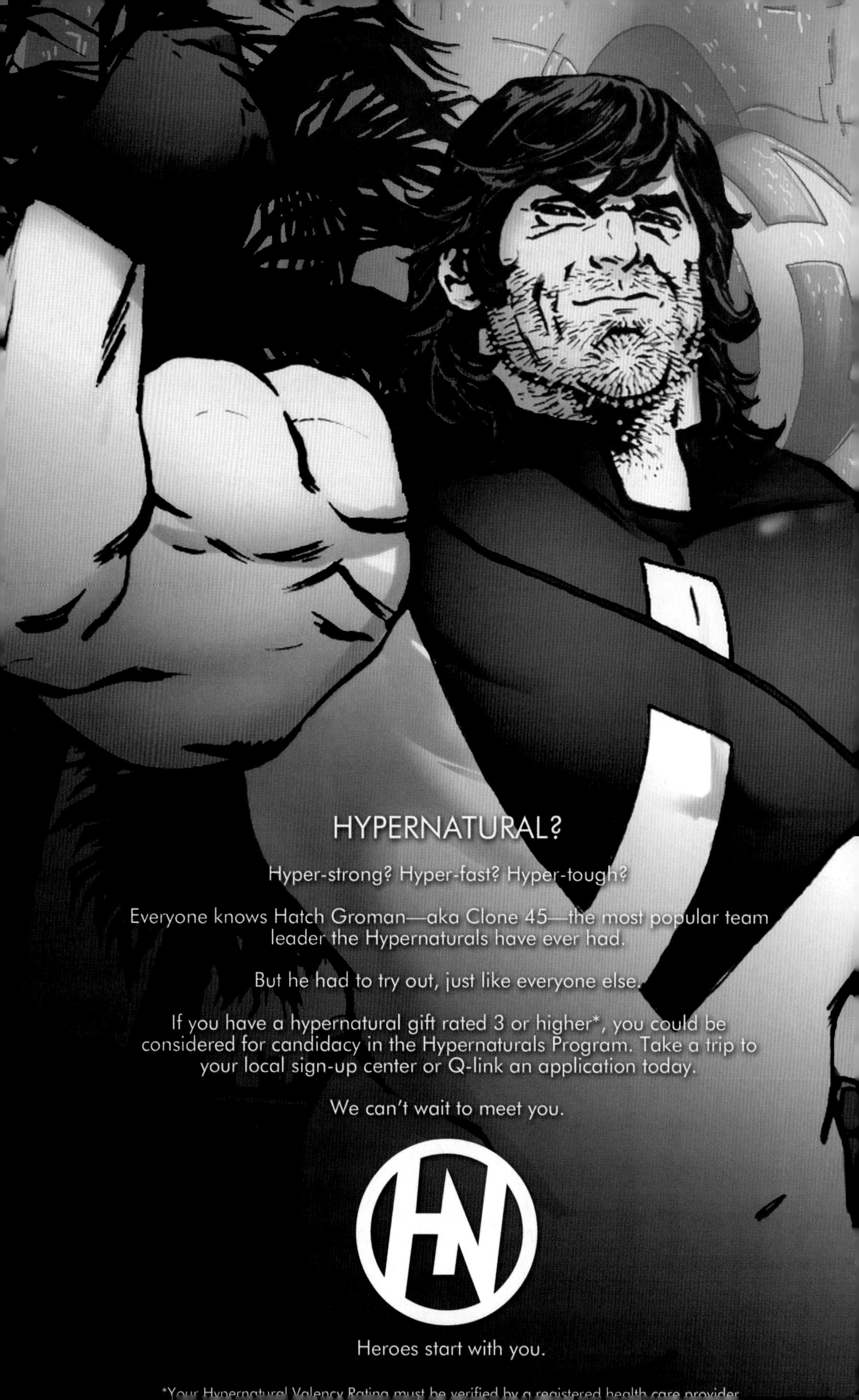
HYPERNATURAL?
Hyper-strong? Hyper-fast? Hyper-tough?
Everyone knows Hatch Groman—aka Clone 45—the most popular team leader the Hypernaturals have ever had.
But he had to try out, just like everyone else.
If you have a hypernatural gift rated 3 or higher*, you could be considered for candidacy in the Hypernaturals Program. Take a trip to your local sign-up center or Q-link an application today.
We can't wait to meet you.
HN
Heroes start with you.
*Your Hypernatural Valency Rating must be verified by a registered health care provider

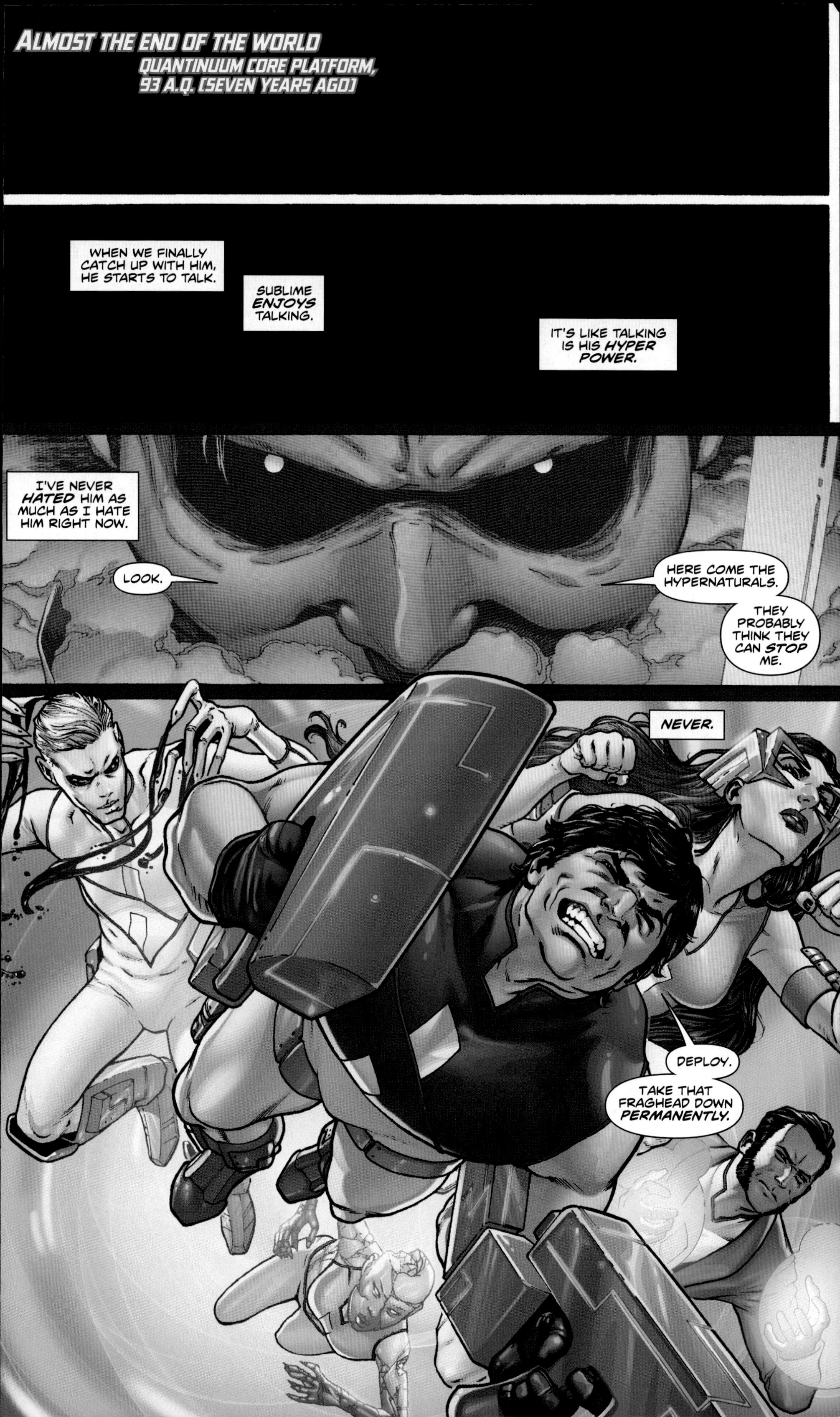
ALMOST THE END OF THE WORLD
QUANTINUUM CORE PLATFORM, 93 A.Q. [SEVEN YEARS AGO]
WHEN WE FINALLY CATCH UP WITH HIM, HE STARTS TO TALK.
SUBLIME *ENJOYS* TALKING.
IT'S LIKE TALKING IS HIS *HYPER POWER.*
I'VE NEVER *HATED* HIM AS MUCH AS I HATE HIM RIGHT NOW.
LOOK.
HERE COME THE HYPERNATURALS.
THEY PROBABLY THINK THEY CAN *STOP* ME.
NEVER.
DEPLOY.
TAKE THAT FRAGHEAD DOWN *PERMANENTLY.*

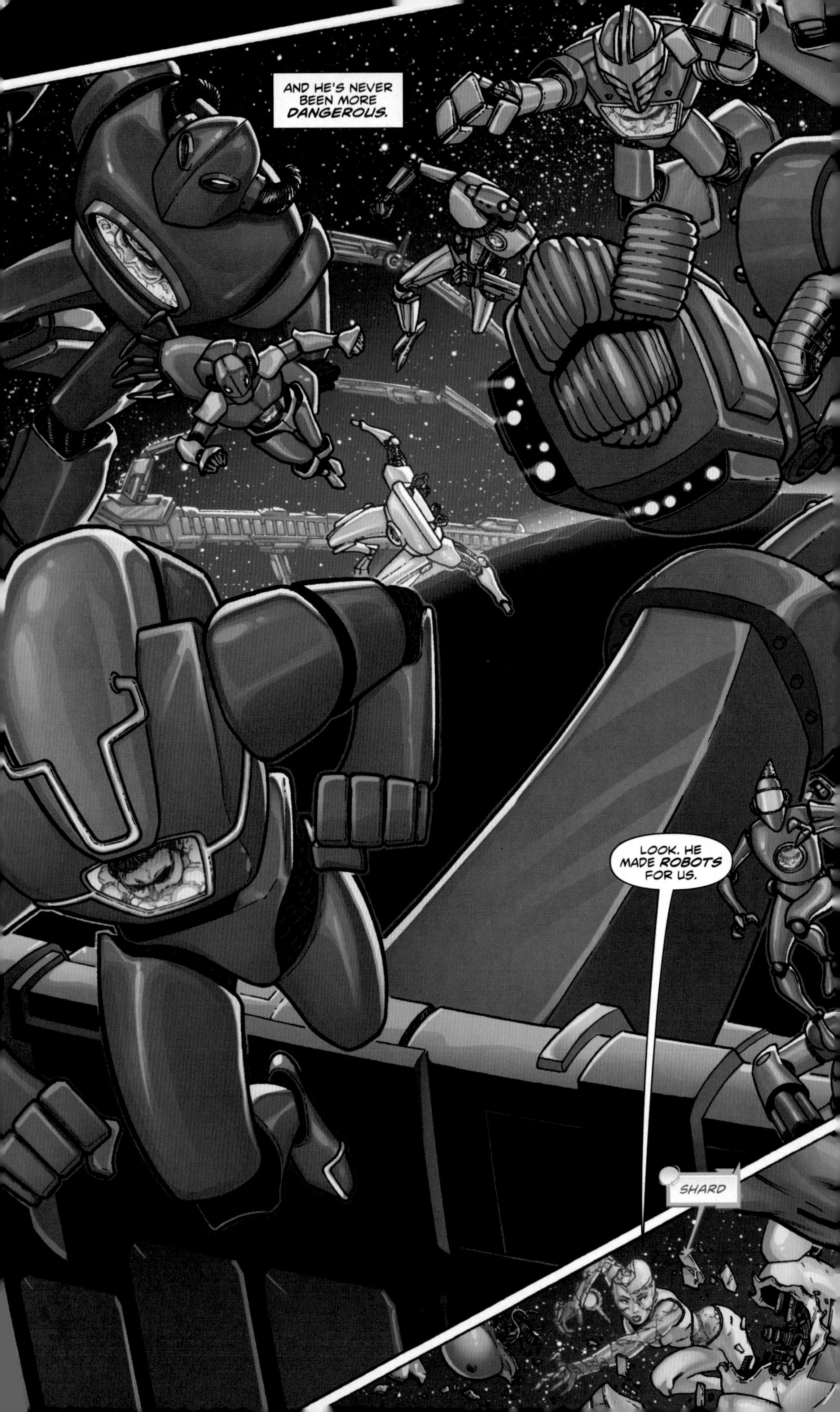
AND HE'S NEVER BEEN MORE DANGEROUS.
LOOK. HE MADE ROBOTS FOR US.
SHARD

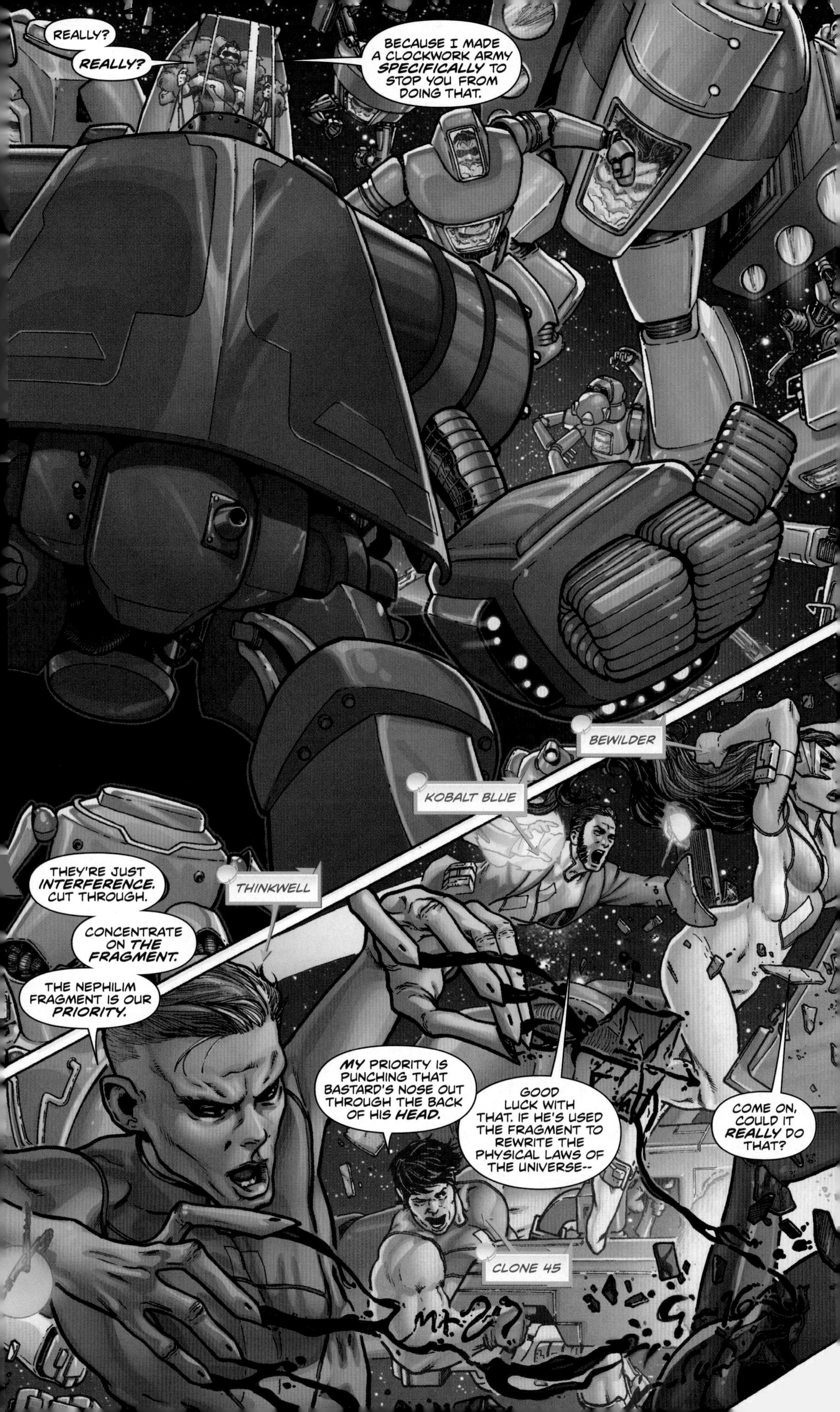

REALLY?
REALLY?
BECAUSE I MADE A CLOCKWORK ARMY SPECIFICALLY TO STOP YOU FROM DOING THAT.
BEWILDER
KOBALT BLUE
THINKWELL
THEY'RE JUST INTERFERENCE. CUT THROUGH.
CONCENTRATE ON THE FRAGMENT.
THE NEPHILIM FRAGMENT IS OUR PRIORITY.
MY PRIORITY IS PUNCHING THAT BASTARD'S NOSE OUT THROUGH THE BACK OF HIS HEAD.
GOOD LUCK WITH THAT. IF HE'S USED THE FRAGMENT TO REWRITE THE PHYSICAL LAWS OF THE UNIVERSE--
COME ON, COULD IT REALLY DO THAT?
CLONE 45

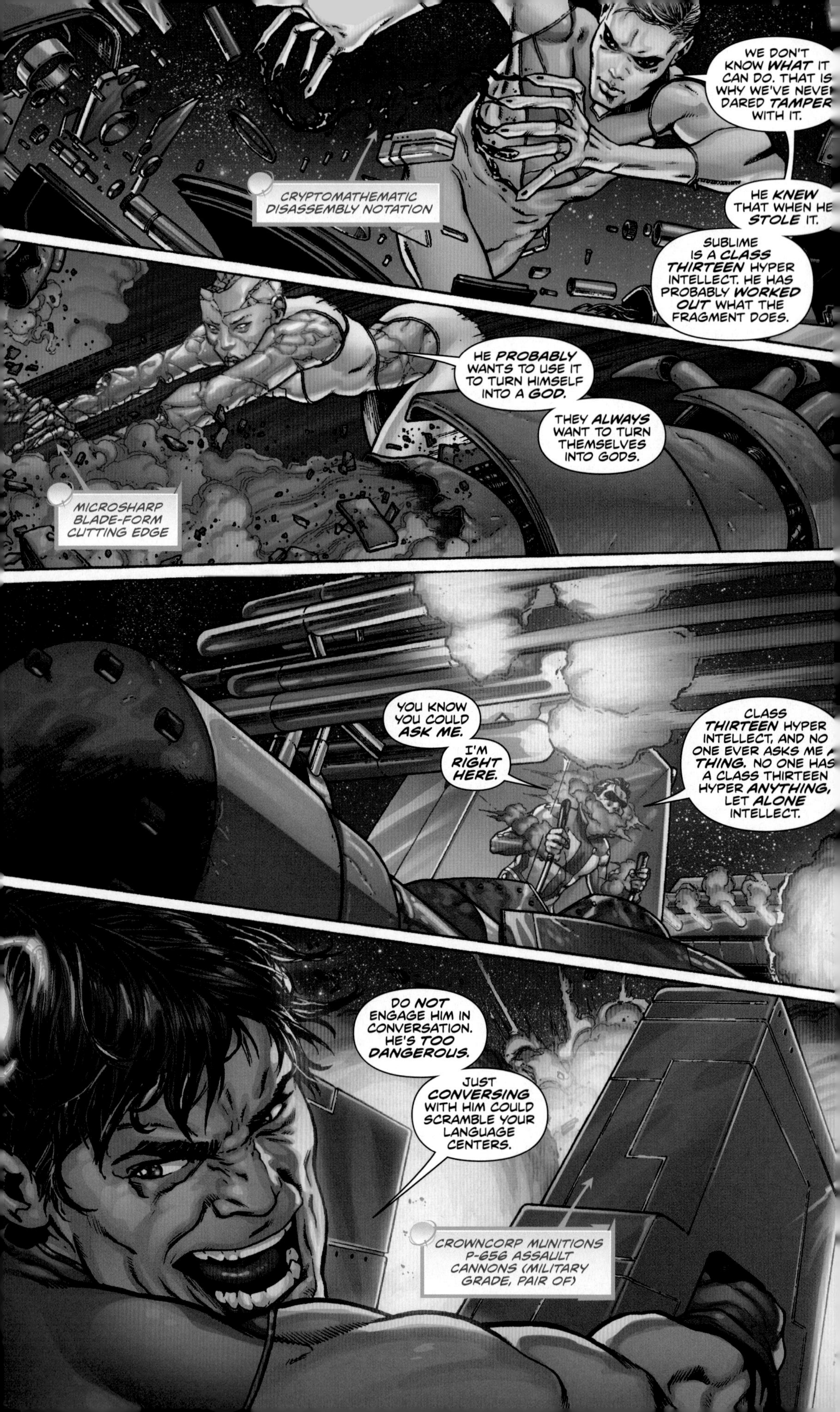

WE DON'T KNOW WHAT IT CAN DO. THAT IS WHY WE'VE NEVER DARED TAMPER WITH IT.
CRYPTOMATHEMATIC DISASSEMBLY NOTATION
HE KNEW THAT WHEN HE STOLE IT.
SUBLIME IS A CLASS THIRTEEN HYPER INTELLECT. HE HAS PROBABLY WORKED OUT WHAT THE FRAGMENT DOES.
HE PROBABLY WANTS TO USE IT TO TURN HIMSELF INTO A GOD.
THEY ALWAYS WANT TO TURN THEMSELVES INTO GODS.
MICROSHARP BLADE-FORM CUTTING EDGE
YOU KNOW YOU COULD ASK ME.
I'M RIGHT HERE.
CLASS THIRTEEN HYPER INTELLECT, AND NO ONE EVER ASKS ME A THING. NO ONE HAS A CLASS THIRTEEN HYPER ANYTHING, LET ALONE INTELLECT.
DO NOT ENGAGE HIM IN CONVERSATION. HE'S TOO DANGEROUS.
JUST CONVERSING WITH HIM COULD SCRAMBLE YOUR LANGUAGE CENTERS.
CROWNCORP MUNITIONS P-656 ASSAULT CANNONS (MILITARY GRADE, PAIR OF)

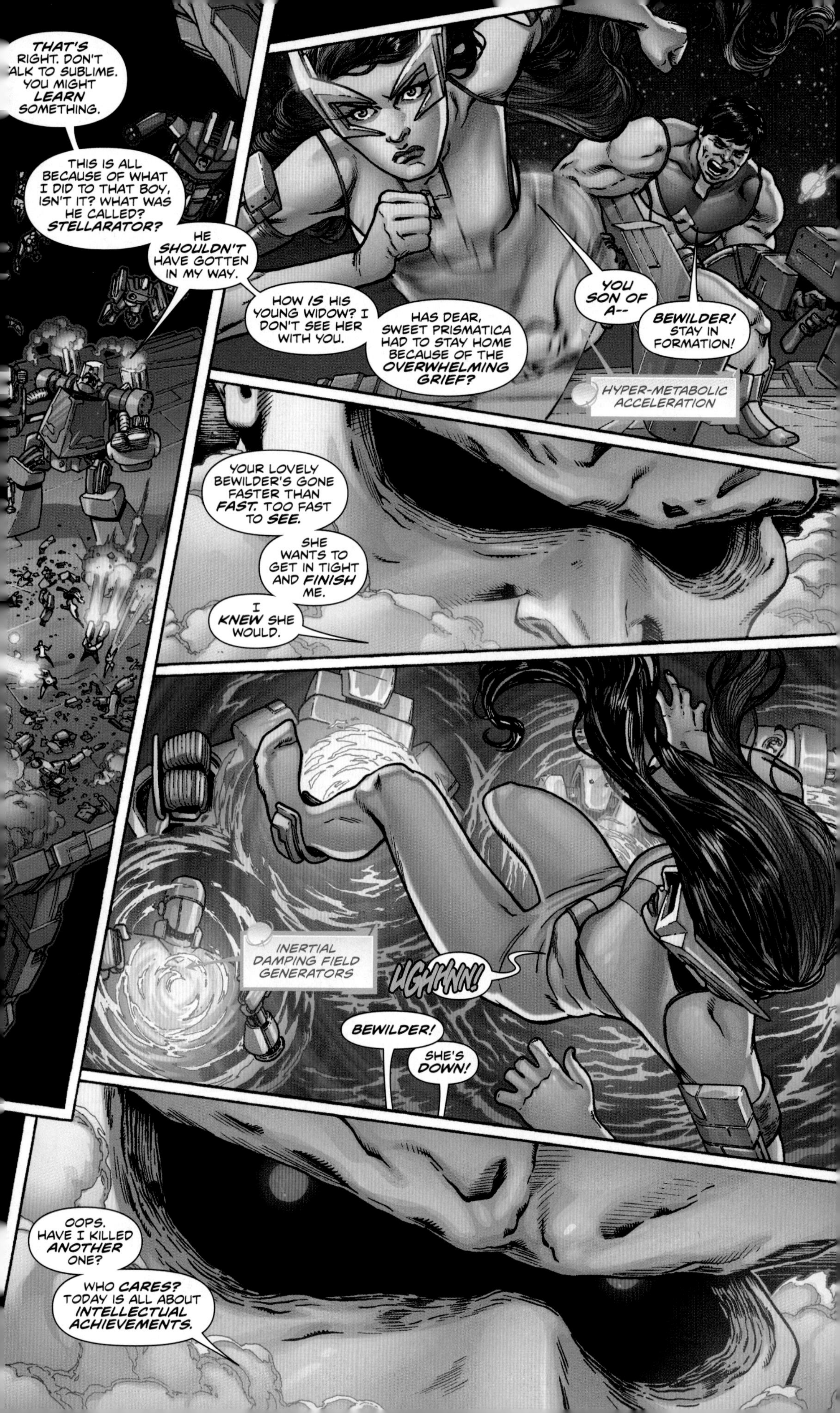
THAT'S RIGHT. DON'T TALK TO SUBLIME. YOU MIGHT LEARN SOMETHING.
THIS IS ALL BECAUSE OF WHAT I DID TO THAT BOY, ISN'T IT? WHAT WAS HE CALLED? STELLARATOR?
HE SHOULDN'T HAVE GOTTEN IN MY WAY.
HOW IS HIS YOUNG WIDOW? I DON'T SEE HER WITH YOU.
HAS DEAR, SWEET PRISMATICA HAD TO STAY HOME BECAUSE OF THE OVERWHELMING GRIEF?
YOU SON OF A--
BEWILDER! STAY IN FORMATION!
HYPER-METABOLIC ACCELERATION
YOUR LOVELY BEWILDER'S GONE FASTER THAN FAST. TOO FAST TO SEE.
SHE WANTS TO GET IN TIGHT AND FINISH ME.
I KNEW SHE WOULD.
INERTIAL DAMPING FIELD GENERATORS
UGHHNN!
BEWILDER!
SHE'S DOWN!
OOPS. HAVE I KILLED ANOTHER ONE?
WHO CARES? TODAY IS ALL ABOUT INTELLECTUAL ACHIEVEMENTS.

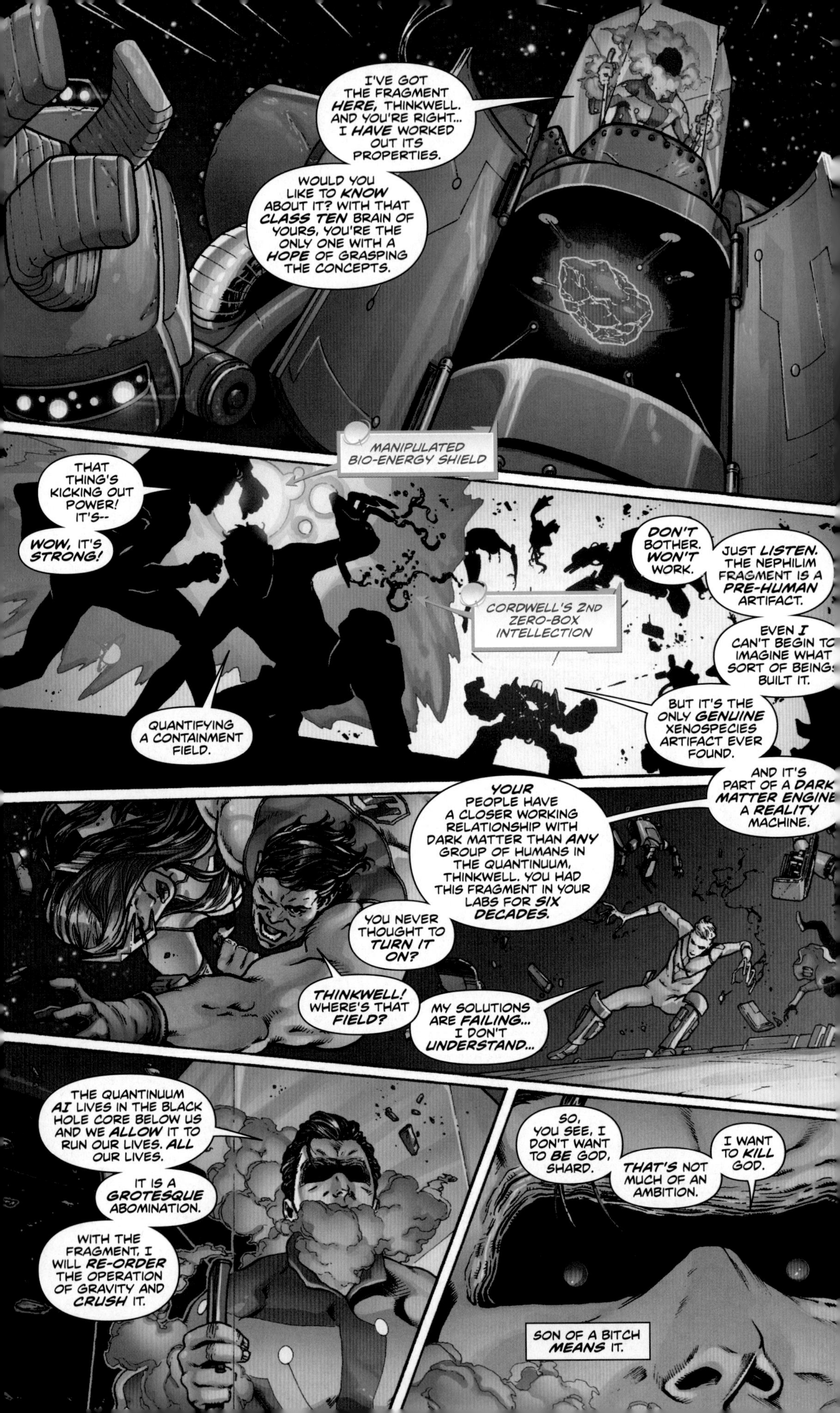

I'VE GOT THE FRAGMENT HERE, THINKWELL. AND YOU'RE RIGHT... I HAVE WORKED OUT ITS PROPERTIES.
WOULD YOU LIKE TO KNOW ABOUT IT? WITH THAT CLASS TEN BRAIN OF YOURS, YOU'RE THE ONLY ONE WITH A HOPE OF GRASPING THE CONCEPTS.
MANIPULATED BIO-ENERGY SHIELD
THAT THING'S KICKING OUT POWER! IT'S--
WOW, IT'S STRONG!
CORDWELL'S 2ND ZERO-BOX INTELLECTION
QUANTIFYING A CONTAINMENT FIELD.
DON'T BOTHER. WON'T WORK.
JUST LISTEN. THE NEPHILIM FRAGMENT IS A PRE-HUMAN ARTIFACT.
EVEN I CAN'T BEGIN TO IMAGINE WHAT SORT OF BEING BUILT IT.
BUT IT'S THE ONLY GENUINE XENOSPECIES ARTIFACT EVER FOUND.
AND IT'S PART OF A DARK MATTER ENGINE. A REALITY MACHINE.
YOUR PEOPLE HAVE A CLOSER WORKING RELATIONSHIP WITH DARK MATTER THAN ANY GROUP OF HUMANS IN THE QUANTINUUM, THINKWELL. YOU HAD THIS FRAGMENT IN YOUR LABS FOR SIX DECADES.
YOU NEVER THOUGHT TO TURN IT ON?
THINKWELL! WHERE'S THAT FIELD?
MY SOLUTIONS ARE FAILING... I DON'T UNDERSTAND...
THE QUANTINUUM AI LIVES IN THE BLACK HOLE CORE BELOW US AND WE ALLOW IT TO RUN OUR LIVES. ALL OUR LIVES.
IT IS A GROTESQUE ABOMINATION.
WITH THE FRAGMENT, I WILL RE-ORDER THE OPERATION OF GRAVITY AND CRUSH IT.
SO, YOU SEE, I DON'T WANT TO BE GOD, SHARD.
THAT'S NOT MUCH OF AN AMBITION.
I WANT TO KILL GOD.
SON OF A BITCH MEANS IT.

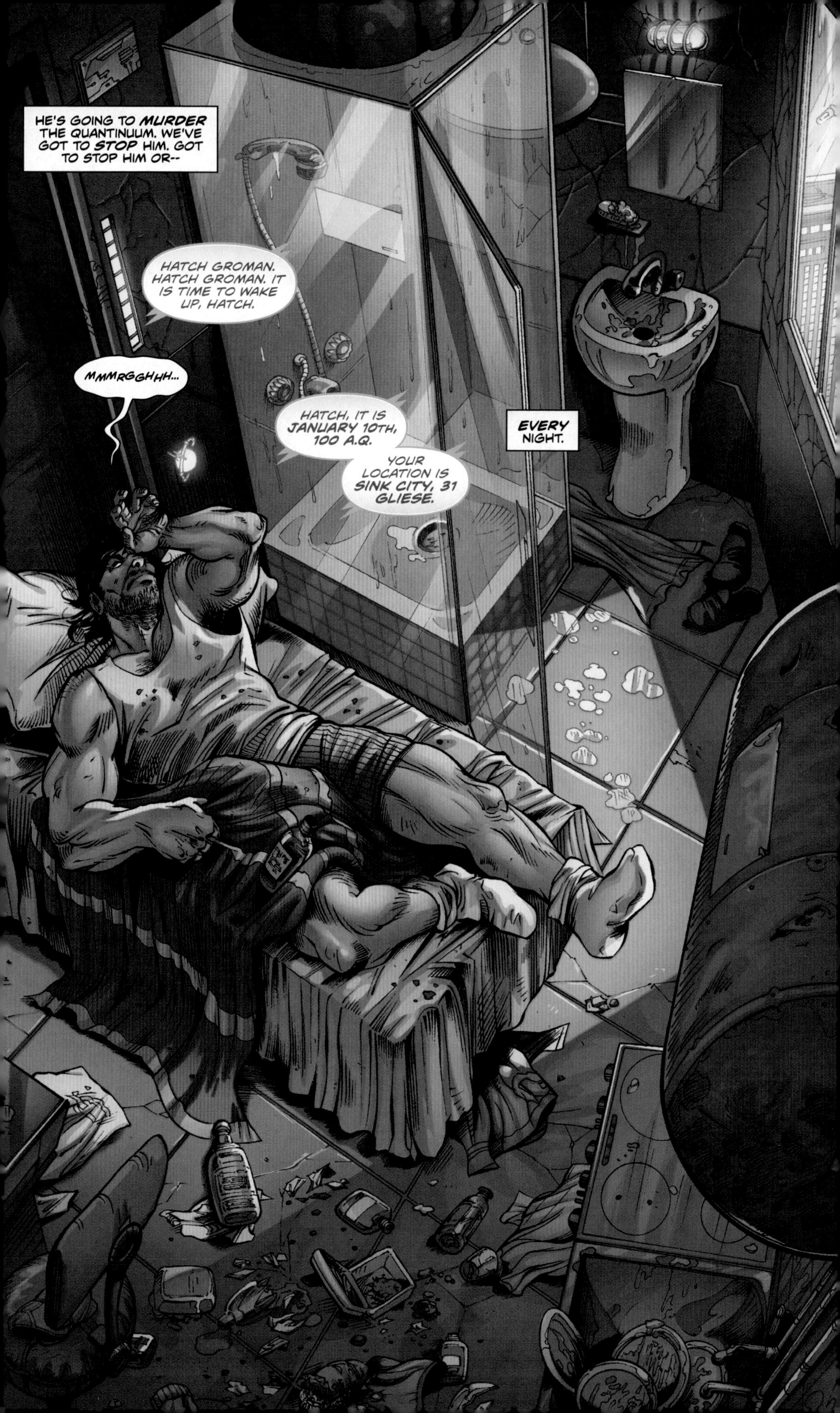
HE'S GOING TO MURDER THE QUANTINUUM. WE'VE GOT TO STOP HIM. GOT TO STOP HIM OR--
HATCH GROMAN. HATCH GROMAN. IT IS TIME TO WAKE UP, HATCH.
MMMRGGHHH...
HATCH, IT IS JANUARY 10TH, 100 A.Q.
YOUR LOCATION IS SINK CITY, 31 GLIESE.
EVERY NIGHT.

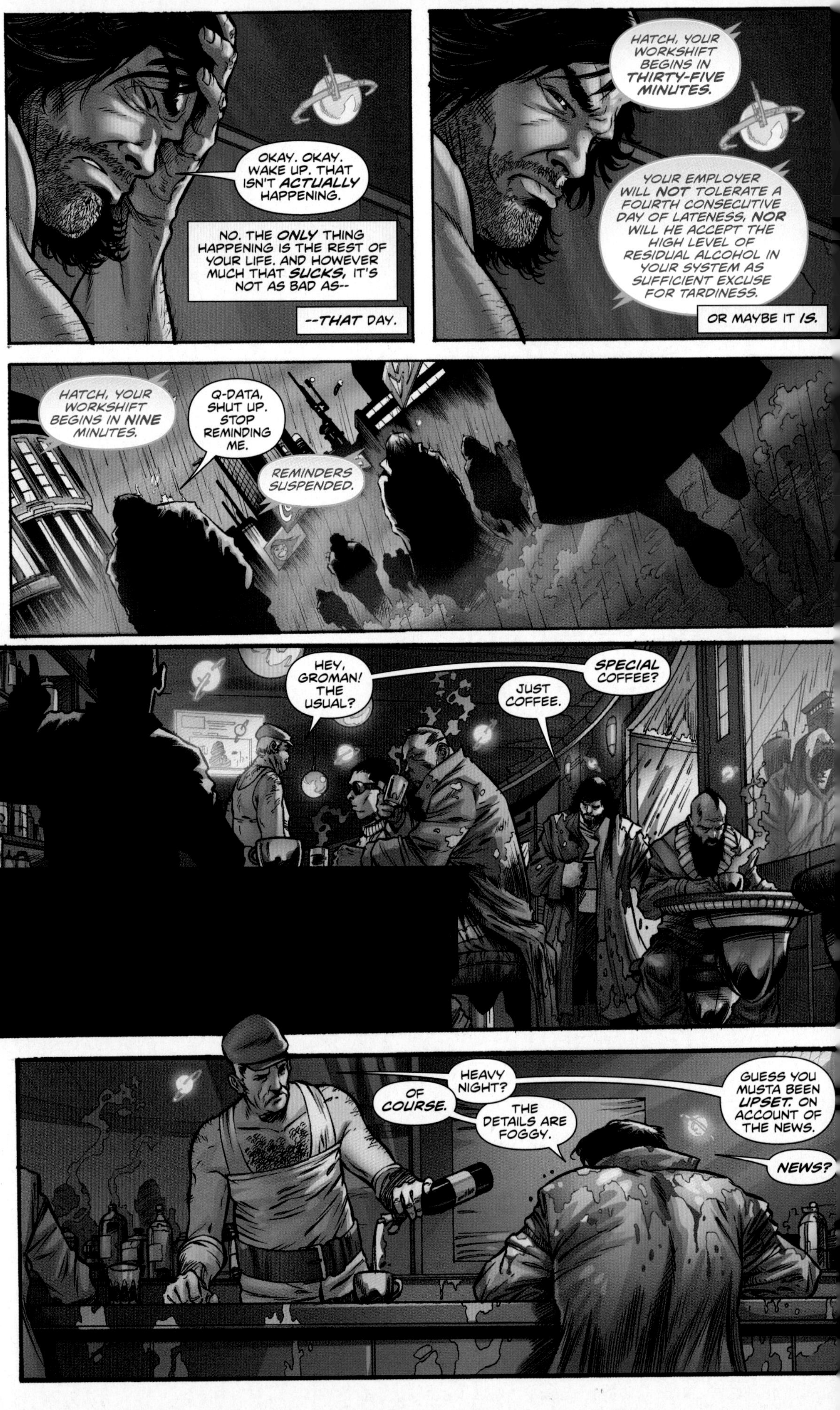
OKAY. OKAY. WAKE UP. THAT ISN'T ACTUALLY HAPPENING.
NO. THE ONLY THING HAPPENING IS THE REST OF YOUR LIFE. AND HOWEVER MUCH THAT SUCKS, IT'S NOT AS BAD AS--
--THAT DAY.
HATCH, YOUR WORKSHIFT BEGINS IN THIRTY-FIVE MINUTES.
YOUR EMPLOYER WILL NOT TOLERATE A FOURTH CONSECUTIVE DAY OF LATENESS, NOR WILL HE ACCEPT THE HIGH LEVEL OF RESIDUAL ALCOHOL IN YOUR SYSTEM AS SUFFICIENT EXCUSE FOR TARDINESS.
OR MAYBE IT IS.
HATCH, YOUR WORKSHIFT BEGINS IN NINE MINUTES.
Q-DATA, SHUT UP. STOP REMINDING ME.
REMINDERS SUSPENDED.
HEY, GROMAN! THE USUAL?
SPECIAL COFFEE?
JUST COFFEE.
HEAVY NIGHT?
OF COURSE.
THE DETAILS ARE FOGGY.
GUESS YOU MUSTA BEEN UPSET. ON ACCOUNT OF THE NEWS.
NEWS?

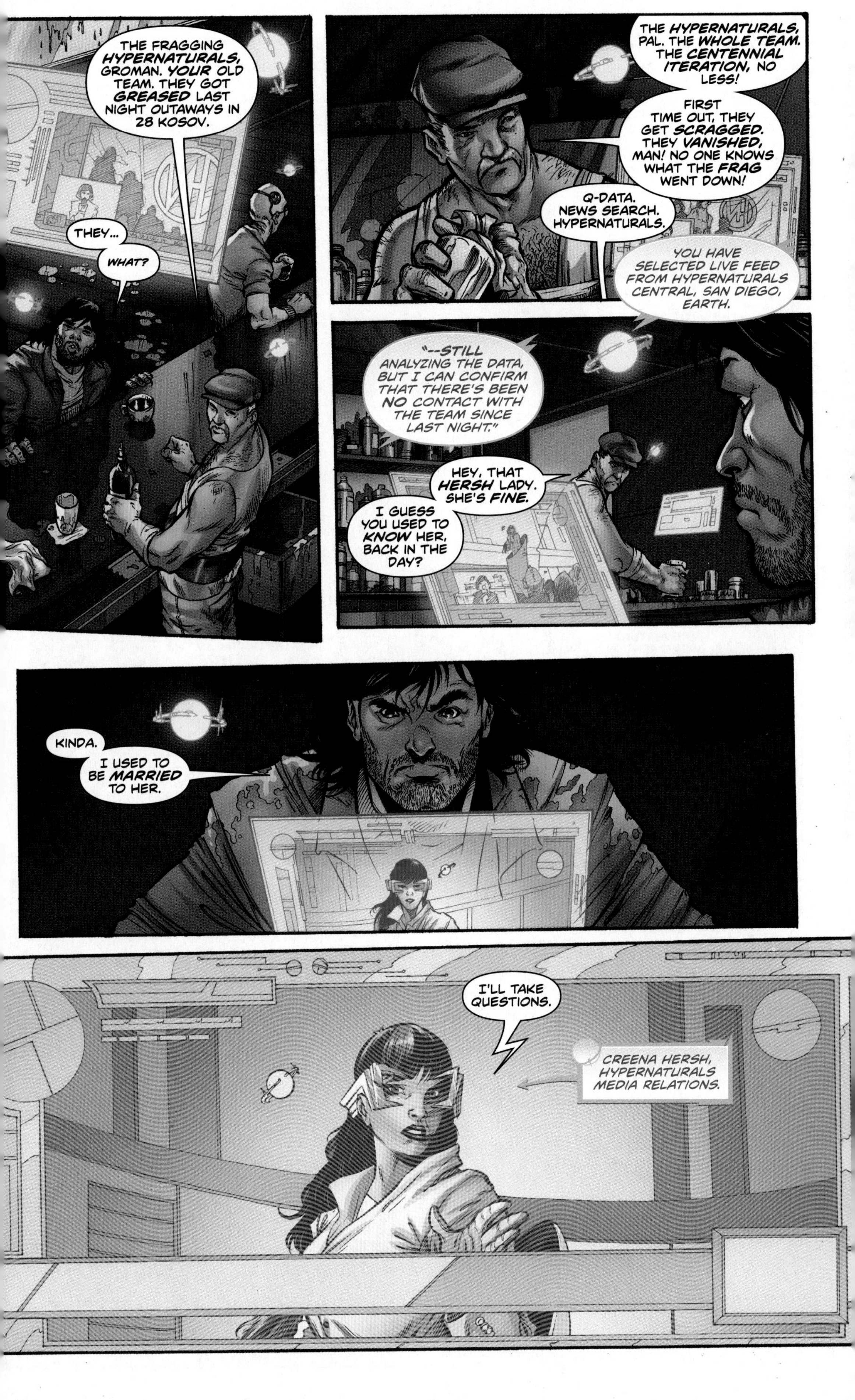
THE FRAGGING HYPERNATURALS, GROMAN. YOUR OLD TEAM. THEY GOT GREASED LAST NIGHT OUTAWAYS IN 28 KOSOV.
THEY...
WHAT?
THE HYPERNATURALS, PAL. THE WHOLE TEAM. THE CENTENNIAL ITERATION, NO LESS!
FIRST TIME OUT, THEY GET SCRAGGED. THEY VANISHED, MAN! NO ONE KNOWS WHAT THE FRAG WENT DOWN!
Q-DATA. NEWS SEARCH. HYPERNATURALS.
YOU HAVE SELECTED LIVE FEED FROM HYPERNATURALS CENTRAL, SAN DIEGO, EARTH.
"--STILL ANALYZING THE DATA, BUT I CAN CONFIRM THAT THERE'S BEEN NO CONTACT WITH THE TEAM SINCE LAST NIGHT."
HEY, THAT HERSH LADY. SHE'S FINE.
I GUESS YOU USED TO KNOW HER, BACK IN THE DAY?
KINDA.
I USED TO BE MARRIED TO HER.
I'LL TAKE QUESTIONS.
CREENA HERSH, HYPERNATURALS MEDIA RELATIONS.

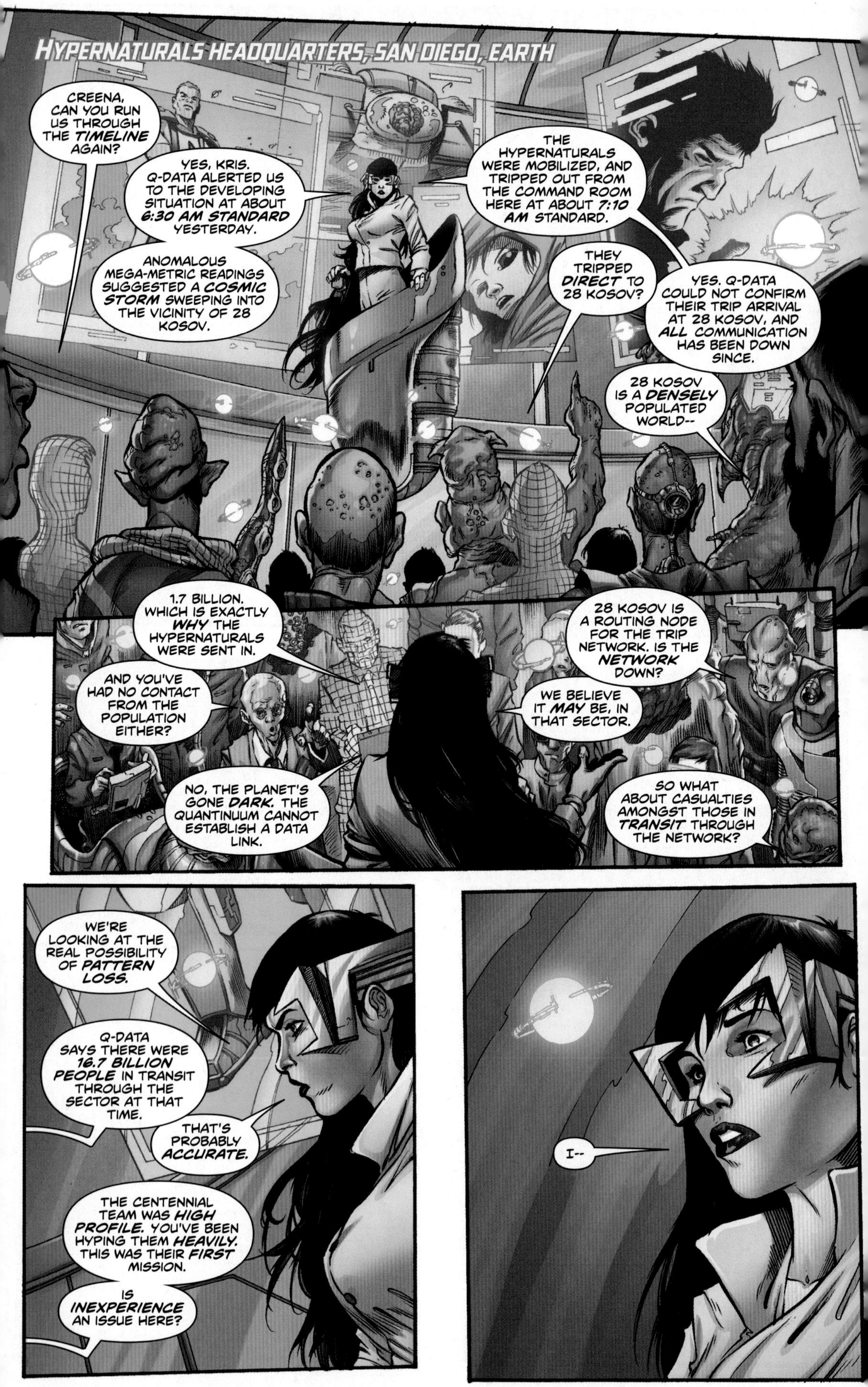
HYPERNATURALS HEADQUARTERS, SAN DIEGO, EARTH
CREENA, CAN YOU RUN US THROUGH THE TIMELINE AGAIN?
YES, KRIS. Q-DATA ALERTED US TO THE DEVELOPING SITUATION AT ABOUT 6:30 AM STANDARD YESTERDAY.
ANOMALOUS MEGA-METRIC READINGS SUGGESTED A COSMIC STORM SWEEPING INTO THE VICINITY OF 28 KOSOV.
THE HYPERNATURALS WERE MOBILIZED, AND TRIPPED OUT FROM THE COMMAND ROOM HERE AT ABOUT 7:10 AM STANDARD.
THEY TRIPPED DIRECT TO 28 KOSOV?
YES. Q-DATA COULD NOT CONFIRM THEIR TRIP ARRIVAL AT 28 KOSOV, AND ALL COMMUNICATION HAS BEEN DOWN SINCE.
28 KOSOV IS A DENSELY POPULATED WORLD--
1.7 BILLION. WHICH IS EXACTLY WHY THE HYPERNATURALS WERE SENT IN.
AND YOU'VE HAD NO CONTACT FROM THE POPULATION EITHER?
NO, THE PLANET'S GONE DARK. THE QUANTINUUM CANNOT ESTABLISH A DATA LINK.
28 KOSOV IS A ROUTING NODE FOR THE TRIP NETWORK. IS THE NETWORK DOWN?
WE BELIEVE IT MAY BE, IN THAT SECTOR.
SO WHAT ABOUT CASUALTIES AMONGST THOSE IN TRANSIT THROUGH THE NETWORK?
WE'RE LOOKING AT THE REAL POSSIBILITY OF PATTERN LOSS.
Q-DATA SAYS THERE WERE 16.7 BILLION PEOPLE IN TRANSIT THROUGH THE SECTOR AT THAT TIME.
THAT'S PROBABLY ACCURATE.
THE CENTENNIAL TEAM WAS HIGH PROFILE. YOU'VE BEEN HYPING THEM HEAVILY. THIS WAS THEIR FIRST MISSION.
IS INEXPERIENCE AN ISSUE HERE?
I--

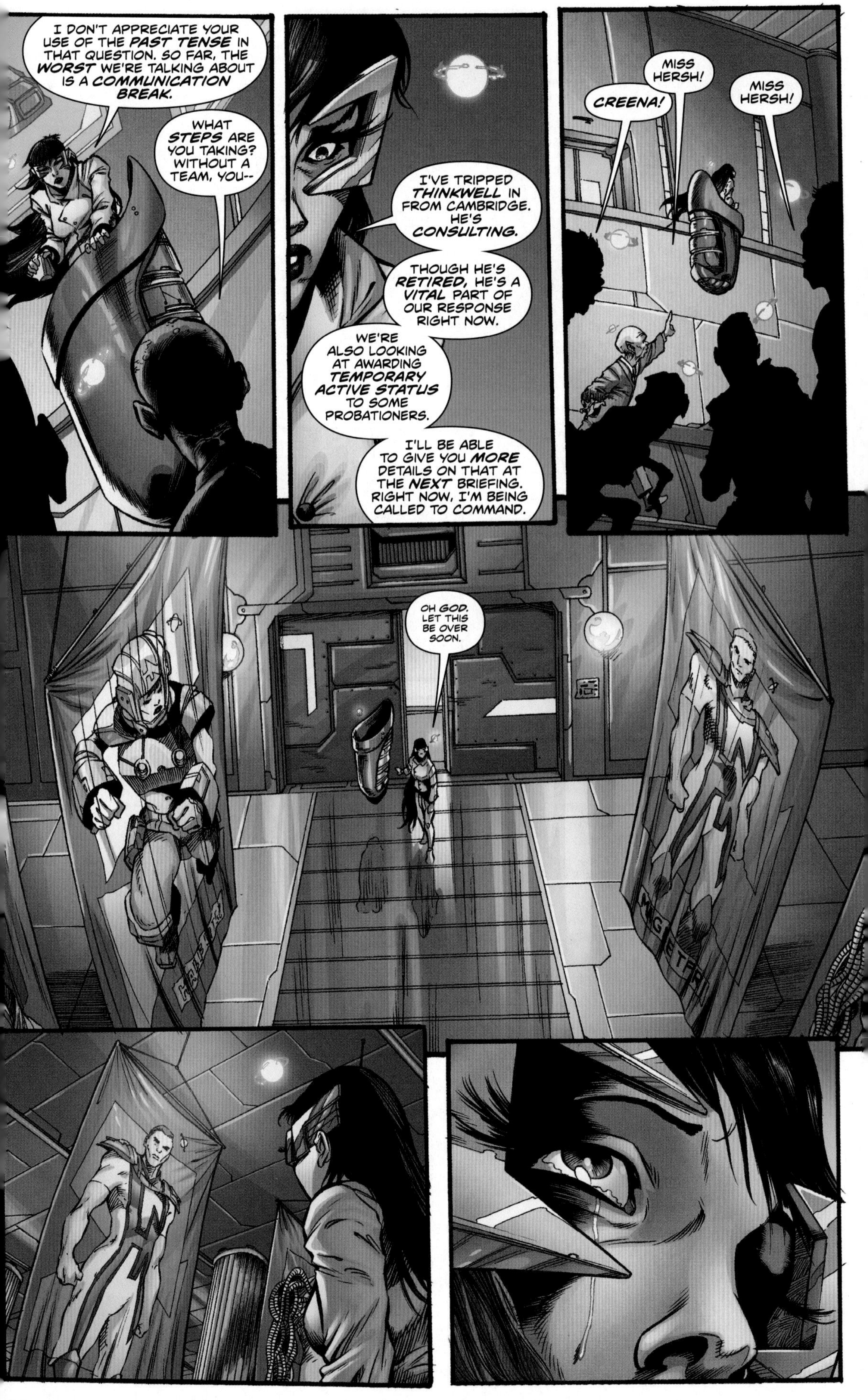
I DON'T APPRECIATE YOUR USE OF THE PAST TENSE IN THAT QUESTION. SO FAR, THE WORST WE'RE TALKING ABOUT IS A COMMUNICATION BREAK.
WHAT STEPS ARE YOU TAKING? WITHOUT A TEAM, YOU--
I'VE TRIPPED THINKWELL IN FROM CAMBRIDGE. HE'S CONSULTING.
THOUGH HE'S RETIRED, HE'S A VITAL PART OF OUR RESPONSE RIGHT NOW.
WE'RE ALSO LOOKING AT AWARDING TEMPORARY ACTIVE STATUS TO SOME PROBATIONERS.
I'LL BE ABLE TO GIVE YOU MORE DETAILS ON THAT AT THE NEXT BRIEFING. RIGHT NOW, I'M BEING CALLED TO COMMAND.
CREENA!
MISS HERSH!
MISS HERSH!
OH GOD. LET THIS BE OVER SOON.

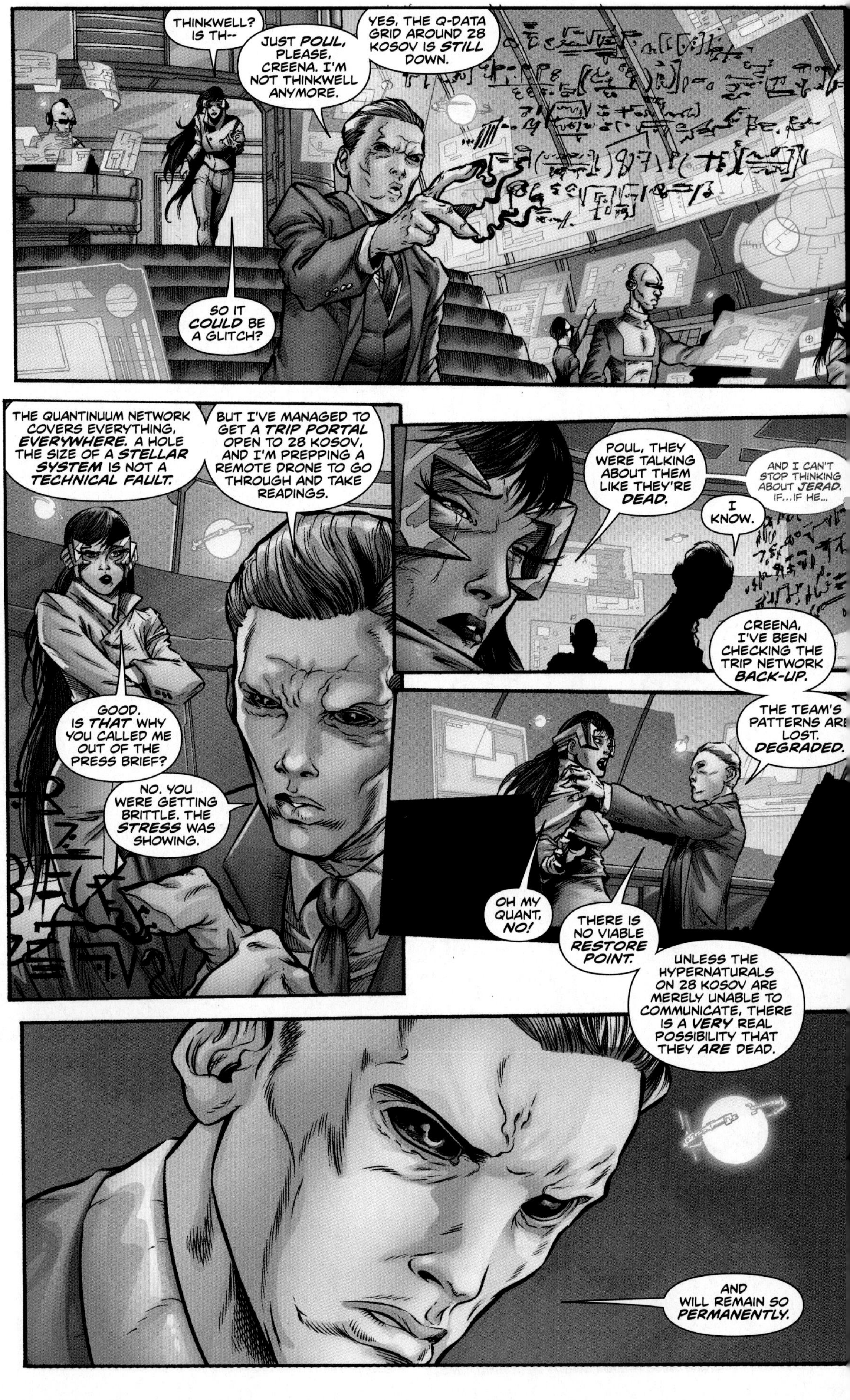
THINKWELL? IS TH--
JUST POUL, PLEASE, CREENA. I'M NOT THINKWELL ANYMORE.
YES, THE Q-DATA GRID AROUND 28 KOSOV IS STILL DOWN.
SO IT COULD BE A GLITCH?
THE QUANTINUUM NETWORK COVERS EVERYTHING, EVERYWHERE. A HOLE THE SIZE OF A STELLAR SYSTEM IS NOT A TECHNICAL FAULT.
BUT I'VE MANAGED TO GET A TRIP PORTAL OPEN TO 28 KOSOV, AND I'M PREPPING A REMOTE DRONE TO GO THROUGH AND TAKE READINGS.
GOOD. IS THAT WHY YOU CALLED ME OUT OF THE PRESS BRIEF?
NO. YOU WERE GETTING BRITTLE. THE STRESS WAS SHOWING.
POUL, THEY WERE TALKING ABOUT THEM LIKE THEY'RE DEAD.
AND I CAN'T STOP THINKING ABOUT JERAD. IF...IF HE...
I KNOW.
CREENA, I'VE BEEN CHECKING THE TRIP NETWORK BACK-UP.
THE TEAM'S PATTERNS ARE LOST. DEGRADED.
OH MY QUANT, NO!
THERE IS NO VIABLE RESTORE POINT.
UNLESS THE HYPERNATURALS ON 28 KOSOV ARE MERELY UNABLE TO COMMUNICATE, THERE IS A VERY REAL POSSIBILITY THAT THEY ARE DEAD.
AND WILL REMAIN SO PERMANENTLY.

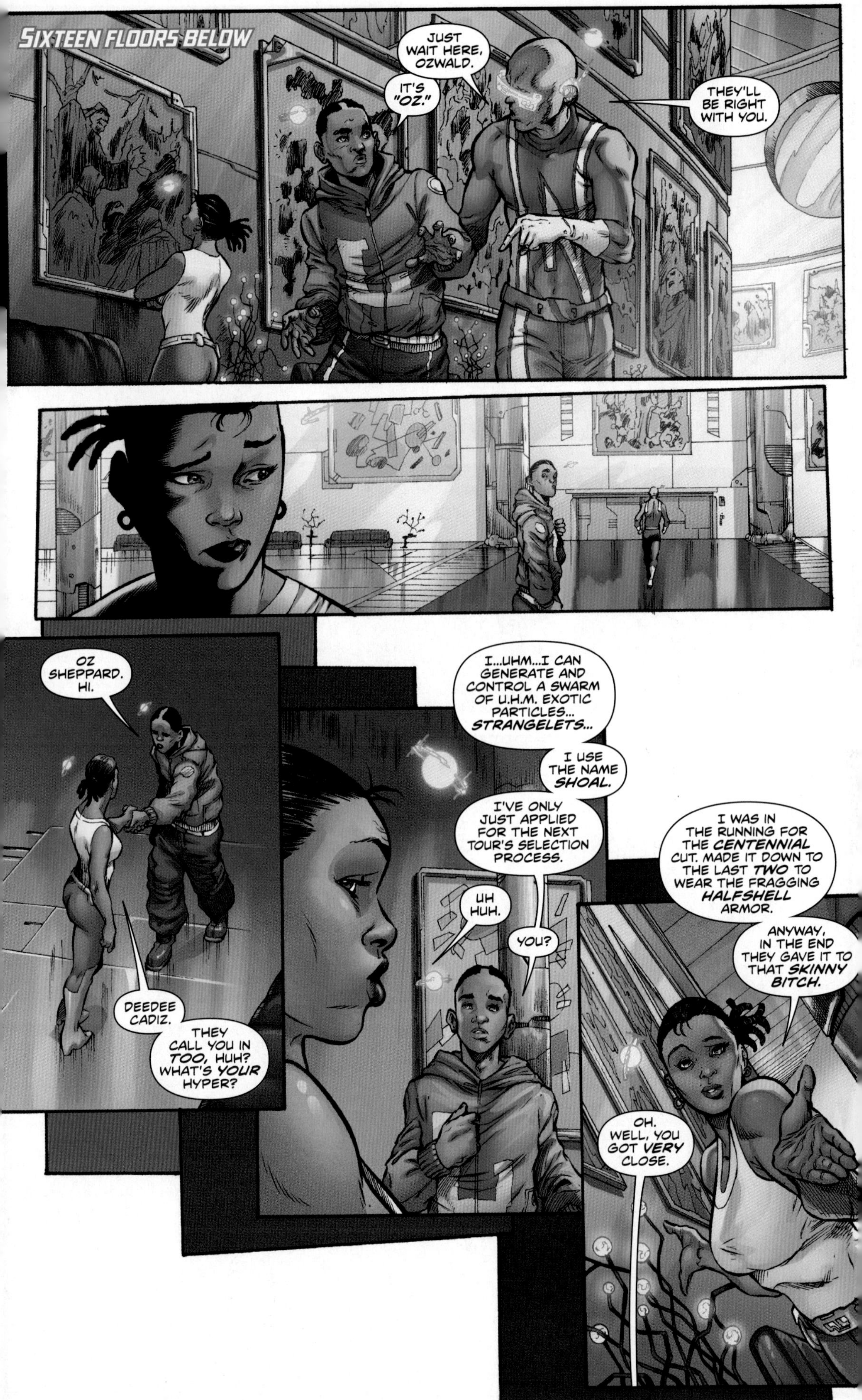
SIXTEEN FLOORS BELOW
JUST WAIT HERE, OZWALD.
IT'S "OZ."
THEY'LL BE RIGHT WITH YOU.
OZ SHEPPARD. HI.
DEEDEE CADIZ.
THEY CALL YOU IN TOO, HUH? WHAT'S YOUR HYPER?
I...UHM...I CAN GENERATE AND CONTROL A SWARM OF U.H.M. EXOTIC PARTICLES... STRANGELETS...
I USE THE NAME SHOAL.
I'VE ONLY JUST APPLIED FOR THE NEXT TOUR'S SELECTION PROCESS.
UH HUH.
YOU?
I WAS IN THE RUNNING FOR THE CENTENNIAL CUT. MADE IT DOWN TO THE LAST TWO TO WEAR THE FRAGGING HALFSHELL ARMOR.
ANYWAY, IN THE END THEY GAVE IT TO THAT SKINNY BITCH.
OH. WELL, YOU GOT VERY CLOSE.

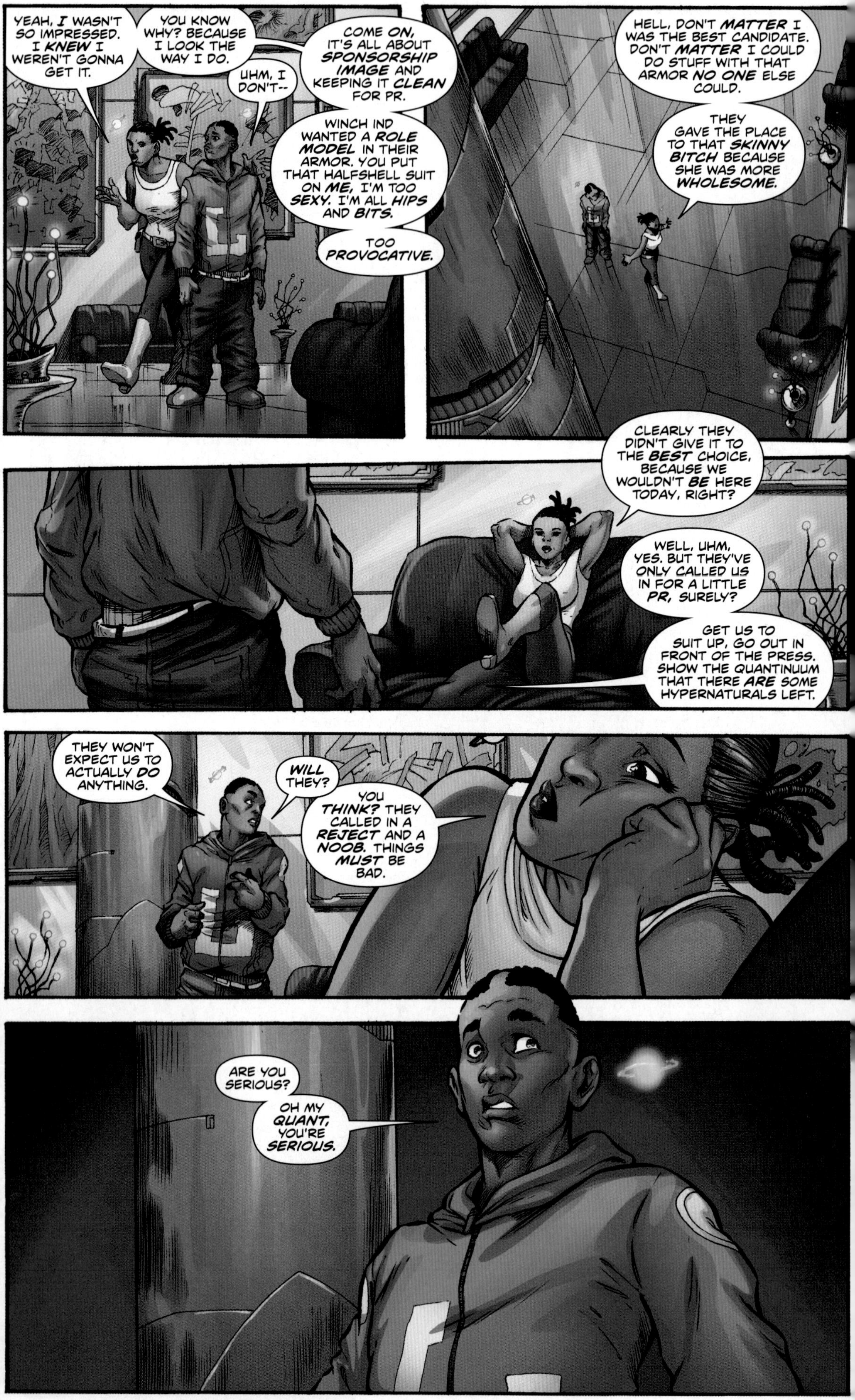
YEAH, I WASN'T SO IMPRESSED. I KNEW I WEREN'T GONNA GET IT.
YOU KNOW WHY? BECAUSE I LOOK THE WAY I DO.
UHM, I DON'T--
COME ON, IT'S ALL ABOUT SPONSORSHIP IMAGE AND KEEPING IT CLEAN FOR PR.
WINCH IND WANTED A ROLE MODEL IN THEIR ARMOR. YOU PUT THAT HALFSHELL SUIT ON ME, I'M TOO SEXY. I'M ALL HIPS AND BITS.
TOO PROVOCATIVE.
HELL, DON'T MATTER I WAS THE BEST CANDIDATE. DON'T MATTER I COULD DO STUFF WITH THAT ARMOR NO ONE ELSE COULD.
THEY GAVE THE PLACE TO THAT SKINNY BITCH BECAUSE SHE WAS MORE WHOLESOME.
CLEARLY THEY DIDN'T GIVE IT TO THE BEST CHOICE, BECAUSE WE WOULDN'T BE HERE TODAY, RIGHT?
WELL, UHM, YES. BUT THEY'VE ONLY CALLED US IN FOR A LITTLE PR, SURELY?
GET US TO SUIT UP, GO OUT IN FRONT OF THE PRESS. SHOW THE QUANTINUUM THAT THERE ARE SOME HYPERNATURALS LEFT.
THEY WON'T EXPECT US TO ACTUALLY DO ANYTHING.
WILL THEY?
YOU THINK? THEY CALLED IN A REJECT AND A NOOB. THINGS MUST BE BAD.
ARE YOU SERIOUS?
OH MY QUANT, YOU'RE SERIOUS.

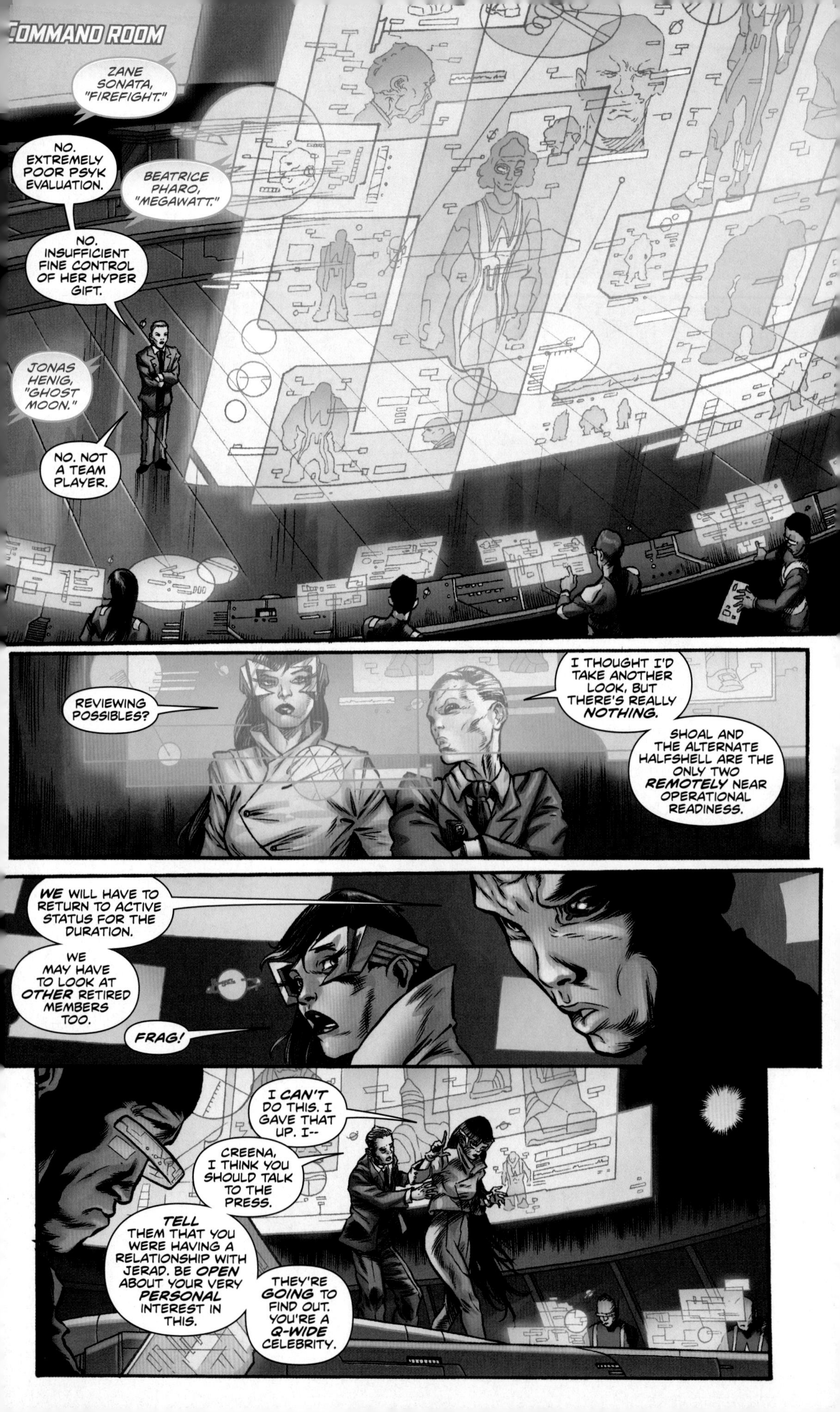
COMMAND ROOM
ZANE SONATA, "FIREFIGHT."
NO. EXTREMELY POOR PSYK EVALUATION.
BEATRICE PHARO, "MEGAWATT."
NO. INSUFFICIENT FINE CONTROL OF HER HYPER GIFT.
JONAS HENIG, "GHOST MOON."
NO. NOT A TEAM PLAYER.
REVIEWING POSSIBLES?
I THOUGHT I'D TAKE ANOTHER LOOK, BUT THERE'S REALLY NOTHING.
SHOAL AND THE ALTERNATE HALFSHELL ARE THE ONLY TWO REMOTELY NEAR OPERATIONAL READINESS.
WE WILL HAVE TO RETURN TO ACTIVE STATUS FOR THE DURATION.
WE MAY HAVE TO LOOK AT OTHER RETIRED MEMBERS TOO.
FRAG!
I CAN'T DO THIS. I GAVE THAT UP. I--
CREENA, I THINK YOU SHOULD TALK TO THE PRESS.
TELL THEM THAT YOU WERE HAVING A RELATIONSHIP WITH JERAD. BE OPEN ABOUT YOUR VERY PERSONAL INTEREST IN THIS.
THEY'RE GOING TO FIND OUT. YOU'RE A Q-WIDE CELEBRITY.

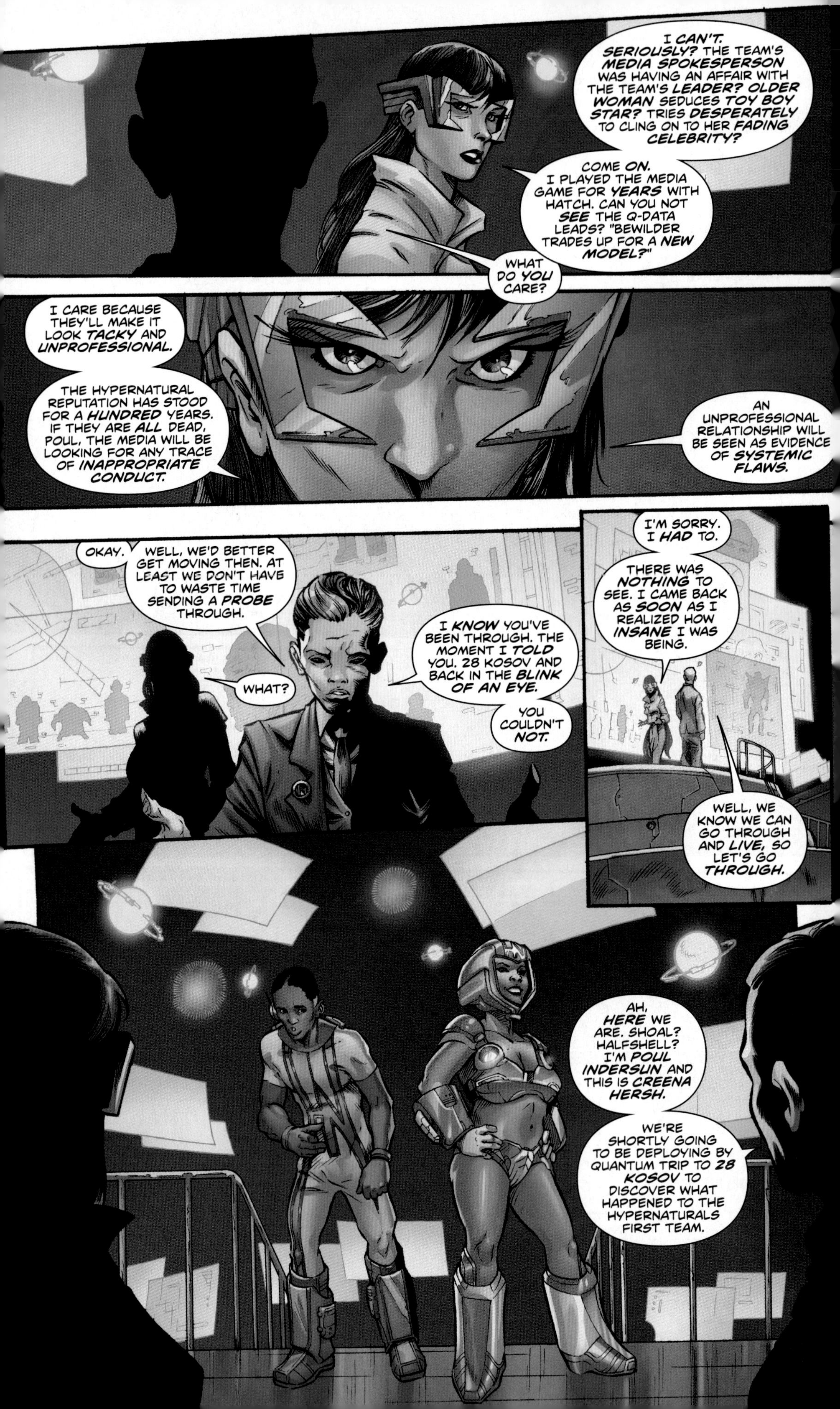

I CAN'T. SERIOUSLY? THE TEAM'S MEDIA SPOKESPERSON WAS HAVING AN AFFAIR WITH THE TEAM'S LEADER? OLDER WOMAN SEDUCES TOY BOY STAR? TRIES DESPERATELY TO CLING ON TO HER FADING CELEBRITY?
COME ON. I PLAYED THE MEDIA GAME FOR YEARS WITH HATCH. CAN YOU NOT SEE THE Q-DATA LEADS? "BEWILDER TRADES UP FOR A NEW MODEL?"
WHAT DO YOU CARE?
I CARE BECAUSE THEY'LL MAKE IT LOOK TACKY AND UNPROFESSIONAL.
THE HYPERNATURAL REPUTATION HAS STOOD FOR A HUNDRED YEARS. IF THEY ARE ALL DEAD, POUL, THE MEDIA WILL BE LOOKING FOR ANY TRACE OF INAPPROPRIATE CONDUCT.
AN UNPROFESSIONAL RELATIONSHIP WILL BE SEEN AS EVIDENCE OF SYSTEMIC FLAWS.
OKAY.
WELL, WE'D BETTER GET MOVING THEN. AT LEAST WE DON'T HAVE TO WASTE TIME SENDING A PROBE THROUGH.
WHAT?
I KNOW YOU'VE BEEN THROUGH. THE MOMENT I TOLD YOU. 28 KOSOV AND BACK IN THE BLINK OF AN EYE.
YOU COULDN'T NOT.
I'M SORRY. I HAD TO.
THERE WAS NOTHING TO SEE. I CAME BACK AS SOON AS I REALIZED HOW INSANE I WAS BEING.
WELL, WE KNOW WE CAN GO THROUGH AND LIVE, SO LET'S GO THROUGH.
AH, HERE WE ARE. SHOAL? HALFSHELL? I'M POUL INDERSUN AND THIS IS CREENA HERSH.
WE'RE SHORTLY GOING TO BE DEPLOYING BY QUANTUM TRIP TO 28 KOSOV TO DISCOVER WHAT HAPPENED TO THE HYPERNATURALS FIRST TEAM.

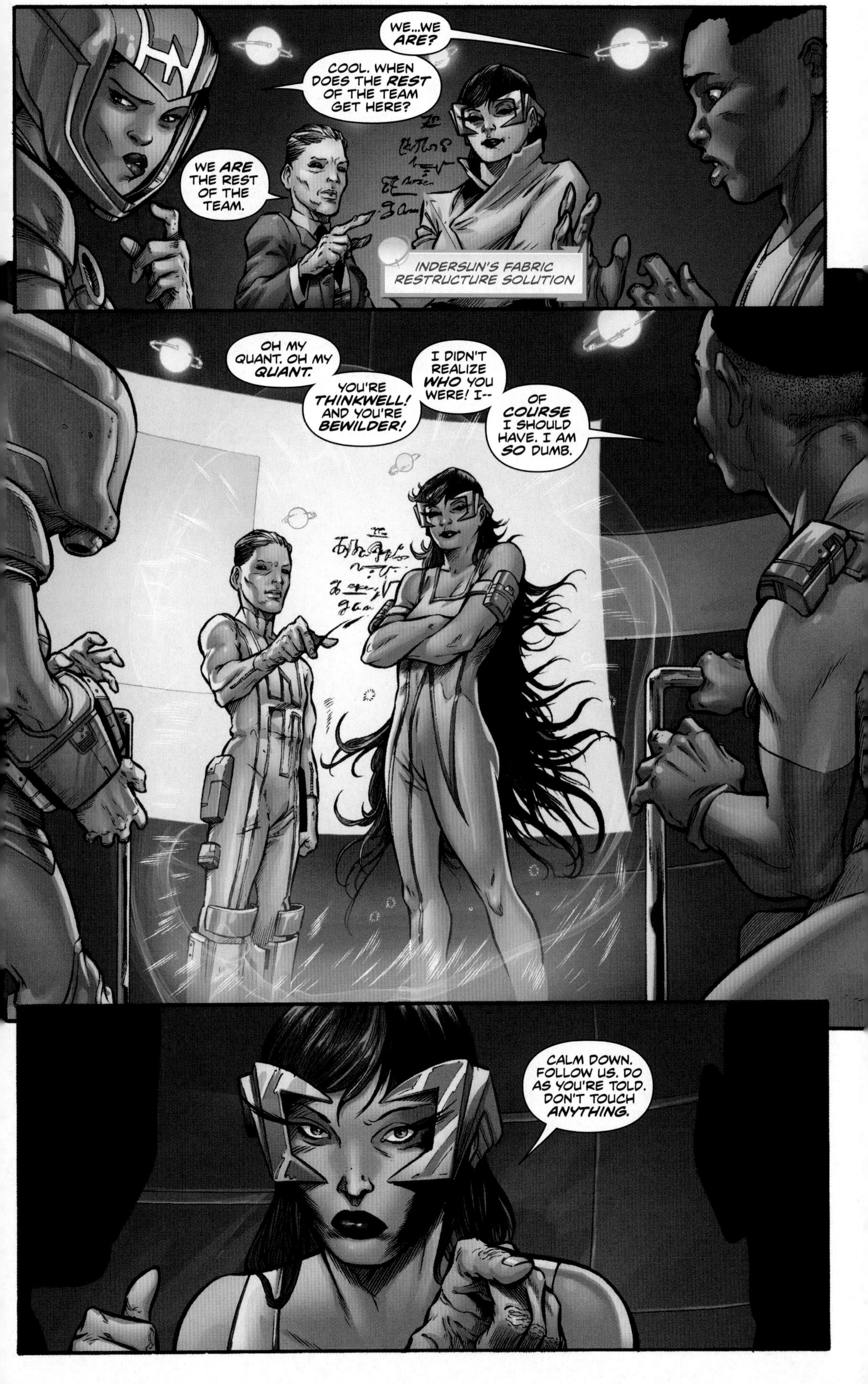
WE...WE ARE?
COOL. WHEN DOES THE REST OF THE TEAM GET HERE?
WE ARE THE REST OF THE TEAM.
INDERSUN'S FABRIC RESTRUCTURE SOLUTION
OH MY QUANT. OH MY QUANT.
YOU'RE THINKWELL! AND YOU'RE BEWILDER!
I DIDN'T REALIZE WHO YOU WERE! I--
OF COURSE I SHOULD HAVE. I AM SO DUMB.
CALM DOWN. FOLLOW US. DO AS YOU'RE TOLD. DON'T TOUCH ANYTHING.

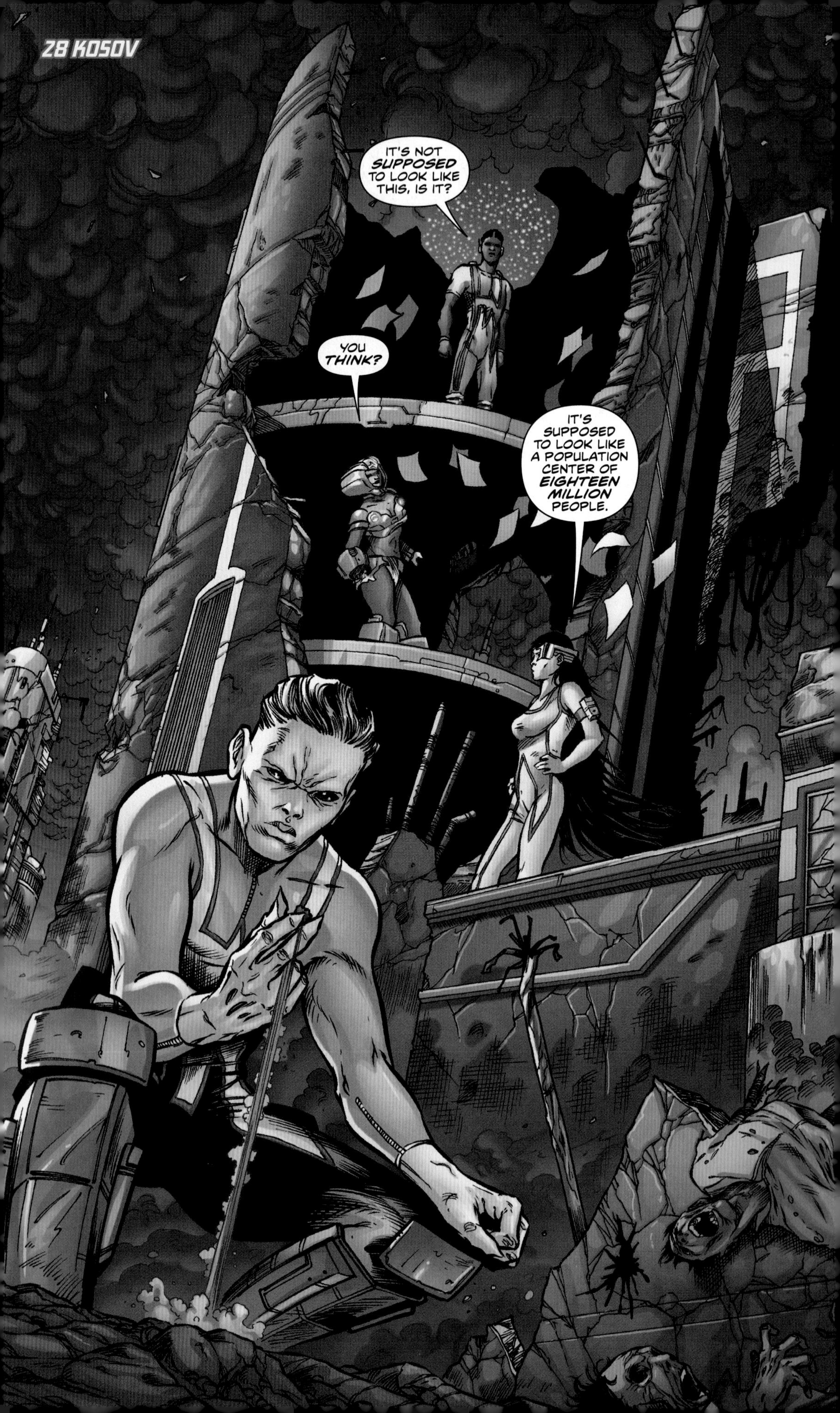
IT'S NOT SUPPOSED TO LOOK LIKE THIS, IS IT?
YOU THINK?
IT'S SUPPOSED TO LOOK LIKE A POPULATION CENTER OF EIGHTEEN MILLION PEOPLE.

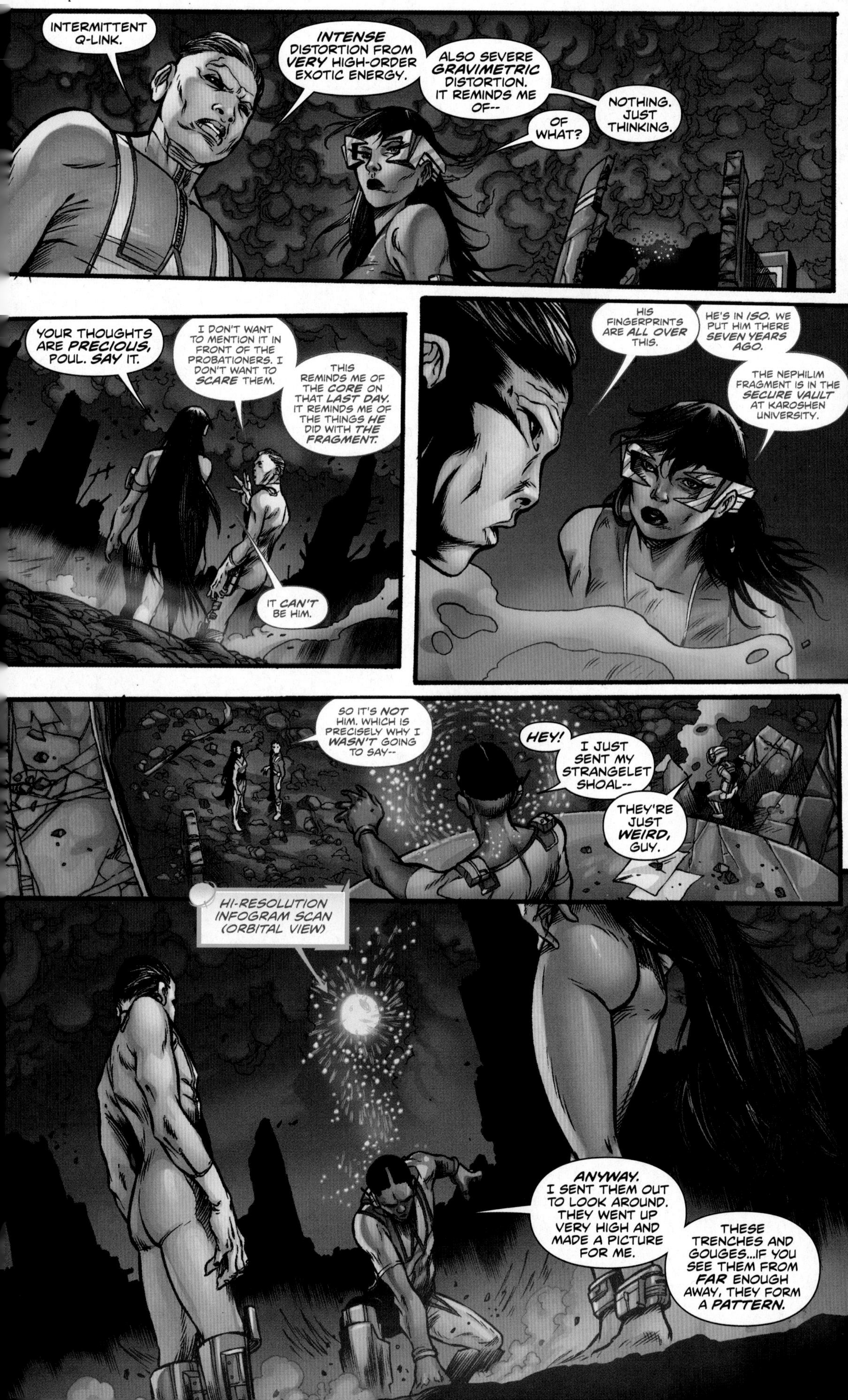
INTERMITTENT Q-LINK.
INTENSE DISTORTION FROM VERY HIGH-ORDER EXOTIC ENERGY.
ALSO SEVERE GRAVIMETRIC DISTORTION. IT REMINDS ME OF--
OF WHAT?
NOTHING. JUST THINKING.
YOUR THOUGHTS ARE PRECIOUS, POUL. SAY IT.
I DON'T WANT TO MENTION IT IN FRONT OF THE PROBATIONERS. I DON'T WANT TO SCARE THEM.
THIS REMINDS ME OF THE CORE ON THAT LAST DAY. IT REMINDS ME OF THE THINGS HE DID WITH THE FRAGMENT.
IT CAN'T BE HIM.
HIS FINGERPRINTS ARE ALL OVER THIS.
HE'S IN ISO. WE PUT HIM THERE SEVEN YEARS AGO.
THE NEPHILIM FRAGMENT IS IN THE SECURE VAULT AT KAROSHEN UNIVERSITY.
SO IT'S NOT HIM. WHICH IS PRECISELY WHY I WASN'T GOING TO SAY--
HEY! I JUST SENT MY STRANGELET SHOAL--
THEY'RE JUST WEIRD, GUY.
HI-RESOLUTION INFOGRAM SCAN (ORBITAL VIEW)
ANYWAY. I SENT THEM OUT TO LOOK AROUND. THEY WENT UP VERY HIGH AND MADE A PICTURE FOR ME.
THESE TRENCHES AND GOUGES...IF YOU SEE THEM FROM FAR ENOUGH AWAY, THEY FORM A PATTERN.

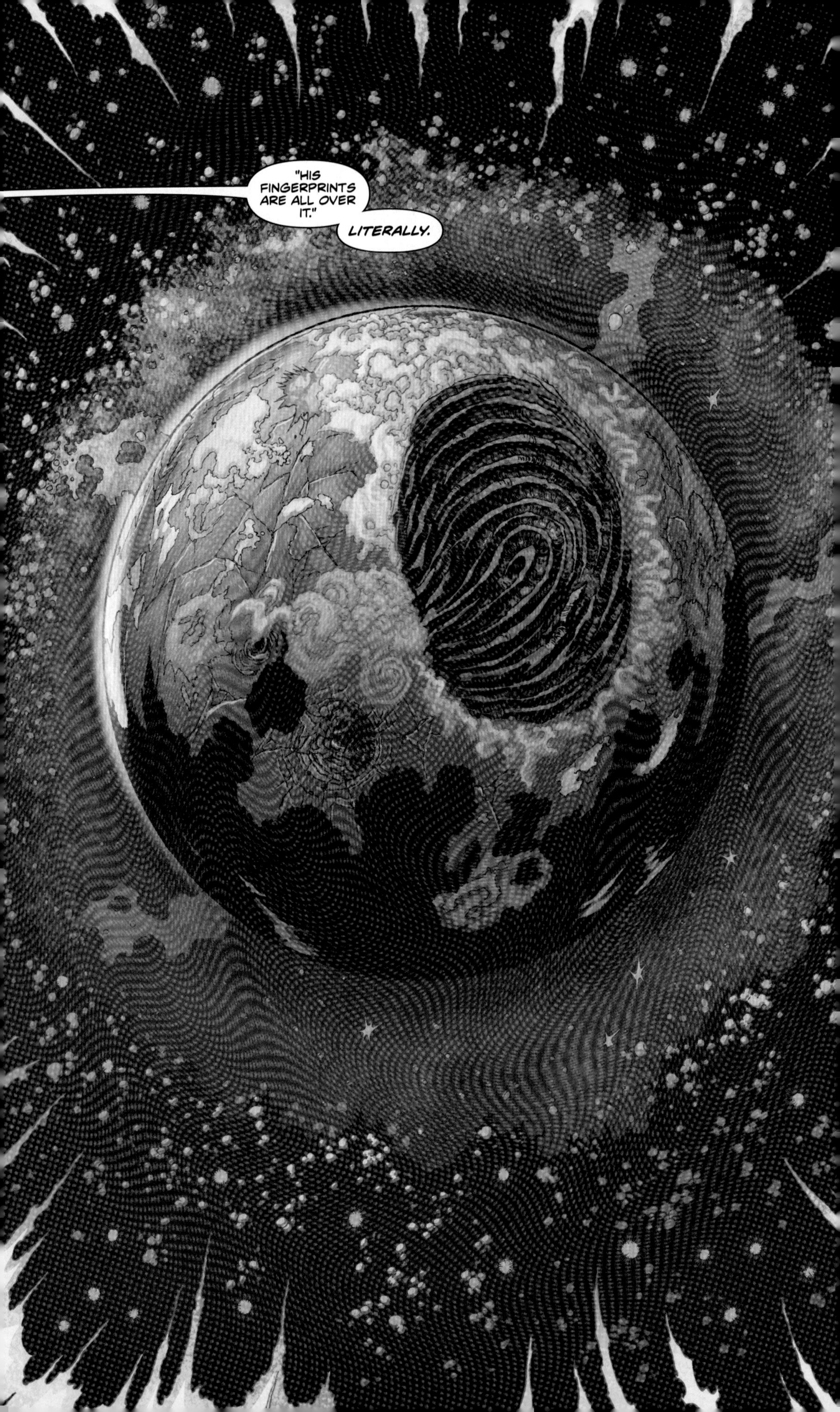
"HIS FINGERPRINTS ARE ALL OVER IT."
LITERALLY.

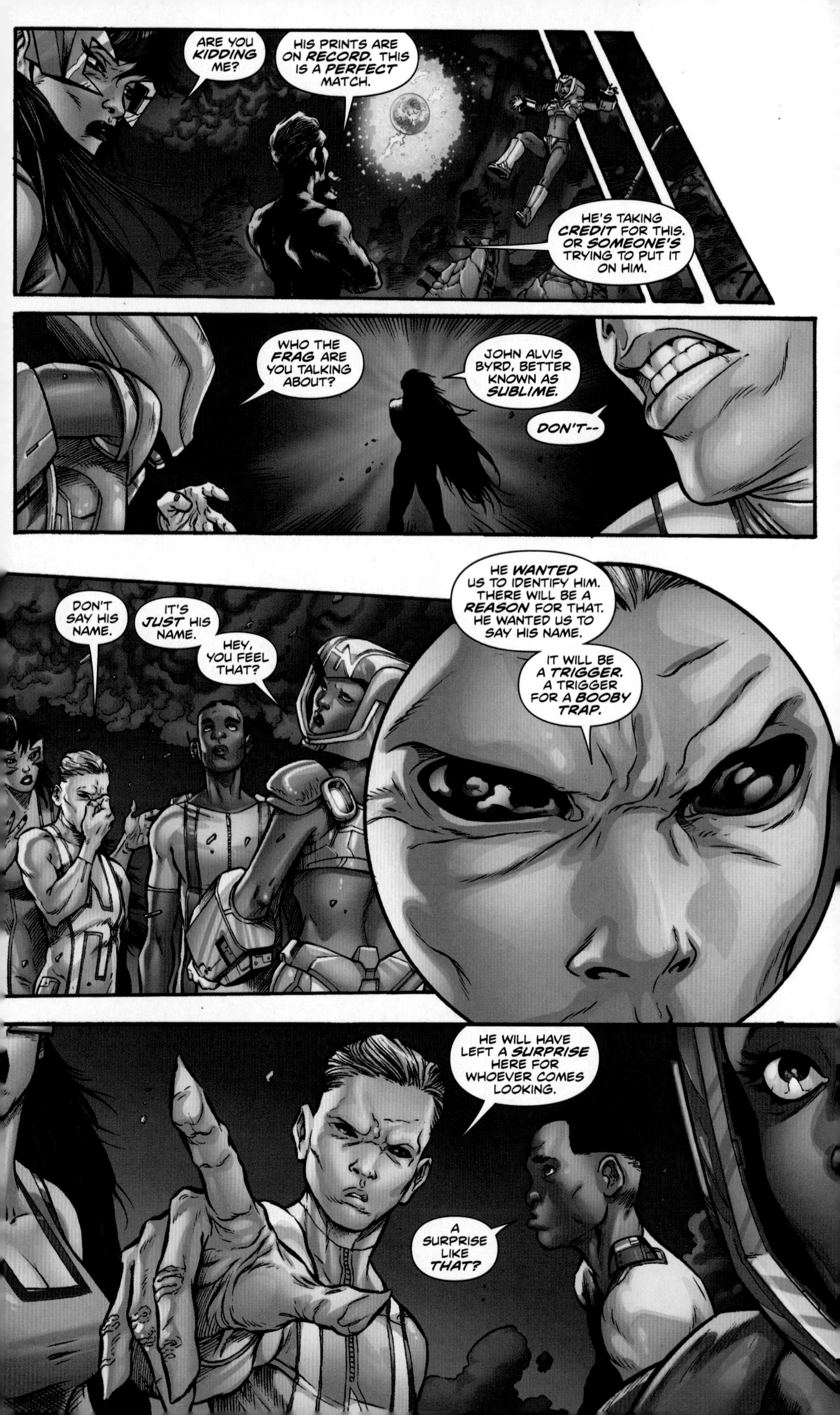
ARE YOU KIDDING ME?
HIS PRINTS ARE ON RECORD. THIS IS A PERFECT MATCH.
HE'S TAKING CREDIT FOR THIS. OR SOMEONE'S TRYING TO PUT IT ON HIM.
WHO THE FRAG ARE YOU TALKING ABOUT?
JOHN ALVIS BYRD, BETTER KNOWN AS SUBLIME.
DON'T--
DON'T SAY HIS NAME.
IT'S JUST HIS NAME.
HEY, YOU FEEL THAT?
HE WANTED US TO IDENTIFY HIM. THERE WILL BE A REASON FOR THAT. HE WANTED US TO SAY HIS NAME.
IT WILL BE A TRIGGER. A TRIGGER FOR A BOOBY TRAP.
HE WILL HAVE LEFT A SURPRISE HERE FOR WHOEVER COMES LOOKING.
A SURPRISE LIKE THAT?

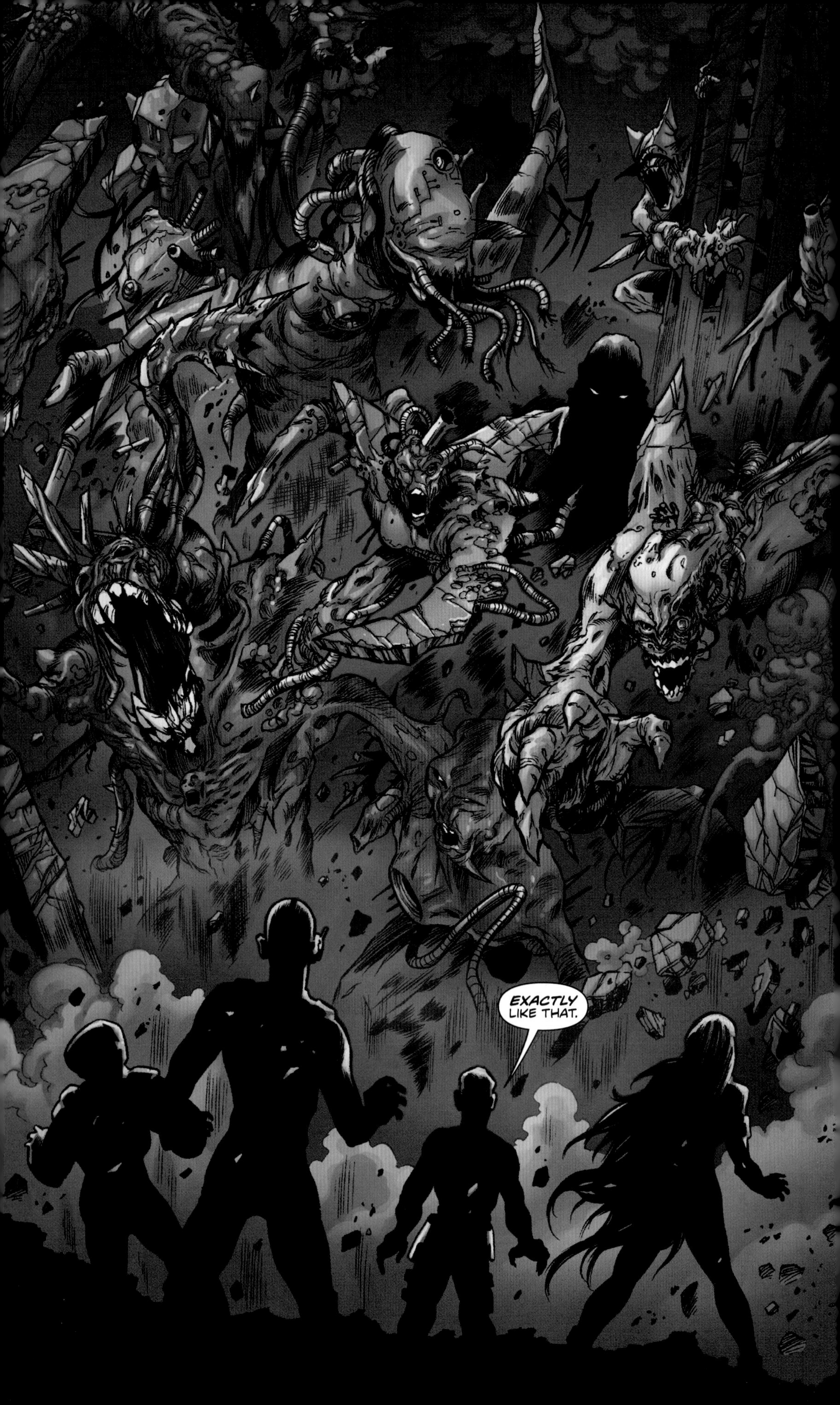
EXACTLY LIKE THAT.

Zastrugi

Pure ice world. Pure ice water.

Quench the Quantinuum.

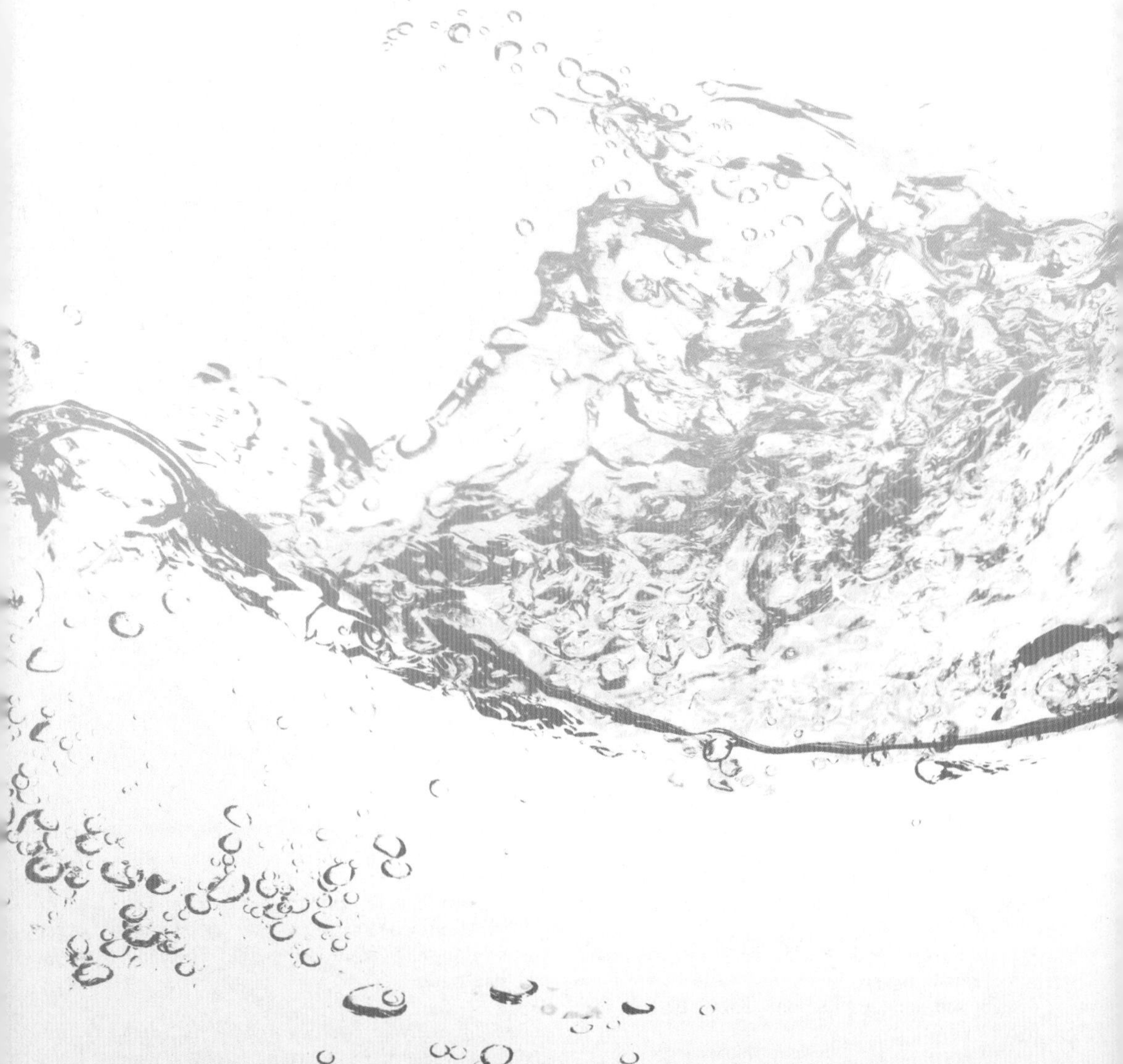

Zastrugi ® trademark of the 77 Zastrugi Water Bottling Company

BEWILDERED

> **" I NEVER THOUGHT I'D BE THE PERSON I AM. I STILL HAVE TO PINCH MYSELF. "**

For Altar Image, Sasha Zwanel in conversation with Creena Hersh.

Creena Hersh was born on 99 Cygnus in 66 A.Q. and is one of the most famous faces in the Quantinuum. She is the model of choice for several of the industry's top designers, and was voted The Face of Quantinuum in the 99 Fashion Choice Awards. As a style icon, she is without parallel. Her hypernatural gifts won her a place in the Hypernatural Program in her early twenties, and she served with the team with distinction during its illustrious "Nineteenth Tour" (90-95). As Bewilder, she was part of perhaps the most famous and beloved line-up in the team's history. She retired after one term, and has served ever since as the team's Media Relations Coordinator.

I grew up on the road rather than on 99 Cygnus. My family were teamsters in the cargo federation and they worked a lot off-world in hi-grav environments.

I guess I was born hyper-metabolic. Three generations of my family worked in hi-grav, so there are bone density and muscle mutations. I was the first true hyper.

They call it super-speed, but it's more than speed. It's short bursts of acceleration, where the world seems to stop moving for me, and I live in the blink of an eye or the beat of a heart.

It burns me out fast—I eat like a pig! After a meta-burst, I tend to gorge on max-cal snacks. I really don't eat like other supermodels! You'd be horrified!

My tour with the team was an amazing experience. It was a whirlwind. I've been told we were the "favorite line-up", but I think kids today forget some of the all-time greats back in the '20s and '30s. I mean, Warpstar? Clone 40? Hard Cell? Come on.

Being a high profile couple was tough. Clone 45 and I were on every cover and every link. It's like we lived our lives in public. That was a lot of pressure for a relationship.

I'll always love Hatch. There's no animosity. It just didn't work out.

I never thought I'd be the person I am. I still have to pinch myself. I came from a very poor, very honest working class family. I thought I'd be handling cargo as a trade.

Being a hyper took me out of that and gave me opportunities, but I haven't forgotten where I came from. I go visit whenever I can. Family is everything to me. I am close to my mom, and my sisters and brother.

I don't have a beauty regime. I know that makes people hate me when I say that! I'm kinda hard wearing. The muscle and bone density that allow me to endure the bursts of hyper-velocity also seem to keep away the signs of aging.

The secret of looking good is simple. Eat well, sleep well, hydrate, and stay rested. It's easy for me to say that because I don't, but I have an excuse. If I wasn't a hyper, my lifestyle would not have been kind to me.

One tour was enough. It was amazing, but it was enough. We did some huge things in those five years. If nothing else, we stopped Sublime. I will always be proud of that, but it came at a price for the team, and I couldn't go on when the tour finished.

I love my job now. I feel like a mother to the team. Maybe "guardian angel" is better. Or "big sister"!

I'm the public face of the Hypernaturals. And I'm one of the people who get to select the team. It's a big responsibility. I'm glad to be doing this, to be giving back to the team and the program that gave me so much.

The Centennial Iteration is the best Hypernaturals squad ever. There, I said it. And I was on the Nineteenth. This team is special.

The Quantinuum is a hundred years old, and so is the Hypernaturals Program. This team is the twenty-first line-up. It has to be good. It's a showcase for the next century.

Magnetar is a superb leader. I've seen the team come together and I've seen it train. It's more complete than we ever were.

" I'VE LIVED FAST AND PARTS OF MY LIFE HAVE BEEN VERY FAST! "

I don't worry that only one member of the new team has served before. I know the press have talked about the lack of field experience. Kobalt Blue brings a veteran wisdom to the squad, but the rest aren't kids.

Program training is a great deal more thorough today than it ever was for us. We've seen things like Sublime, Bioerror and Orange Krush. We've built that knowledge into the prep. Today's team is ready to go. When they go out on their debut mission, they'll be better equipped than we were after ten.

I thank Quant every day for the life I have. It's been amazing, and I know I'm lucky.

The media relations role can be very demanding. I trip everywhere, all the time. I'm never at home as much as I want. I have no time for a private life right now.

I want kids, maybe in another few years. I'm too busy right now, and there's no one special in my life, no matter what the press likes to imagine! One day, maybe.

Maybe if I had a child, it would be hypernatural too. Maybe my hyper is heritable. I don't know if I'd recommend they went into the program. That would always be their choice. I'd like to think I'd be able to give them good advice, thanks to my own experiences.

I've lived fast—and parts of my life have been very fast! When you're inside a hyper-metabolic burst, you feel very alone. You're in your own universe, where everything else has stopped. That's probably why I don't do it these days unless I have to.

It leaves you very tired and very hungry. Do it too much, and it'll put you in a coma. The truth is, the isolation of those accelerated moments is the worst part. I don't want to be alone in my life. Not forever.

Photographs by Lorn Maxin at Agency Q
Clothes by Gauss
Accessories model's own

CHAPTER TWO

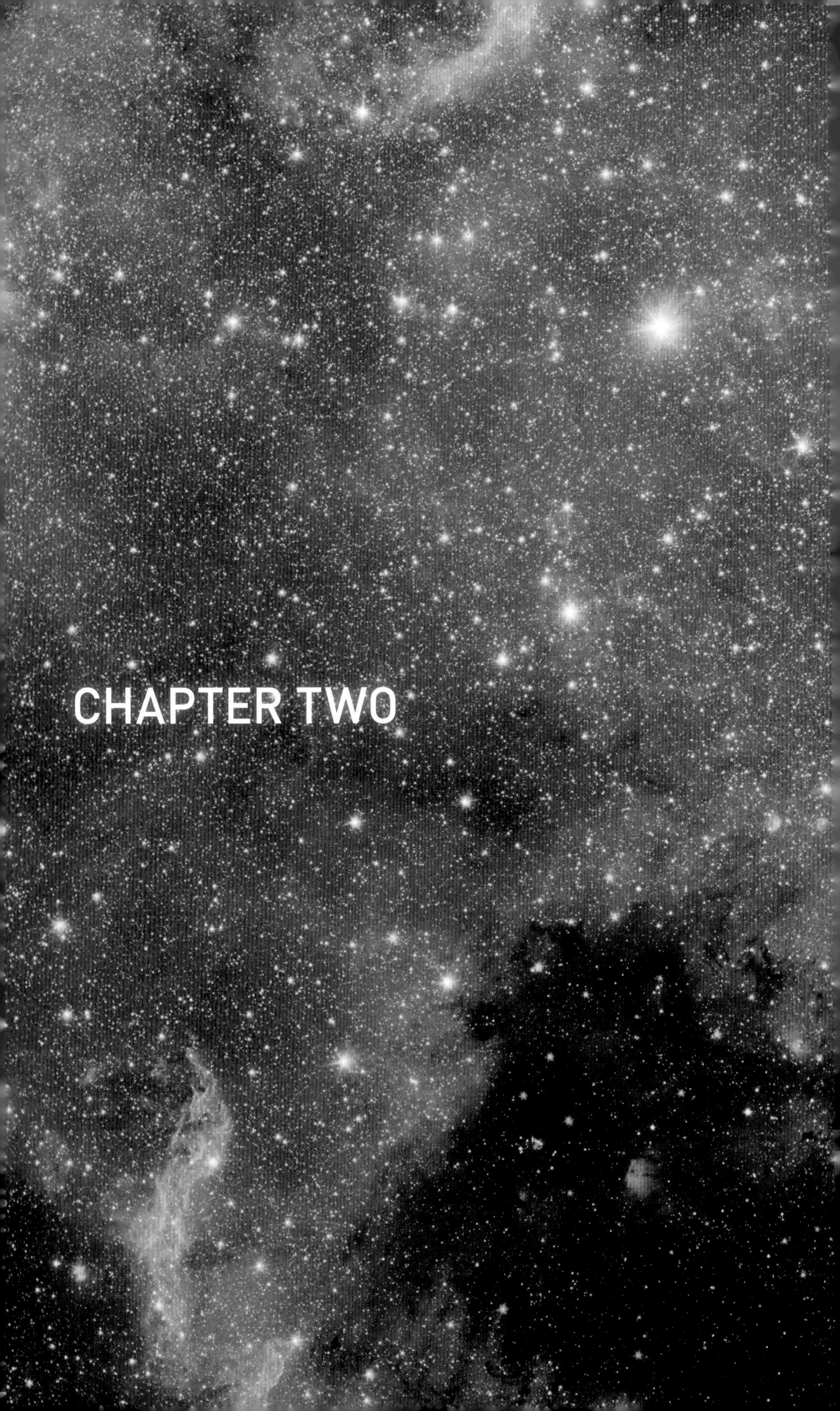

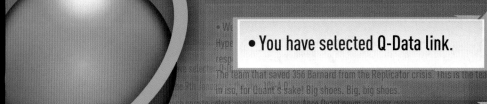

• You have selected Q-Data link.

- It is the 10th of January in the year **100 A.Q.**
  - Touch here to select an alternative to the **Anno Quantinuum** calendar system.
  - Touch here to load local weather reports for your **current cosmic location**.
  - Touch here to access **Q-Data newsflows** from planets near your current cosmic location.
  - Touch here for latest **Quantum Trip transit times**.

- Q-Data entry: The Quantinuum

- The Quantinuum is the name for the human galactic culture, and also for the **artificial intelligence** that controls its function.

- The Quantinuum was created 100 years ago at the start of the **Nanocene Era**. The Nanocene began when the Quantinuum AI achieved Singularity and refashioned human galactic culture. Succeeding the **Holocene Era**, the Nanocene is the next progression of human evolution and...

(to read this entry in full, touch here)

- You have selected live feed newsflow.

- **Rys Harpur** returned as governor of 16 Lassitar for third term, promises to drive home labor bill reforms on Lassitar mine holdings throughout system
- **Winch Ind** confirms acquisition of **Fedorex Nano & Tech**, expected to launch takeover of Crowncorp Munitions before year-end
- **Sy Motter** defeats **Nunos Cladori** in straight sets at Pharoah Sands
- **AI Law** starlet Geenie Gale denies D.U.I. charges
- Concern remains high for fate of the Centennial Year Iteration of the **Hypernaturals Team**, apparently lost during an emergency response mission to 28 Kosov

- The Hypernaturals are the Quantinuum's foremost champions. Famous across the entirety of human galactic culture, the team members are selected on the basis of their hypernatural powers and their strength of character, and serve for five-year terms. In honor of the start of the twenty-first term, the line-up of the team's so-called "Centennial Year Iteration" has recently been announced amid huge publicity and--

...BREAKING NEWS... unconfirmed sources report the entire Hypernaturals Team has vanished on its inaugural mission to 28 Kosov... according to a spokesperson at Hypernaturals Central, San Diego, a special reserve formation of Hypernaturals, including now retired team members Bewilder and Thinkwell from the classic "Nineteenth Tour" line-up, has been dispatched via Quantum Trip to 28 Kosov to investigate...

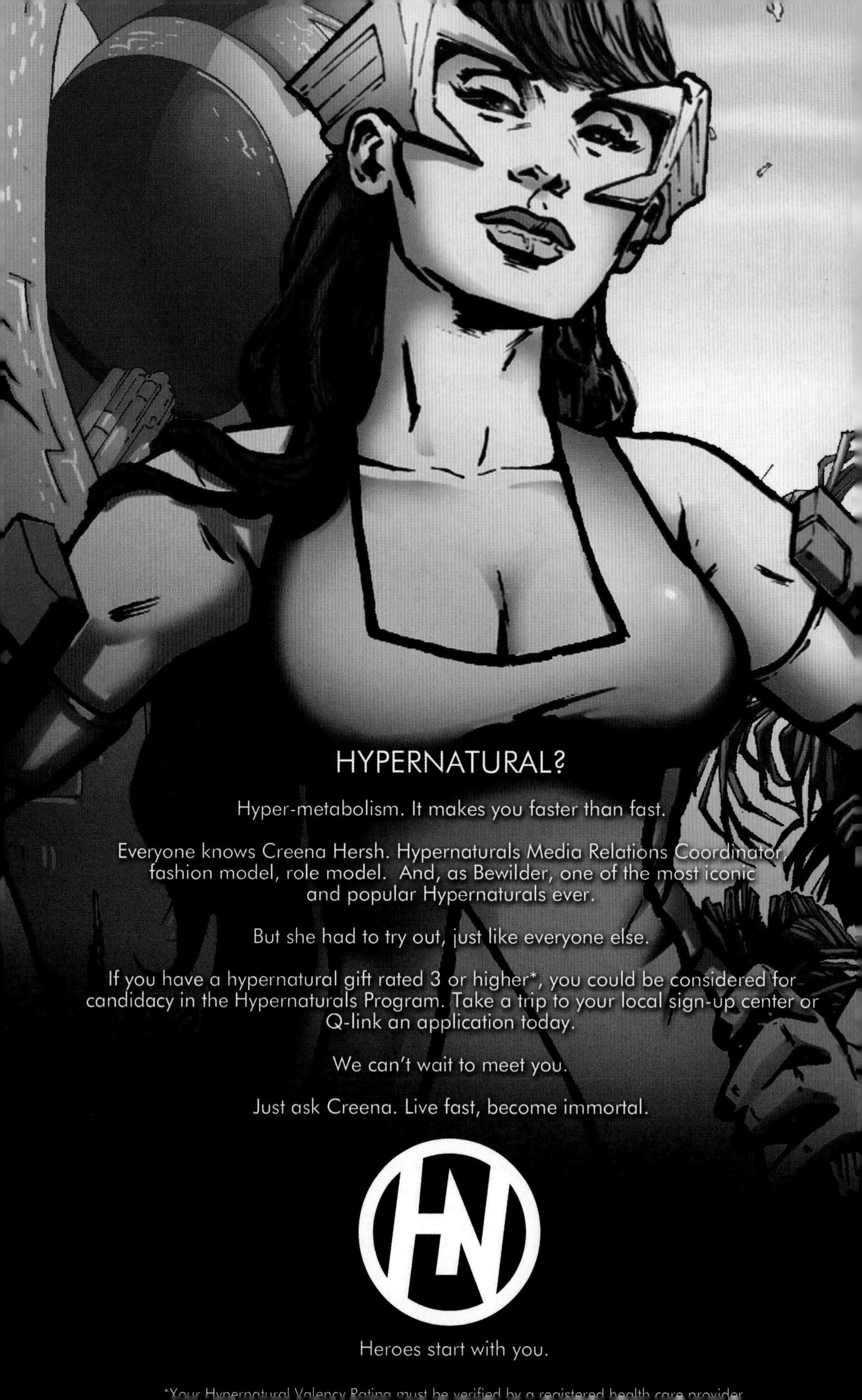
HYPERNATURAL?
Hyper-metabolism. It makes you faster than fast.
Everyone knows Creena Hersh. Hypernaturals Media Relations Coordinator, fashion model, role model. And, as Bewilder, one of the most iconic and popular Hypernaturals ever.
But she had to try out, just like everyone else.
If you have a hypernatural gift rated 3 or higher*, you could be considered for candidacy in the Hypernaturals Program. Take a trip to your local sign-up center or Q-link an application today.
We can't wait to meet you.
Just ask Creena. Live fast, become immortal.
HN
Heroes start with you.
*Your Hypernatural Valency Rating must be verified by a registered health care provider.

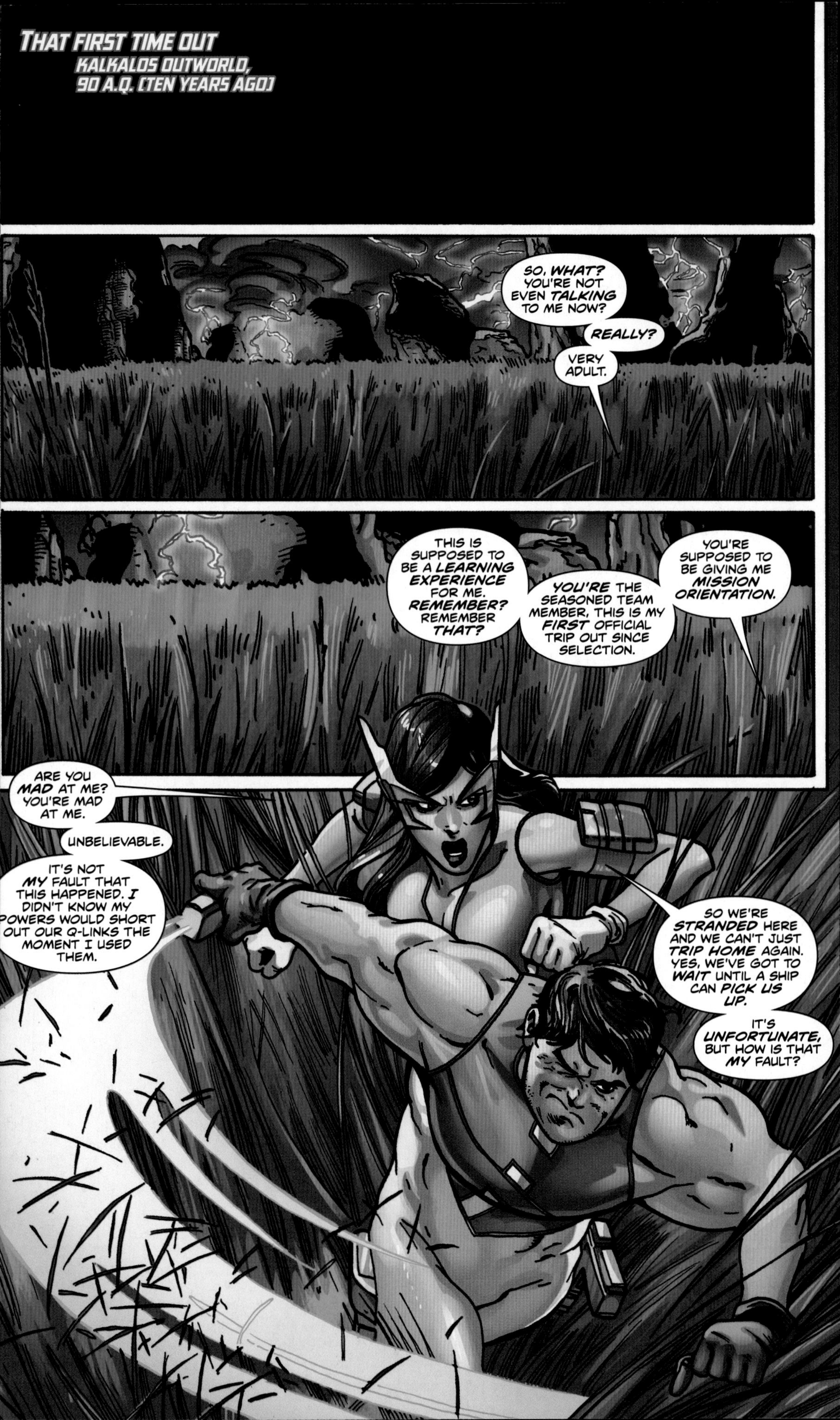

THAT FIRST TIME OUT
KALKALOS OUTWORLD, 90 A.Q. [TEN YEARS AGO]
SO, WHAT? YOU'RE NOT EVEN TALKING TO ME NOW?
REALLY?
VERY ADULT.
THIS IS SUPPOSED TO BE A LEARNING EXPERIENCE FOR ME. REMEMBER? REMEMBER THAT?
YOU'RE THE SEASONED TEAM MEMBER, THIS IS MY FIRST OFFICIAL TRIP OUT SINCE SELECTION.
YOU'RE SUPPOSED TO BE GIVING ME MISSION ORIENTATION.
ARE YOU MAD AT ME? YOU'RE MAD AT ME.
UNBELIEVABLE.
IT'S NOT MY FAULT THAT THIS HAPPENED. I DIDN'T KNOW MY POWERS WOULD SHORT OUT OUR Q-LINKS THE MOMENT I USED THEM.
SO WE'RE STRANDED HERE AND WE CAN'T JUST TRIP HOME AGAIN. YES, WE'VE GOT TO WAIT UNTIL A SHIP CAN PICK US UP.
IT'S UNFORTUNATE, BUT HOW IS THAT MY FAULT?

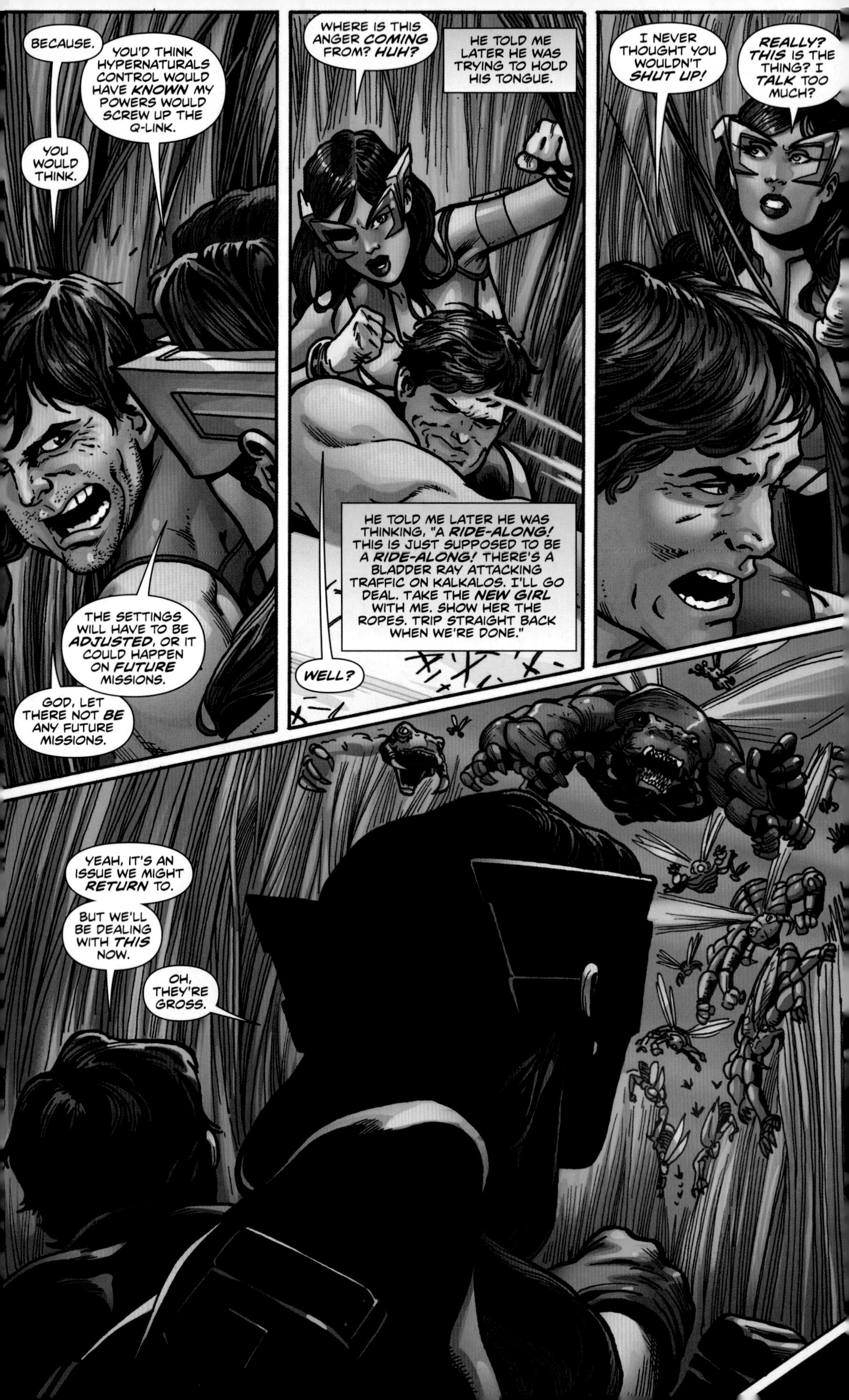
BECAUSE.
YOU'D THINK HYPERNATURALS CONTROL WOULD HAVE KNOWN MY POWERS WOULD SCREW UP THE Q-LINK.
YOU WOULD THINK.
THE SETTINGS WILL HAVE TO BE ADJUSTED, OR IT COULD HAPPEN ON FUTURE MISSIONS.
GOD, LET THERE NOT BE ANY FUTURE MISSIONS.
WHERE IS THIS ANGER COMING FROM? HUH?
HE TOLD ME LATER HE WAS TRYING TO HOLD HIS TONGUE.
HE TOLD ME LATER HE WAS THINKING, "A RIDE-ALONG! THIS IS JUST SUPPOSED TO BE A RIDE-ALONG! THERE'S A BLADDER RAY ATTACKING TRAFFIC ON KALKALOS. I'LL GO DEAL. TAKE THE NEW GIRL WITH ME. SHOW HER THE ROPES. TRIP STRAIGHT BACK WHEN WE'RE DONE."
WELL?
I NEVER THOUGHT YOU WOULDN'T SHUT UP!
REALLY? THIS IS THE THING? I TALK TOO MUCH?
YEAH, IT'S AN ISSUE WE MIGHT RETURN TO.
BUT WE'LL BE DEALING WITH THIS NOW.
OH, THEY'RE GROSS.

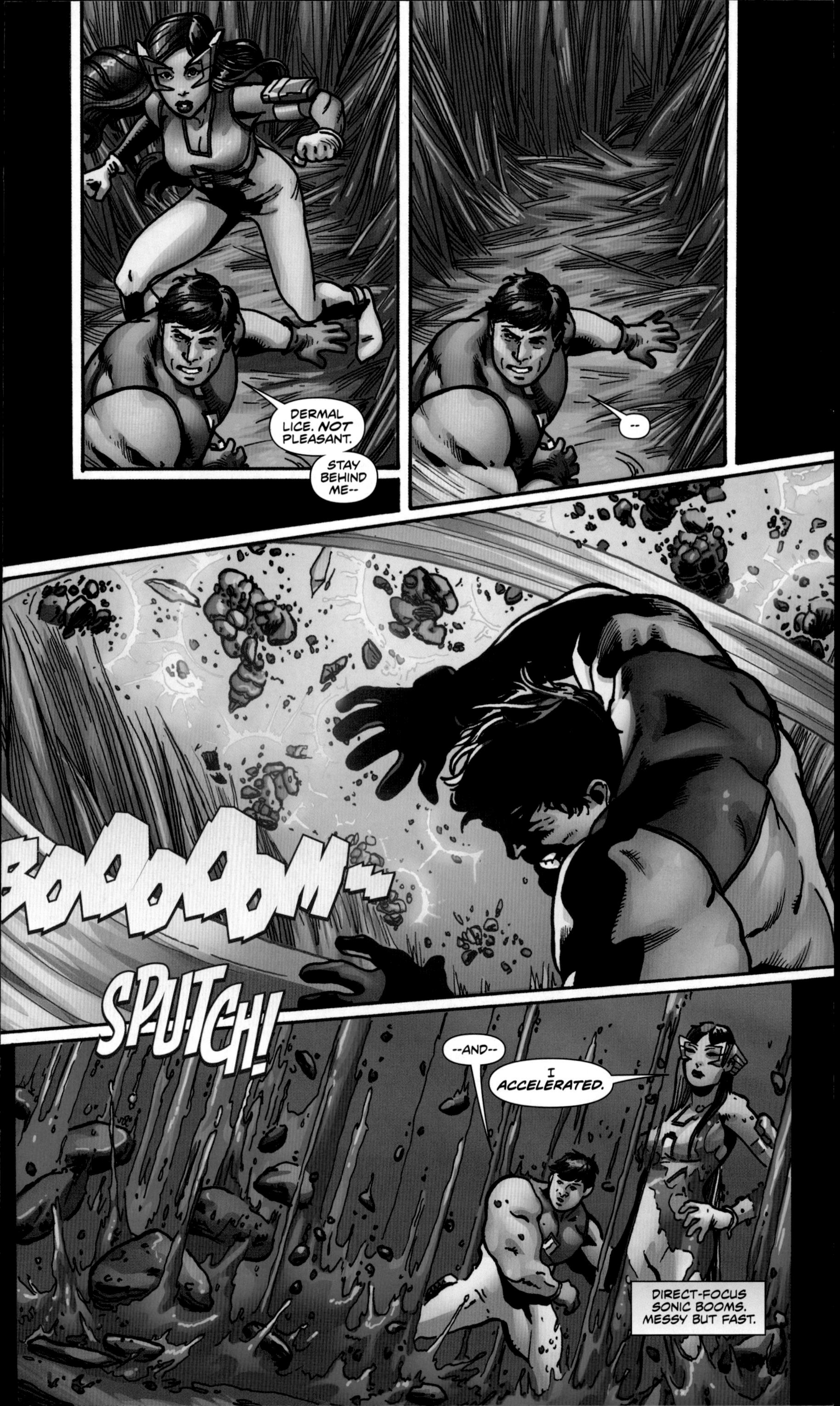
DERMAL LICE. NOT PLEASANT.
STAY BEHIND ME--
--
BOOOOM--
SPLUTCH!
--AND--
I ACCELERATED.
DIRECT-FOCUS SONIC BOOMS. MESSY BUT FAST.

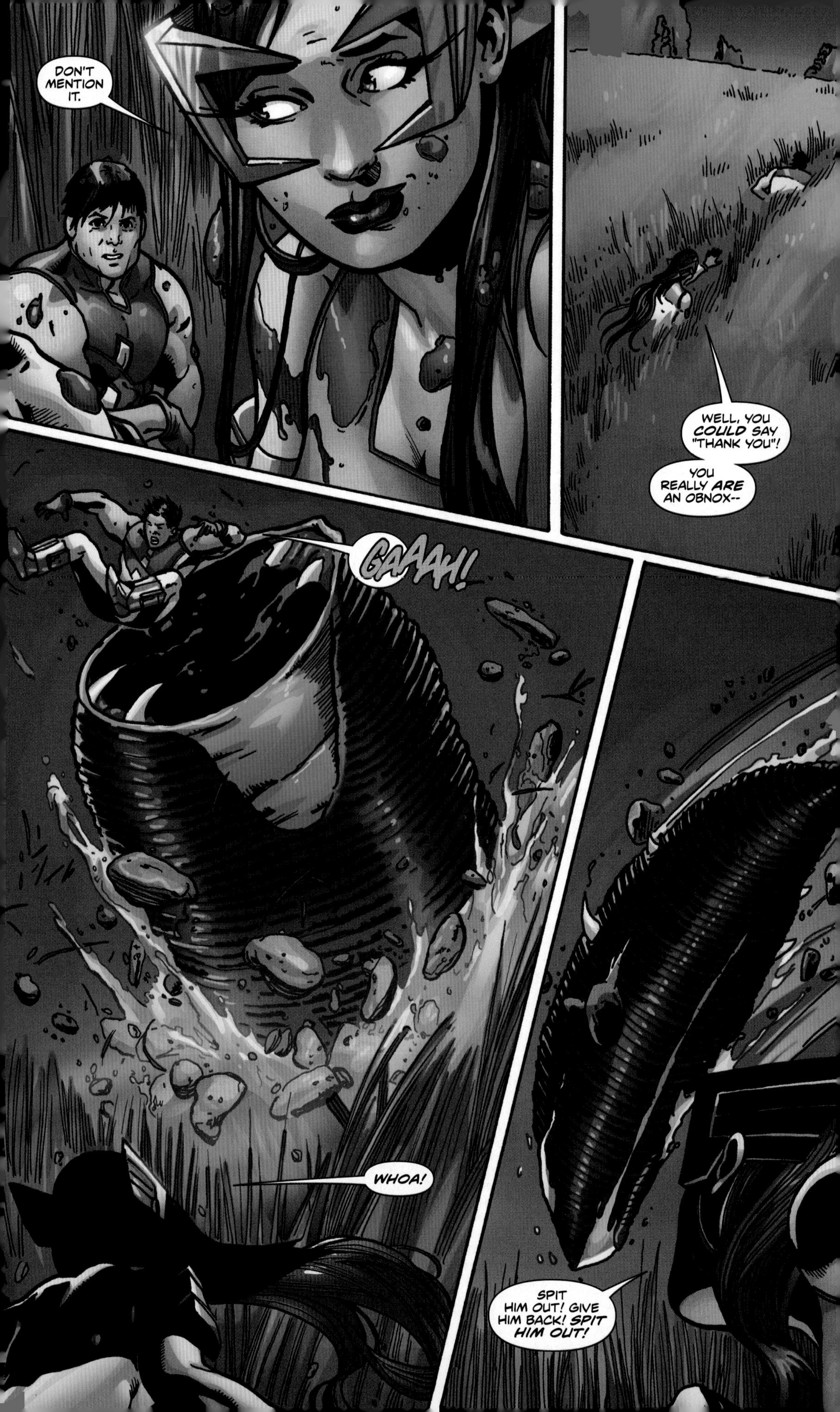
DON'T MENTION IT.
WELL, YOU COULD SAY "THANK YOU"!
YOU REALLY ARE AN OBNOX--
GAAAH!
WHOA!
SPIT HIM OUT! GIVE HIM BACK! SPIT HIM OUT!

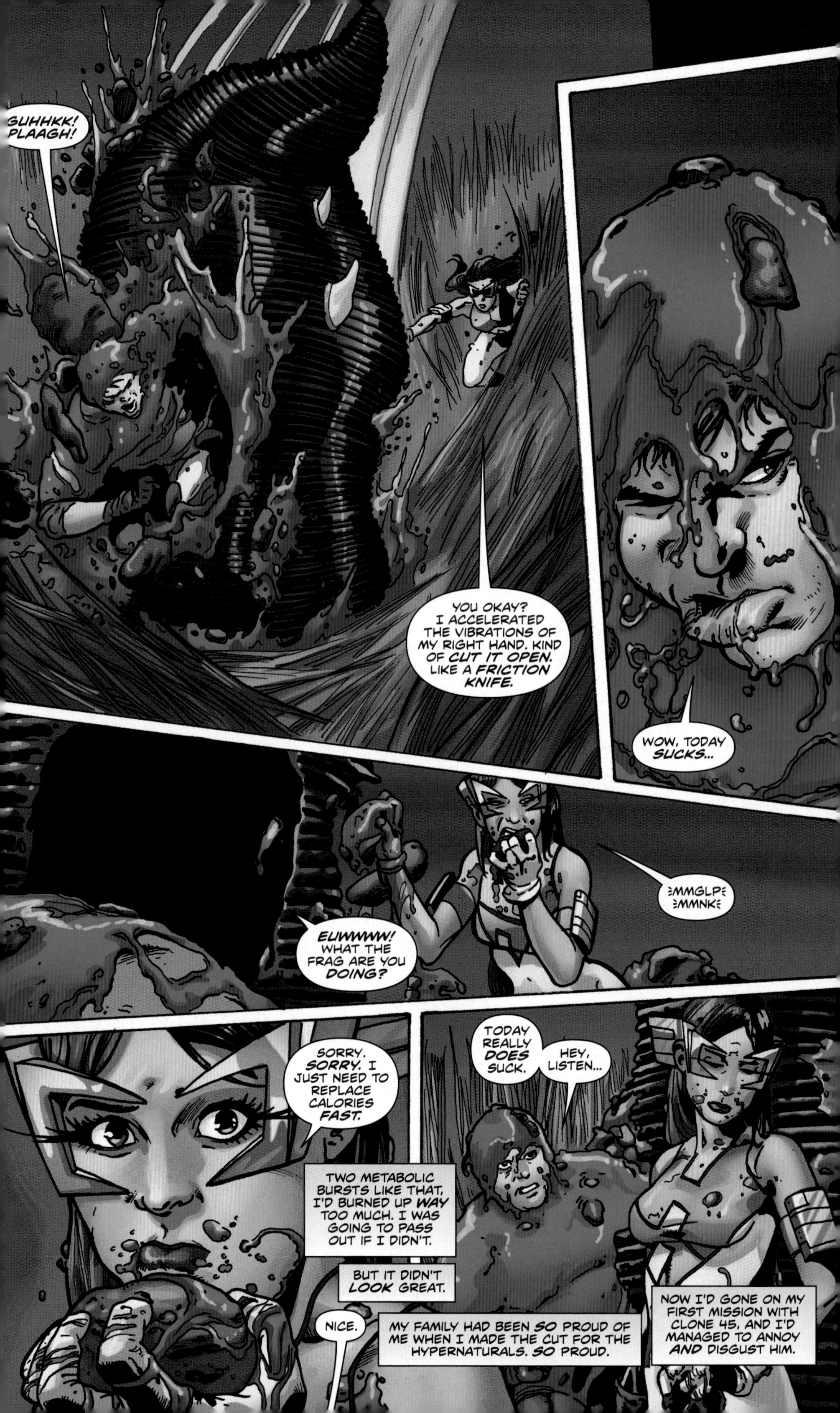
GUHHKK! PLAAGH!
YOU OKAY? I ACCELERATED THE VIBRATIONS OF MY RIGHT HAND. KIND OF CUT IT OPEN. LIKE A FRICTION KNIFE.
WOW, TODAY SUCKS...
MMGLP MMNK
EUWWWW! WHAT THE FRAG ARE YOU DOING?
SORRY. SORRY. I JUST NEED TO REPLACE CALORIES FAST.
TWO METABOLIC BURSTS LIKE THAT, I'D BURNED UP WAY TOO MUCH. I WAS GOING TO PASS OUT IF I DIDN'T.
BUT IT DIDN'T LOOK GREAT.
NICE.
MY FAMILY HAD BEEN SO PROUD OF ME WHEN I MADE THE CUT FOR THE HYPERNATURALS. SO PROUD.
TODAY REALLY DOES SUCK.
HEY, LISTEN...
NOW I'D GONE ON MY FIRST MISSION WITH CLONE 45, AND I'D MANAGED TO ANNOY AND DISGUST HIM.

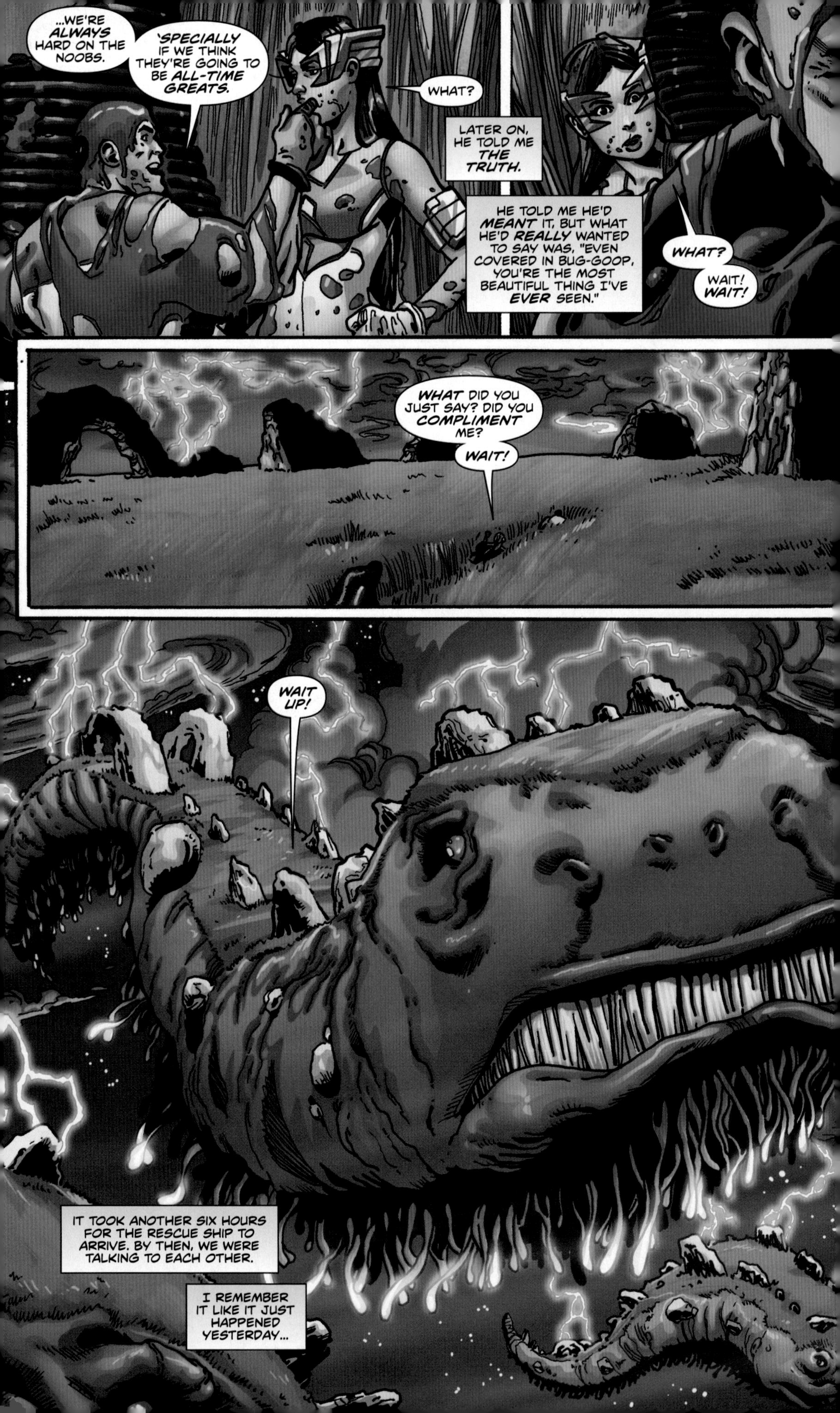
...WE'RE ALWAYS HARD ON THE NOOBS.
'SPECIALLY IF WE THINK THEY'RE GOING TO BE ALL-TIME GREATS.
WHAT?
LATER ON, HE TOLD ME THE TRUTH.
HE TOLD ME HE'D MEANT IT, BUT WHAT HE'D REALLY WANTED TO SAY WAS, "EVEN COVERED IN BUG-GOOP, YOU'RE THE MOST BEAUTIFUL THING I'VE EVER SEEN."
WHAT?
WAIT! WAIT!
WHAT DID YOU JUST SAY? DID YOU COMPLIMENT ME?
WAIT!
WAIT UP!
IT TOOK ANOTHER SIX HOURS FOR THE RESCUE SHIP TO ARRIVE. BY THEN, WE WERE TALKING TO EACH OTHER.
I REMEMBER IT LIKE IT JUST HAPPENED YESTERDAY...

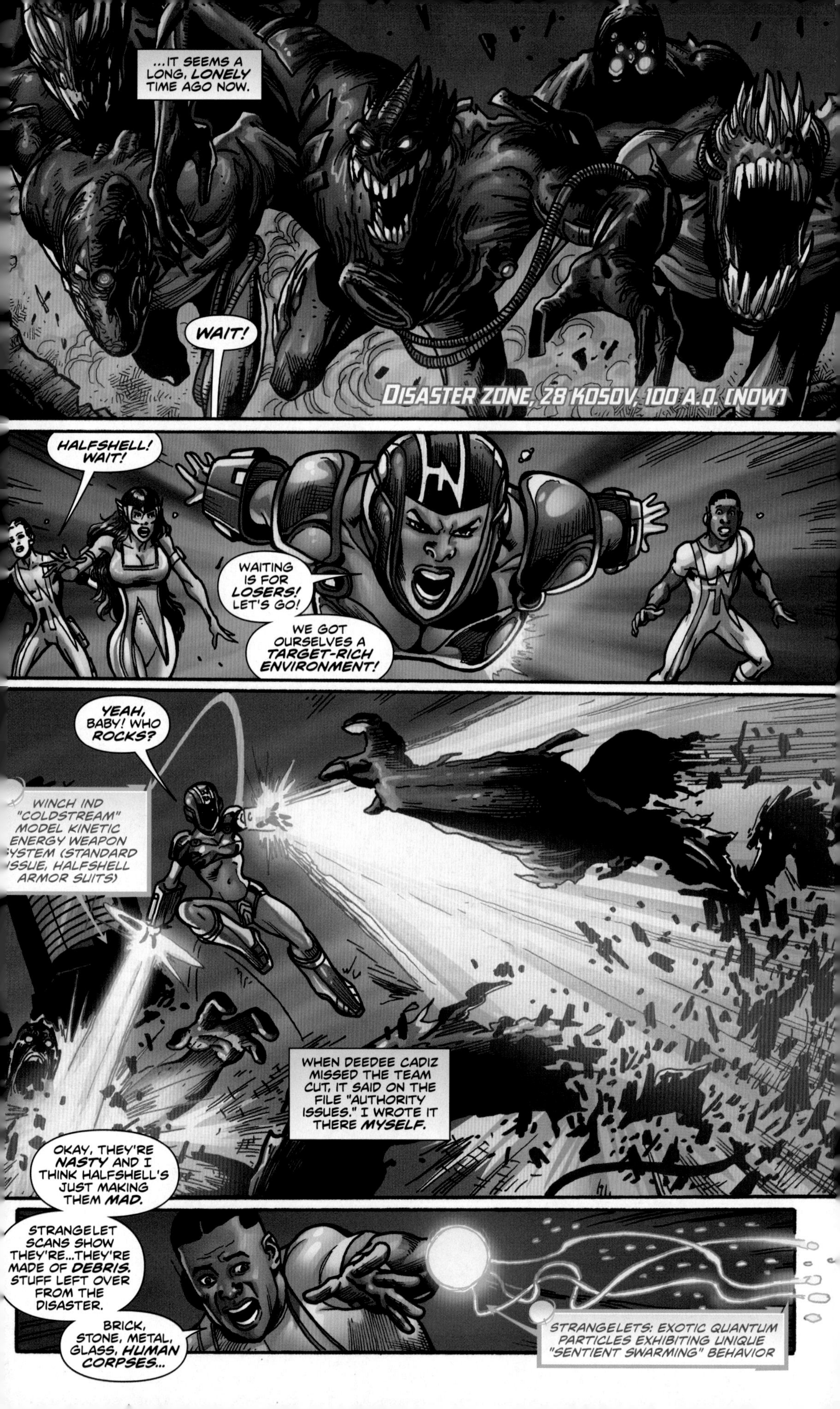

...IT SEEMS A LONG, LONELY TIME AGO NOW.
WAIT!
DISASTER ZONE, 28 KOSOV, 100 A.Q. (NOW)
HALFSHELL! WAIT!
WAITING IS FOR LOSERS! LET'S GO!
WE GOT OURSELVES A TARGET-RICH ENVIRONMENT!
YEAH, BABY! WHO ROCKS?
WINCH IND "COLDSTREAM" MODEL KINETIC ENERGY WEAPON SYSTEM (STANDARD ISSUE, HALFSHELL ARMOR SUITS)
WHEN DEEDEE CADIZ MISSED THE TEAM CUT, IT SAID ON THE FILE "AUTHORITY ISSUES." I WROTE IT THERE MYSELF.
OKAY, THEY'RE NASTY AND I THINK HALFSHELL'S JUST MAKING THEM MAD.
STRANGELET SCANS SHOW THEY'RE...THEY'RE MADE OF DEBRIS. STUFF LEFT OVER FROM THE DISASTER.
BRICK, STONE, METAL, GLASS, HUMAN CORPSES...
STRANGELETS: EXOTIC QUANTUM PARTICLES EXHIBITING UNIQUE "SENTIENT SWARMING" BEHAVIOR

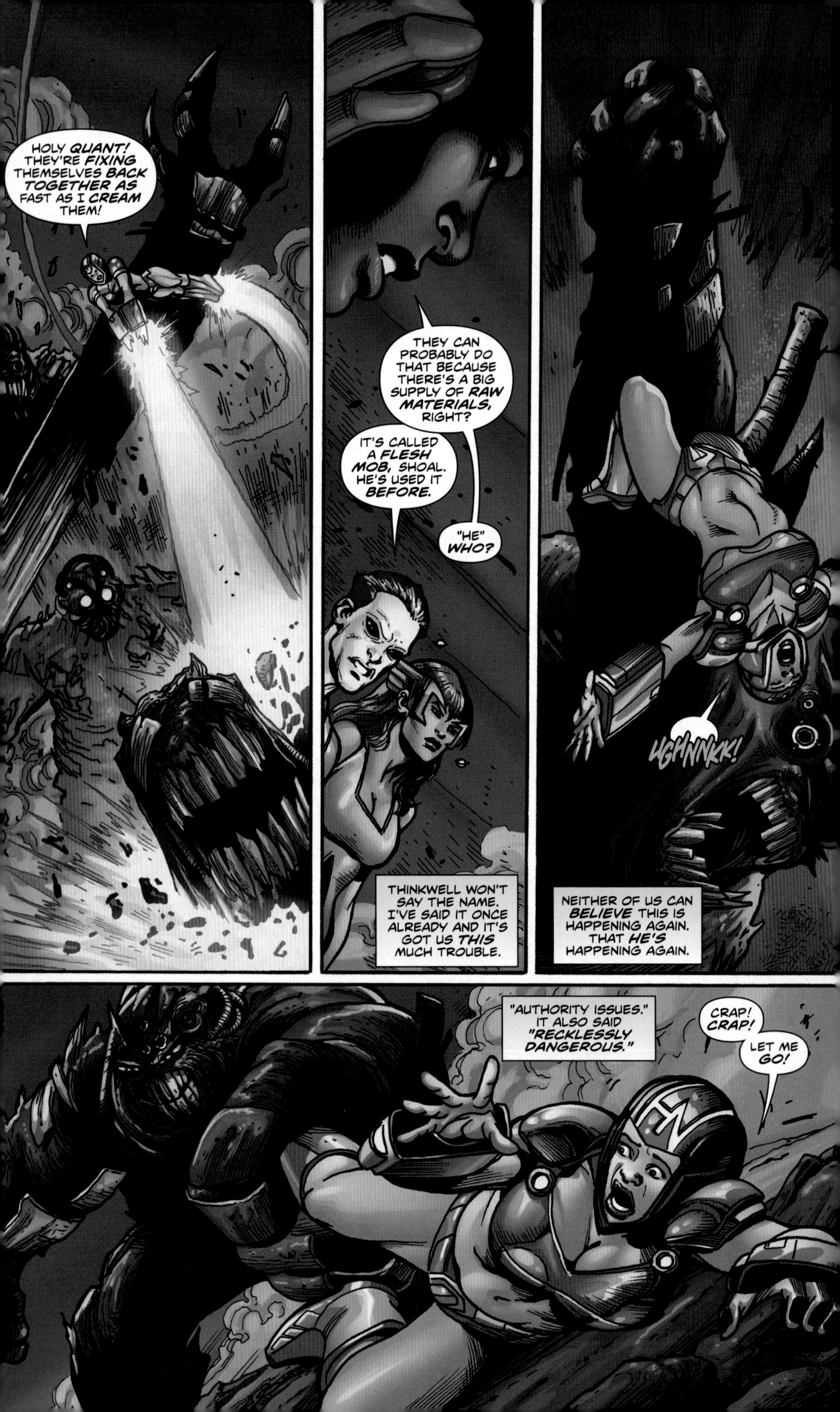
HOLY QUANT! THEY'RE FIXING THEMSELVES BACK TOGETHER AS FAST AS I CREAM THEM!
THEY CAN PROBABLY DO THAT BECAUSE THERE'S A BIG SUPPLY OF RAW MATERIALS, RIGHT?
IT'S CALLED A FLESH MOB, SHOAL. HE'S USED IT BEFORE.
"HE" WHO?
THINKWELL WON'T SAY THE NAME. I'VE SAID IT ONCE ALREADY AND IT'S GOT US THIS MUCH TROUBLE.
UGHNNKK!
NEITHER OF US CAN BELIEVE THIS IS HAPPENING AGAIN. THAT HE'S HAPPENING AGAIN.
"AUTHORITY ISSUES." IT ALSO SAID "RECKLESSLY DANGEROUS."
CRAP! CRAP!
LET ME GO!

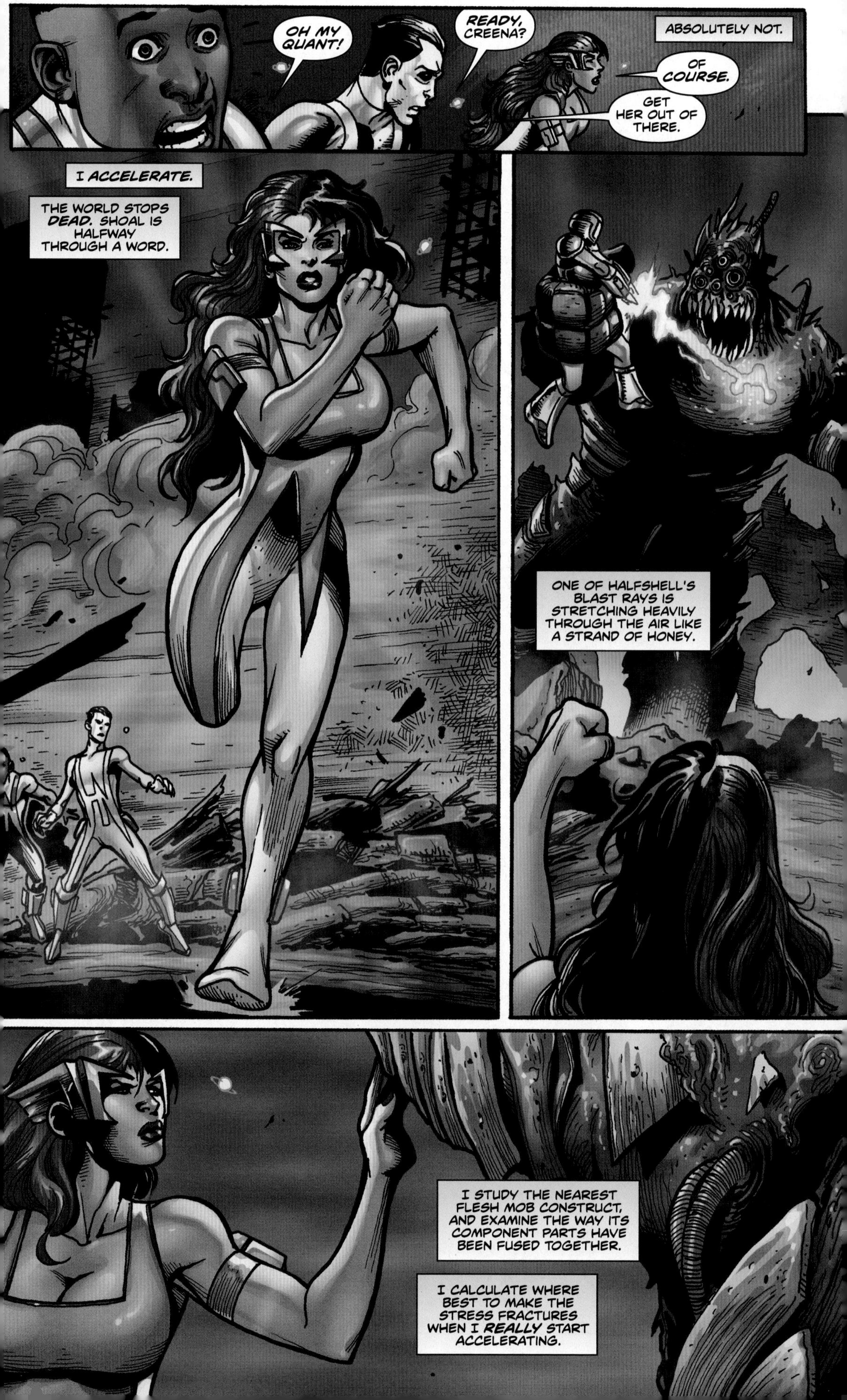
OH MY QUANT!
READY, CREENA?
ABSOLUTELY NOT.
OF COURSE.
GET HER OUT OF THERE.
I ACCELERATE.
THE WORLD STOPS DEAD. SHOAL IS HALFWAY THROUGH A WORD.
ONE OF HALFSHELL'S BLAST RAYS IS STRETCHING HEAVILY THROUGH THE AIR LIKE A STRAND OF HONEY.
I STUDY THE NEAREST FLESH MOB CONSTRUCT, AND EXAMINE THE WAY ITS COMPONENT PARTS HAVE BEEN FUSED TOGETHER.
I CALCULATE WHERE BEST TO MAKE THE STRESS FRACTURES WHEN I REALLY START ACCELERATING.

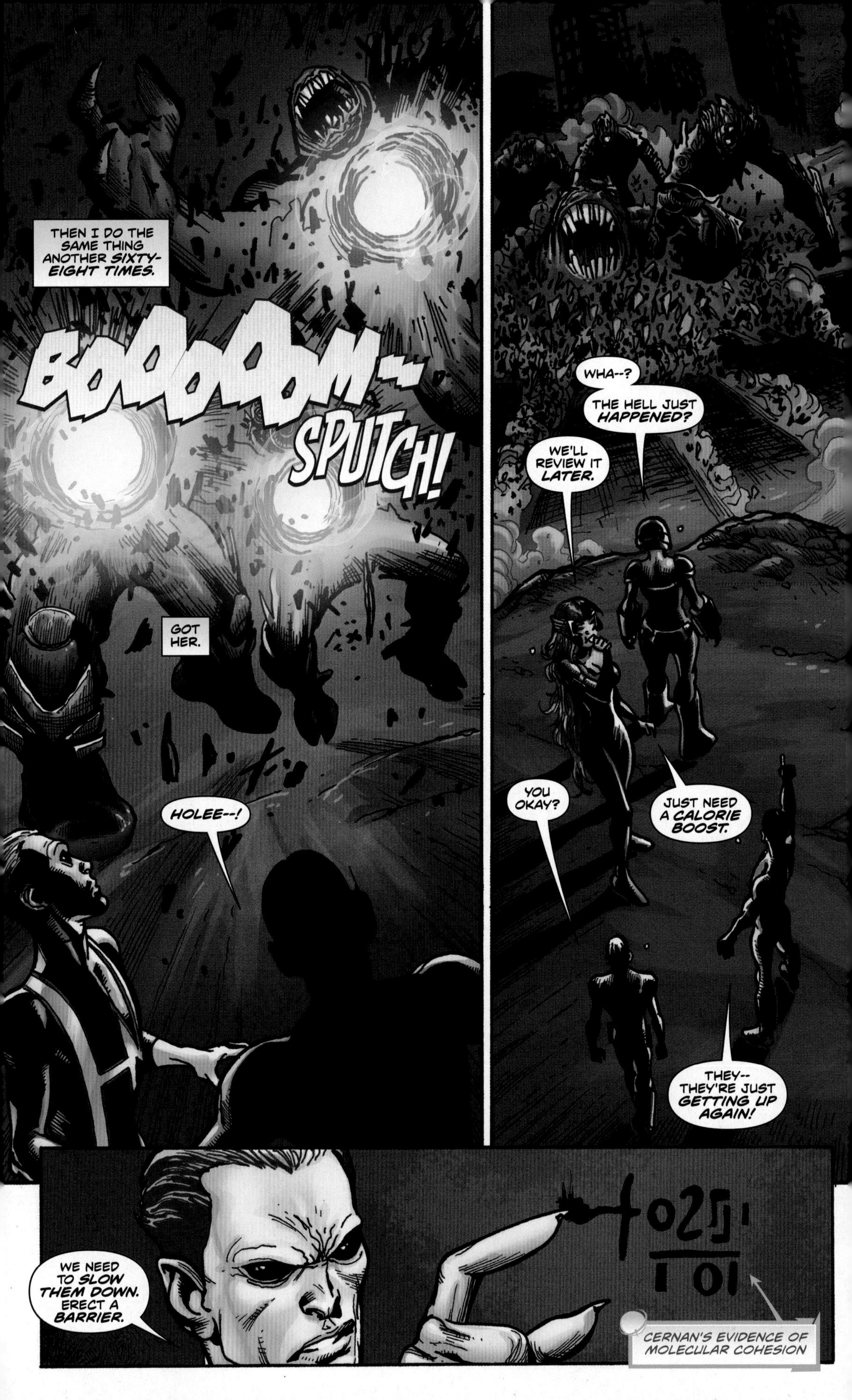
THEN I DO THE SAME THING ANOTHER SIXTY-EIGHT TIMES.
BOOOOOM-SPUTCH!
GOT HER.
HOLEE--!
WHA--?
THE HELL JUST HAPPENED?
WE'LL REVIEW IT LATER.
YOU OKAY?
JUST NEED A CALORIE BOOST.
THEY-- THEY'RE JUST GETTING UP AGAIN!
WE NEED TO SLOW THEM DOWN. ERECT A BARRIER.
CERNAN'S EVIDENCE OF MOLECULAR COHESION

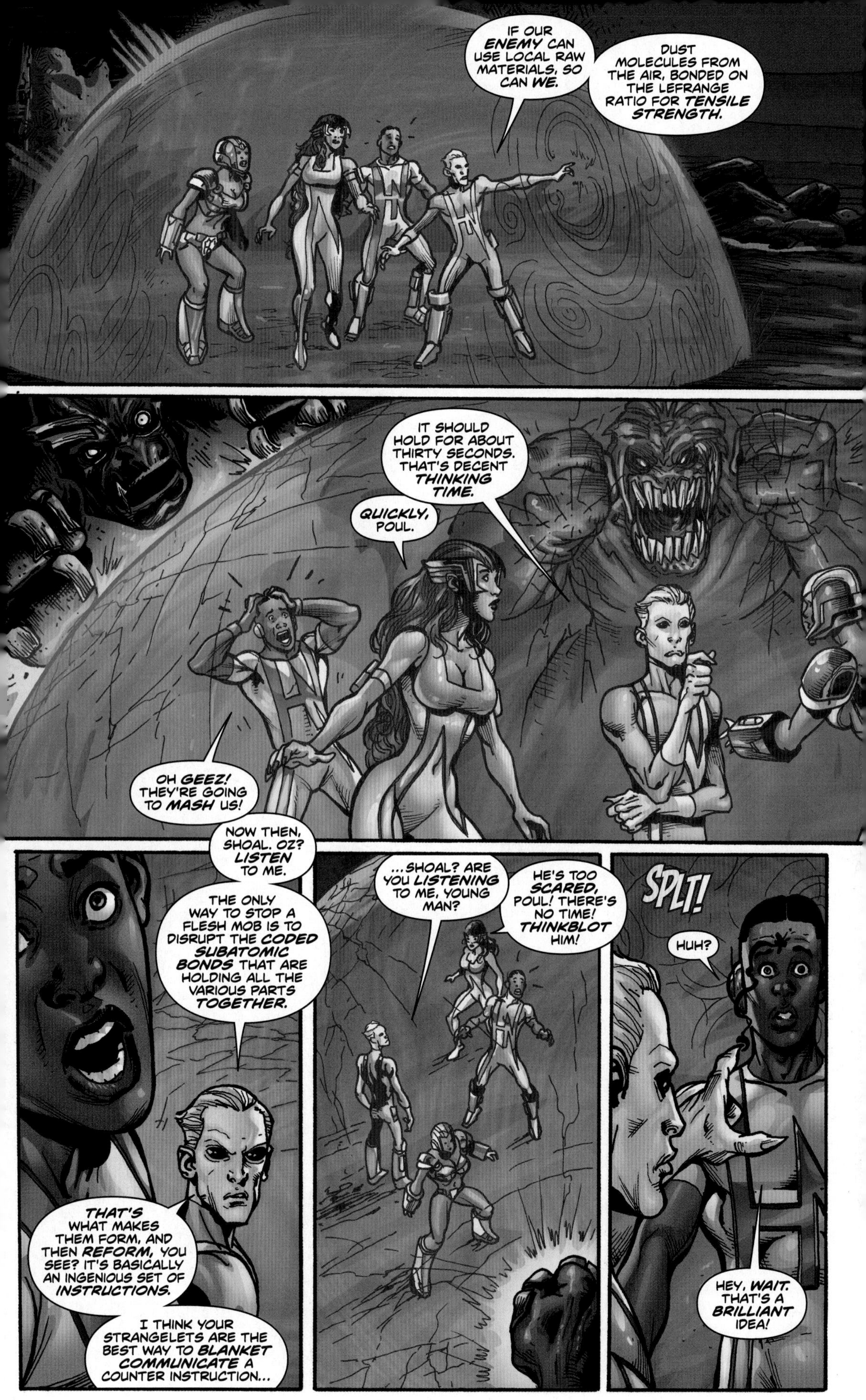
IF OUR ENEMY CAN USE LOCAL RAW MATERIALS, SO CAN WE.
DUST MOLECULES FROM THE AIR, BONDED ON THE LEFRANGE RATIO FOR TENSILE STRENGTH.
IT SHOULD HOLD FOR ABOUT THIRTY SECONDS. THAT'S DECENT THINKING TIME.
QUICKLY, POUL.
OH GEEZ! THEY'RE GOING TO MASH US!
NOW THEN, SHOAL. OZ? LISTEN TO ME.
THE ONLY WAY TO STOP A FLESH MOB IS TO DISRUPT THE CODED SUBATOMIC BONDS THAT ARE HOLDING ALL THE VARIOUS PARTS TOGETHER.
THAT'S WHAT MAKES THEM FORM, AND THEN REFORM, YOU SEE? IT'S BASICALLY AN INGENIOUS SET OF INSTRUCTIONS.
I THINK YOUR STRANGELETS ARE THE BEST WAY TO BLANKET COMMUNICATE A COUNTER INSTRUCTION...
...SHOAL? ARE YOU LISTENING TO ME, YOUNG MAN?
HE'S TOO SCARED, POUL! THERE'S NO TIME! THINKBLOT HIM!
SPLT!
HUH?
HEY, WAIT. THAT'S A BRILLIANT IDEA!

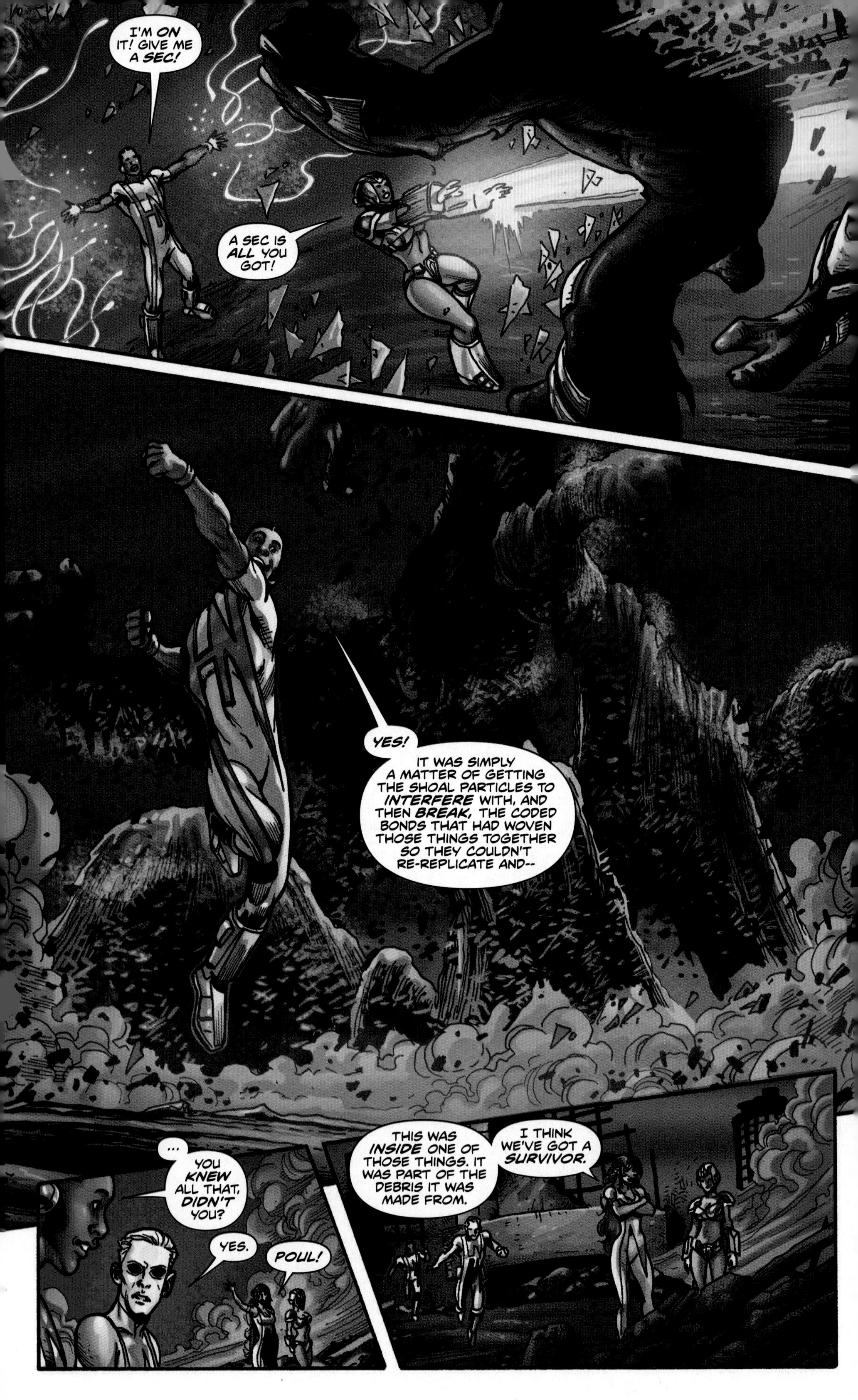
I'M ON IT! GIVE ME A SEC!
A SEC IS ALL YOU GOT!
YES!
IT WAS SIMPLY A MATTER OF GETTING THE SHOAL PARTICLES TO INTERFERE WITH, AND THEN BREAK, THE CODED BONDS THAT HAD WOVEN THOSE THINGS TOGETHER SO THEY COULDN'T RE-REPLICATE AND--
... YOU KNEW ALL THAT, DIDN'T YOU?
YES.
POUL!
THIS WAS INSIDE ONE OF THOSE THINGS. IT WAS PART OF THE DEBRIS IT WAS MADE FROM.
I THINK WE'VE GOT A SURVIVOR.

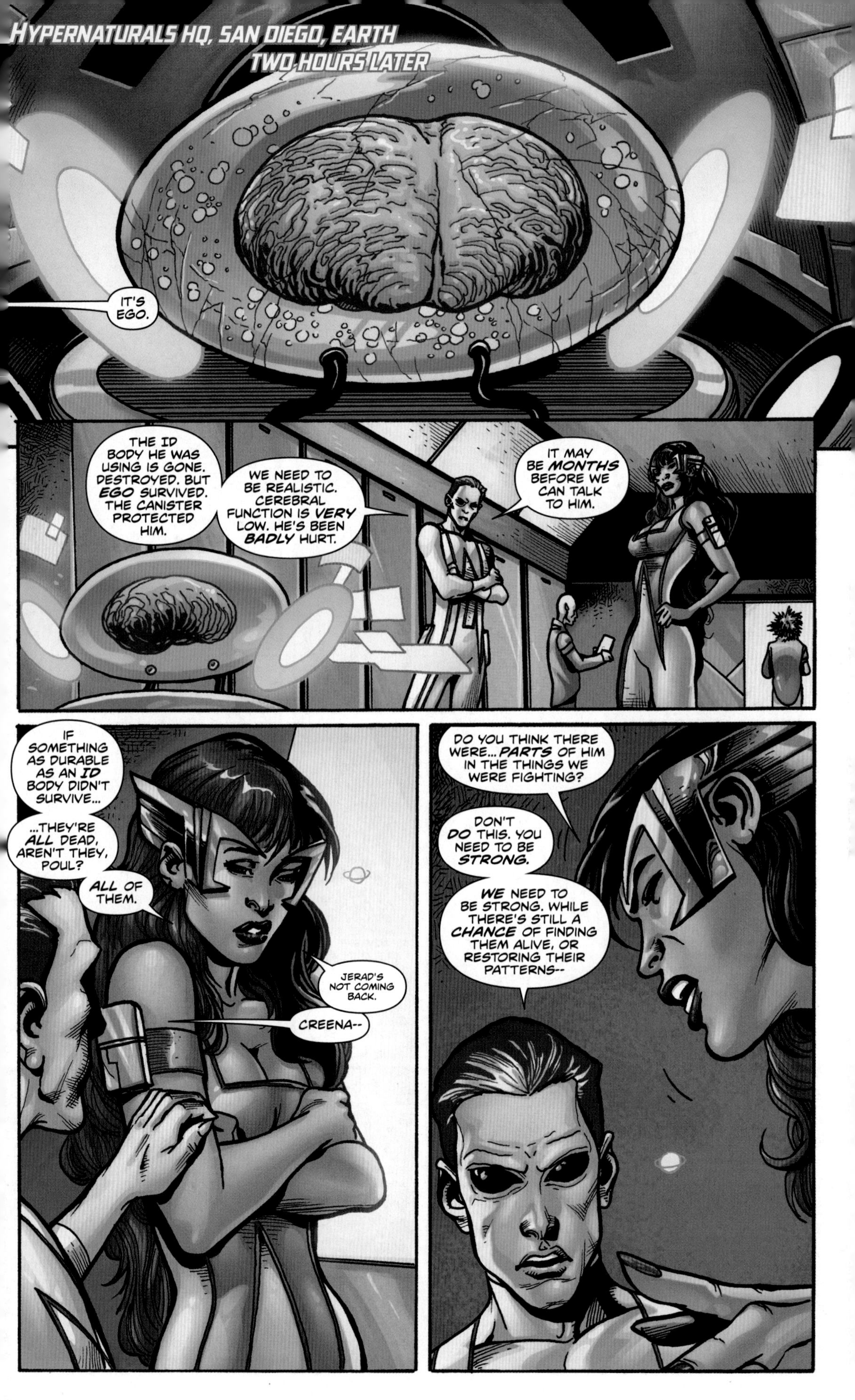
HYPERNATURALS HQ, SAN DIEGO, EARTH
TWO HOURS LATER
IT'S EGO.
THE ID BODY HE WAS USING IS GONE. DESTROYED. BUT EGO SURVIVED. THE CANISTER PROTECTED HIM.
WE NEED TO BE REALISTIC. CEREBRAL FUNCTION IS VERY LOW. HE'S BEEN BADLY HURT.
IT MAY BE MONTHS BEFORE WE CAN TALK TO HIM.
IF SOMETHING AS DURABLE AS AN ID BODY DIDN'T SURVIVE...
...THEY'RE ALL DEAD, AREN'T THEY, POUL?
ALL OF THEM.
JERAD'S NOT COMING BACK.
CREENA--
DO YOU THINK THERE WERE... PARTS OF HIM IN THE THINGS WE WERE FIGHTING?
DON'T DO THIS. YOU NEED TO BE STRONG.
WE NEED TO BE STRONG. WHILE THERE'S STILL A CHANCE OF FINDING THEM ALIVE, OR RESTORING THEIR PATTERNS--

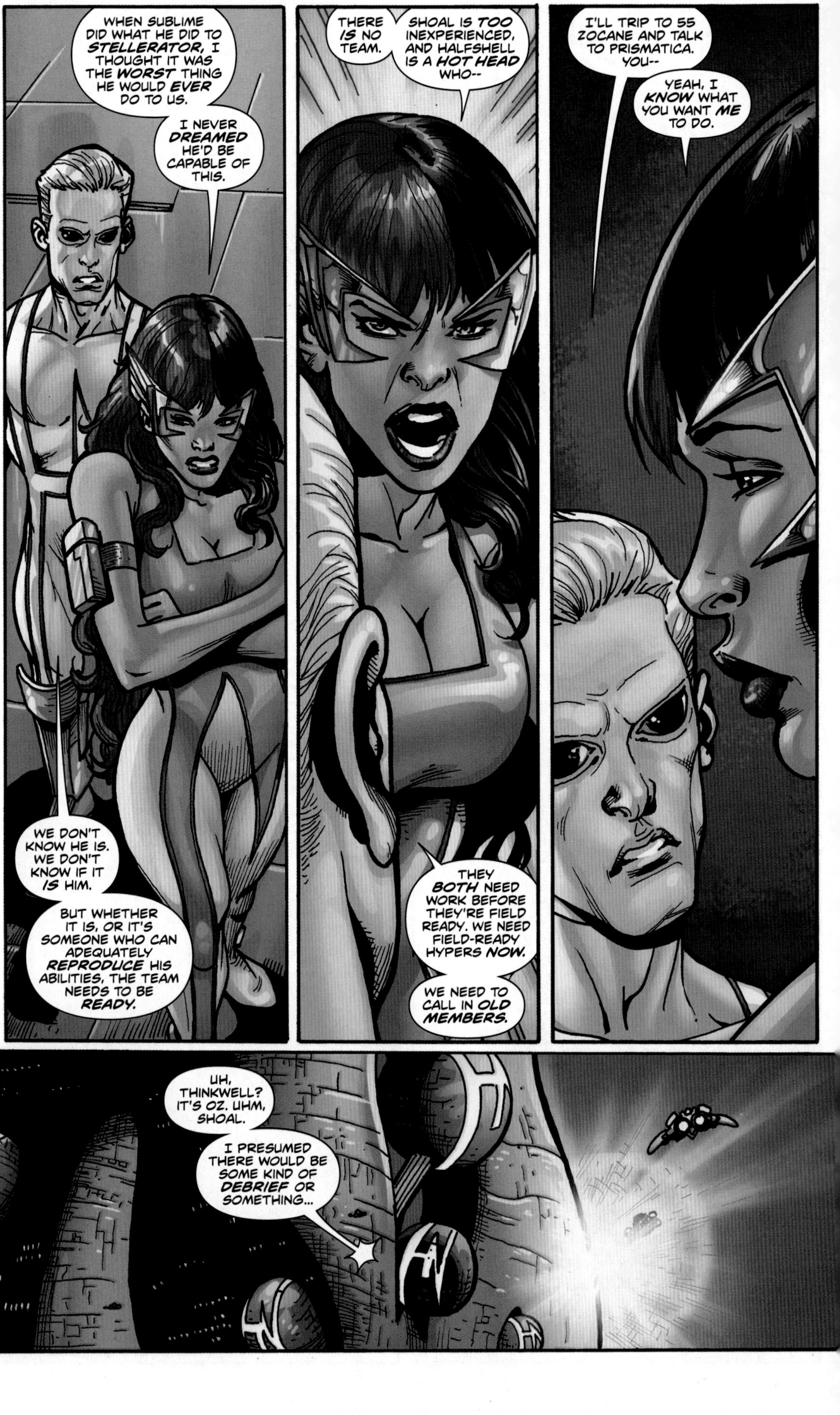
WHEN SUBLIME DID WHAT HE DID TO STELLERATOR, I THOUGHT IT WAS THE WORST THING HE WOULD EVER DO TO US.
I NEVER DREAMED HE'D BE CAPABLE OF THIS.
WE DON'T KNOW HE IS. WE DON'T KNOW IF IT IS HIM.
BUT WHETHER IT IS, OR IT'S SOMEONE WHO CAN ADEQUATELY REPRODUCE HIS ABILITIES, THE TEAM NEEDS TO BE READY.
THERE IS NO TEAM.
SHOAL IS TOO INEXPERIENCED, AND HALFSHELL IS A HOT HEAD WHO--
THEY BOTH NEED WORK BEFORE THEY'RE FIELD READY. WE NEED FIELD-READY HYPERS NOW.
WE NEED TO CALL IN OLD MEMBERS.
I'LL TRIP TO 55 ZOCANE AND TALK TO PRISMATICA. YOU--
YEAH, I KNOW WHAT YOU WANT ME TO DO.
UH, THINKWELL? IT'S OZ. UHM, SHOAL.
I PRESUMED THERE WOULD BE SOME KIND OF DEBRIEF OR SOMETHING...

OF COURSE, WE'LL GET TO IT LATER. BEWILDER AND I HAVE SOME URGENT THINGS TO DEAL WITH.

GO AND FIND HALFSHELL. THE TWO OF YOU SHOULD GET Q-DATA TO RUN YOU SOME MISSION ORIENTATION EXAMS WHILE YOU'RE WAITING FOR US TO GET BACK.

WE...WE DID OKAY, THOUGH, DIDN'T WE?

I MEAN, I KNOW IT COULD'VE GONE BETTER...

THE CIRCUMSTANCES WERE FAR FROM IDEAL. NEITHER OF YOU IS FULLY READY FOR ACTIVE DEPLOYMENT.

THERE IS WORK TO DO, OZ. AND WE'LL GET TO IT.

BUT FOR NOW, WE HAVE OUR HANDS FULL.

OKAY. I UNDERSTAND.

GOOD. DON'T BE DISCOURAGED. FIND HALFSHELL. START RUNNING THOSE ORIENTATION EXERCISES.

ANY TIPS?

YOU TEND TO OVER-THINK, OZ. SHE DOESN'T THINK ENOUGH. YOU COULD START FROM THERE.

OKAY.

Q-MUNICATION ENDED.

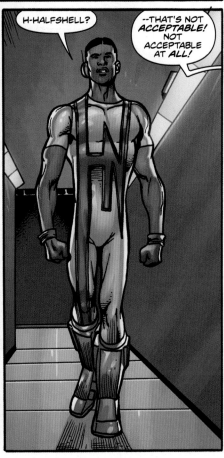

H-HALFSHELL?

--THAT'S NOT ACCEPTABLE! NOT ACCEPTABLE AT ALL!

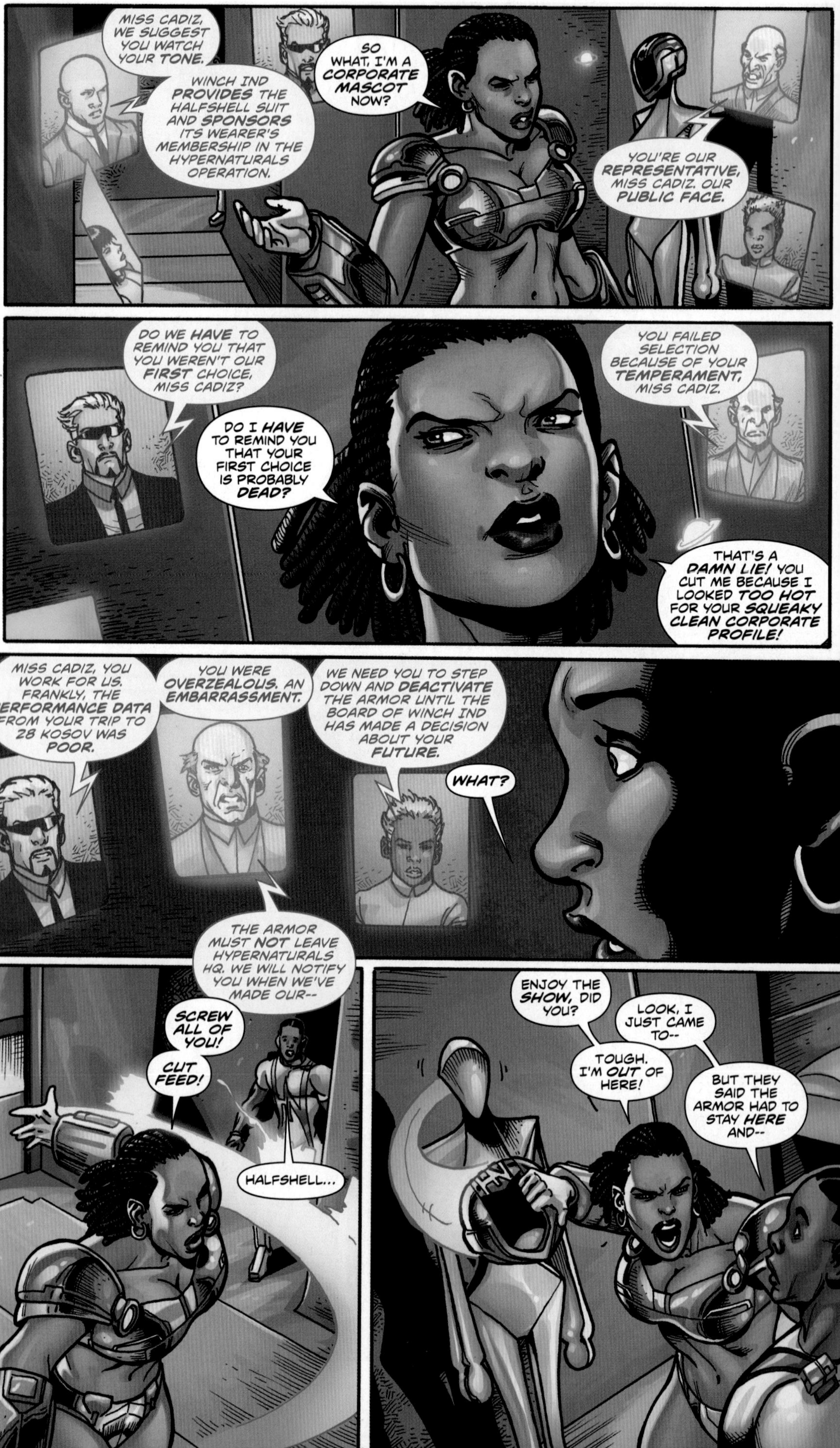
MISS CADIZ, WE SUGGEST YOU WATCH YOUR TONE.
WINCH IND PROVIDES THE HALFSHELL SUIT AND SPONSORS ITS WEARER'S MEMBERSHIP IN THE HYPERNATURALS OPERATION.
SO WHAT, I'M A CORPORATE MASCOT NOW?
YOU'RE OUR REPRESENTATIVE, MISS CADIZ. OUR PUBLIC FACE.
DO WE HAVE TO REMIND YOU THAT YOU WEREN'T OUR FIRST CHOICE, MISS CADIZ?
DO I HAVE TO REMIND YOU THAT YOUR FIRST CHOICE IS PROBABLY DEAD?
YOU FAILED SELECTION BECAUSE OF YOUR TEMPERAMENT, MISS CADIZ.
THAT'S A DAMN LIE! YOU CUT ME BECAUSE I LOOKED TOO HOT FOR YOUR SQUEAKY CLEAN CORPORATE PROFILE!
MISS CADIZ, YOU WORK FOR US. FRANKLY, THE PERFORMANCE DATA FROM YOUR TRIP TO 28 KOSOV WAS POOR.
YOU WERE OVERZEALOUS. AN EMBARRASSMENT.
WE NEED YOU TO STEP DOWN AND DEACTIVATE THE ARMOR UNTIL THE BOARD OF WINCH IND HAS MADE A DECISION ABOUT YOUR FUTURE.
WHAT?
THE ARMOR MUST NOT LEAVE HYPERNATURALS HQ. WE WILL NOTIFY YOU WHEN WE'VE MADE OUR--
SCREW ALL OF YOU!
CUT FEED!
HALFSHELL...
ENJOY THE SHOW, DID YOU?
LOOK, I JUST CAME TO--
TOUGH. I'M OUT OF HERE!
BUT THEY SAID THE ARMOR HAD TO STAY HERE AND--

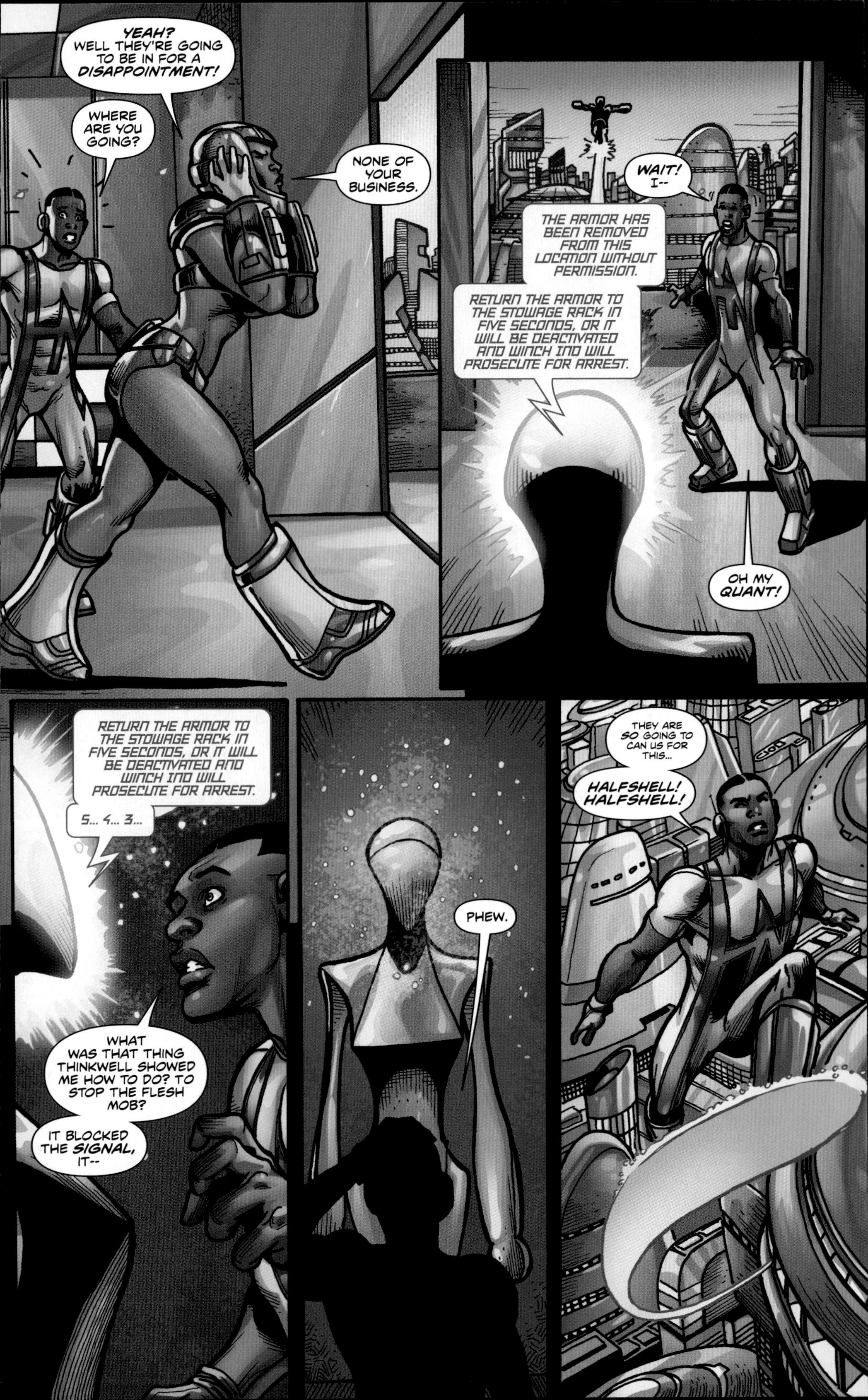
YEAH? WELL THEY'RE GOING TO BE IN FOR A DISAPPOINTMENT!
WHERE ARE YOU GOING?
NONE OF YOUR BUSINESS.
WAIT! I--
THE ARMOR HAS BEEN REMOVED FROM THIS LOCATION WITHOUT PERMISSION.
RETURN THE ARMOR TO THE STOWAGE RACK IN FIVE SECONDS, OR IT WILL BE DEACTIVATED AND WINCH IND WILL PROSECUTE FOR ARREST.
OH MY QUANT!
RETURN THE ARMOR TO THE STOWAGE RACK IN FIVE SECONDS, OR IT WILL BE DEACTIVATED AND WINCH IND WILL PROSECUTE FOR ARREST.
5... 4... 3...
WHAT WAS THAT THING THINKWELL SHOWED ME HOW TO DO? TO STOP THE FLESH MOB?
IT BLOCKED THE SIGNAL, IT--
PHEW.
THEY ARE SO GOING TO CAN US FOR THIS...
HALFSHELL! HALFSHELL!

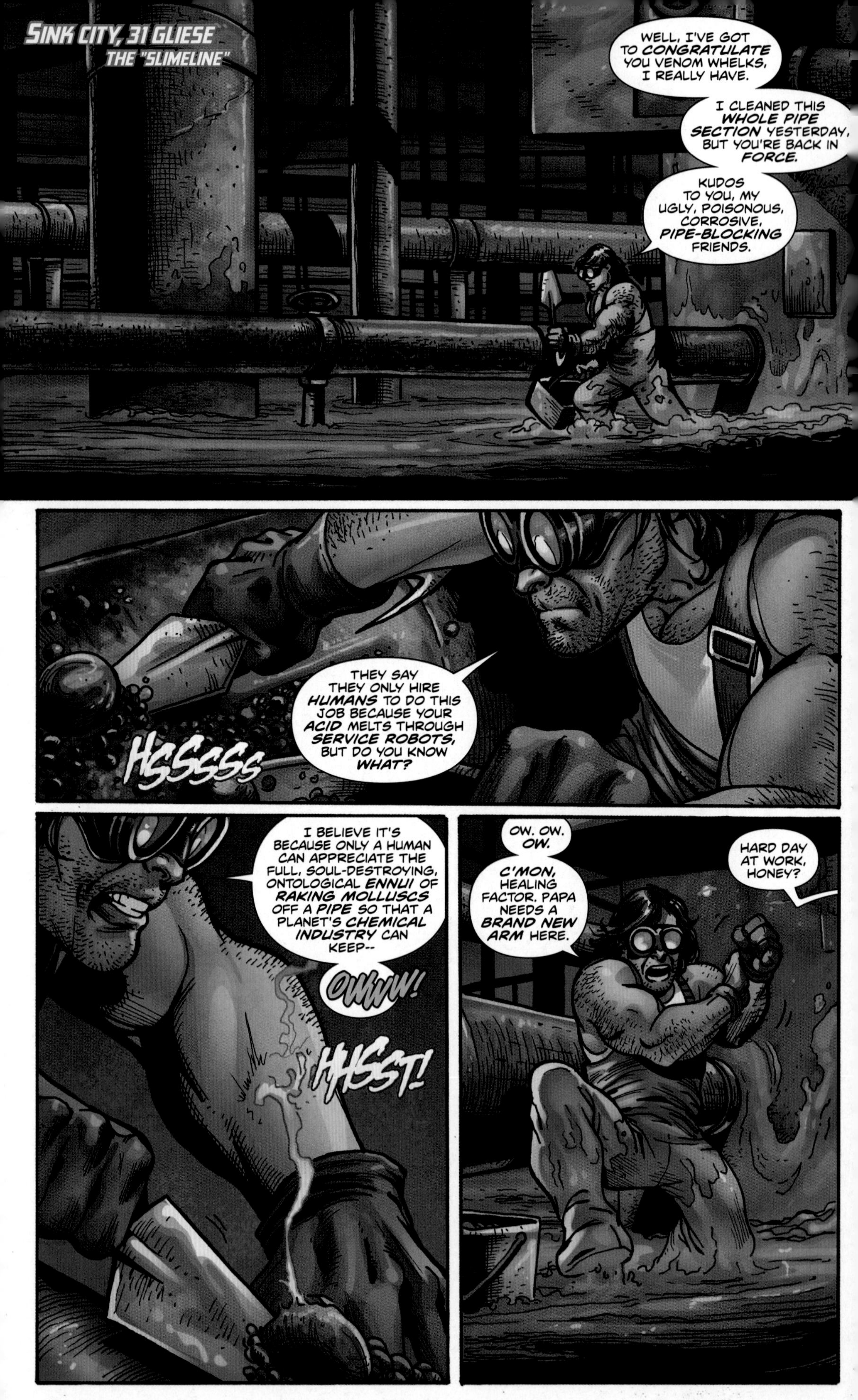
SINK CITY, 31 GLIESE
THE "SLIMELINE"
WELL, I'VE GOT TO CONGRATULATE YOU VENOM WHELKS, I REALLY HAVE.
I CLEANED THIS WHOLE PIPE SECTION YESTERDAY, BUT YOU'RE BACK IN FORCE.
KUDOS TO YOU, MY UGLY, POISONOUS, CORROSIVE, PIPE-BLOCKING FRIENDS.
HSSSSS
THEY SAY THEY ONLY HIRE HUMANS TO DO THIS JOB BECAUSE YOUR ACID MELTS THROUGH SERVICE ROBOTS, BUT DO YOU KNOW WHAT?
I BELIEVE IT'S BECAUSE ONLY A HUMAN CAN APPRECIATE THE FULL, SOUL-DESTROYING, ONTOLOGICAL ENNUI OF RAKING MOLLUSCS OFF A PIPE SO THAT A PLANET'S CHEMICAL INDUSTRY CAN KEEP--
OWWW!
HHSST!
OW. OW. OW.
C'MON, HEALING FACTOR. PAPA NEEDS A BRAND NEW ARM HERE.
HARD DAY AT WORK, HONEY?

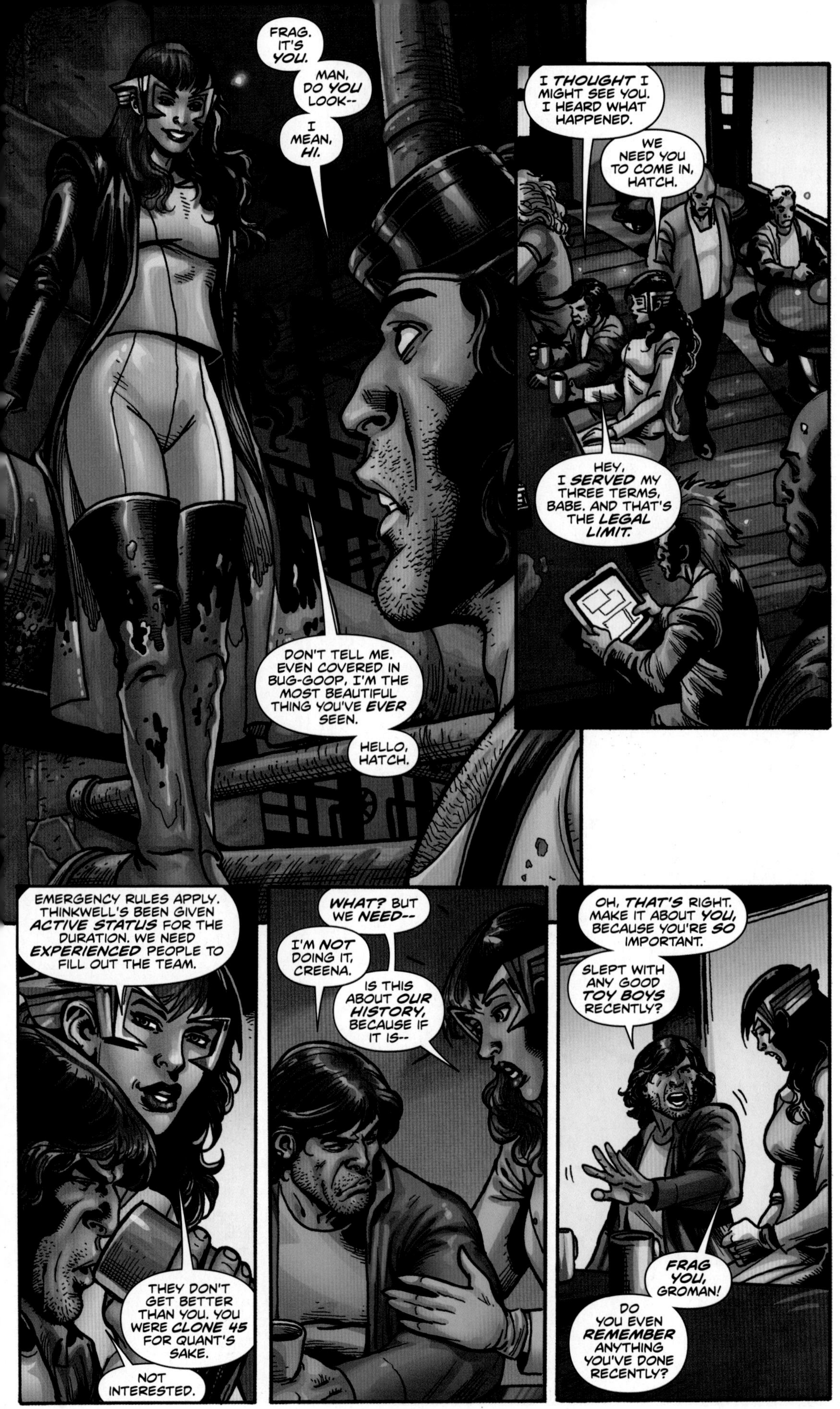
FRAG. IT'S *YOU.*
MAN, DO *YOU* LOOK--
I MEAN, *HI.*
DON'T TELL ME. EVEN COVERED IN BUG-GOOP, I'M THE MOST BEAUTIFUL THING YOU'VE *EVER* SEEN.
HELLO, HATCH.
I *THOUGHT* I MIGHT SEE YOU. I HEARD WHAT HAPPENED.
WE NEED YOU TO COME IN, HATCH.
HEY, I *SERVED* MY THREE TERMS, BABE. AND THAT'S THE *LEGAL LIMIT.*
EMERGENCY RULES APPLY. THINKWELL'S BEEN GIVEN *ACTIVE STATUS* FOR THE DURATION. WE NEED *EXPERIENCED* PEOPLE TO FILL OUT THE TEAM.
THEY DON'T GET BETTER THAN YOU. YOU WERE *CLONE 45* FOR QUANT'S SAKE.
NOT INTERESTED.
WHAT? BUT WE *NEED--*
I'M *NOT* DOING IT, CREENA.
IS THIS ABOUT *OUR HISTORY,* BECAUSE IF IT IS--
OH, *THAT'S* RIGHT. MAKE IT ABOUT *YOU,* BECAUSE YOU'RE *SO* IMPORTANT.
SLEPT WITH ANY GOOD *TOY BOYS* RECENTLY?
FRAG YOU, GROMAN!
DO YOU EVEN *REMEMBER* ANYTHING YOU'VE DONE RECENTLY?

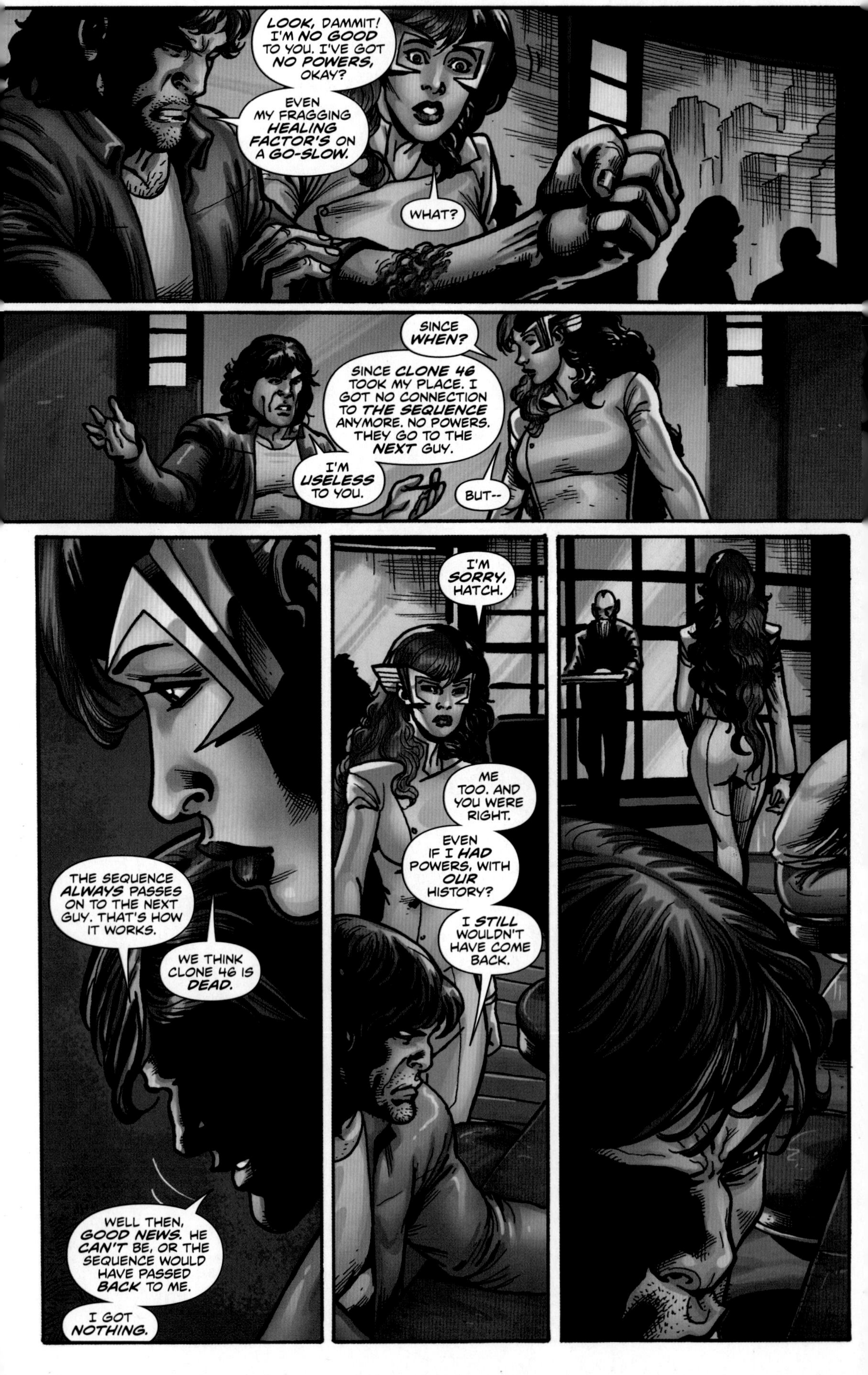
LOOK, DAMMIT! I'M NO GOOD TO YOU. I'VE GOT NO POWERS, OKAY?
EVEN MY FRAGGING HEALING FACTOR'S ON A GO-SLOW.
WHAT?
SINCE WHEN?
SINCE CLONE 46 TOOK MY PLACE. I GOT NO CONNECTION TO THE SEQUENCE ANYMORE. NO POWERS. THEY GO TO THE NEXT GUY.
I'M USELESS TO YOU.
BUT--
THE SEQUENCE ALWAYS PASSES ON TO THE NEXT GUY. THAT'S HOW IT WORKS.
WE THINK CLONE 46 IS DEAD.
WELL THEN, GOOD NEWS. HE CAN'T BE, OR THE SEQUENCE WOULD HAVE PASSED BACK TO ME.
I GOT NOTHING.
I'M SORRY, HATCH.
ME TOO. AND YOU WERE RIGHT.
EVEN IF I HAD POWERS, WITH OUR HISTORY?
I STILL WOULDN'T HAVE COME BACK.

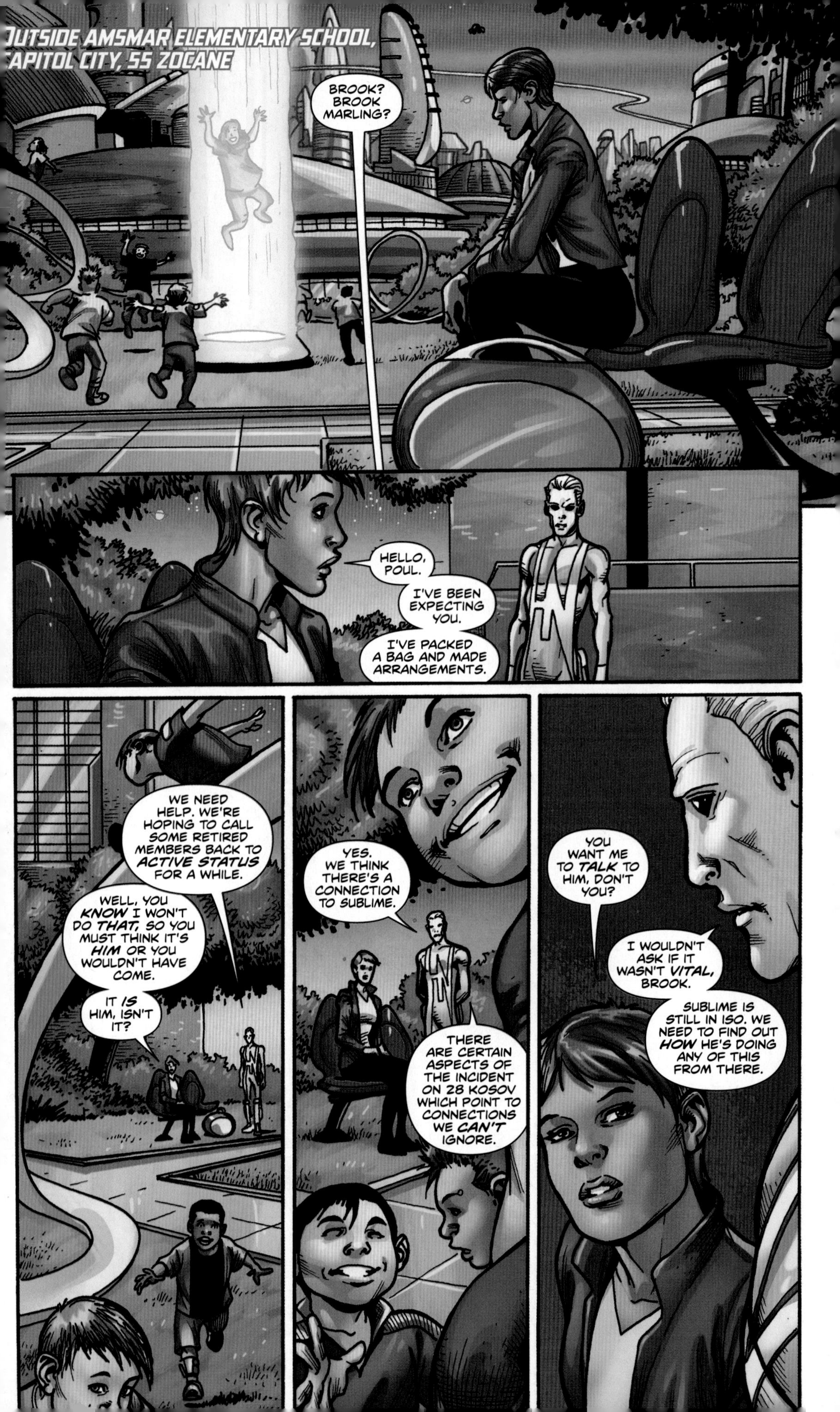
OUTSIDE AMSMAR ELEMENTARY SCHOOL, CAPITOL CITY, 55 ZOCANE
BROOK? BROOK MARLING?
HELLO, POUL.
I'VE BEEN EXPECTING YOU.
I'VE PACKED A BAG AND MADE ARRANGEMENTS.
WE NEED HELP. WE'RE HOPING TO CALL SOME RETIRED MEMBERS BACK TO ACTIVE STATUS FOR A WHILE.
WELL, YOU KNOW I WON'T DO THAT, SO YOU MUST THINK IT'S HIM OR YOU WOULDN'T HAVE COME.
IT IS HIM, ISN'T IT?
YES. WE THINK THERE'S A CONNECTION TO SUBLIME.
THERE ARE CERTAIN ASPECTS OF THE INCIDENT ON 28 KOSOV WHICH POINT TO CONNECTIONS WE CAN'T IGNORE.
YOU WANT ME TO TALK TO HIM, DON'T YOU?
I WOULDN'T ASK IF IT WASN'T VITAL, BROOK.
SUBLIME IS STILL IN ISO. WE NEED TO FIND OUT HOW HE'S DOING ANY OF THIS FROM THERE.

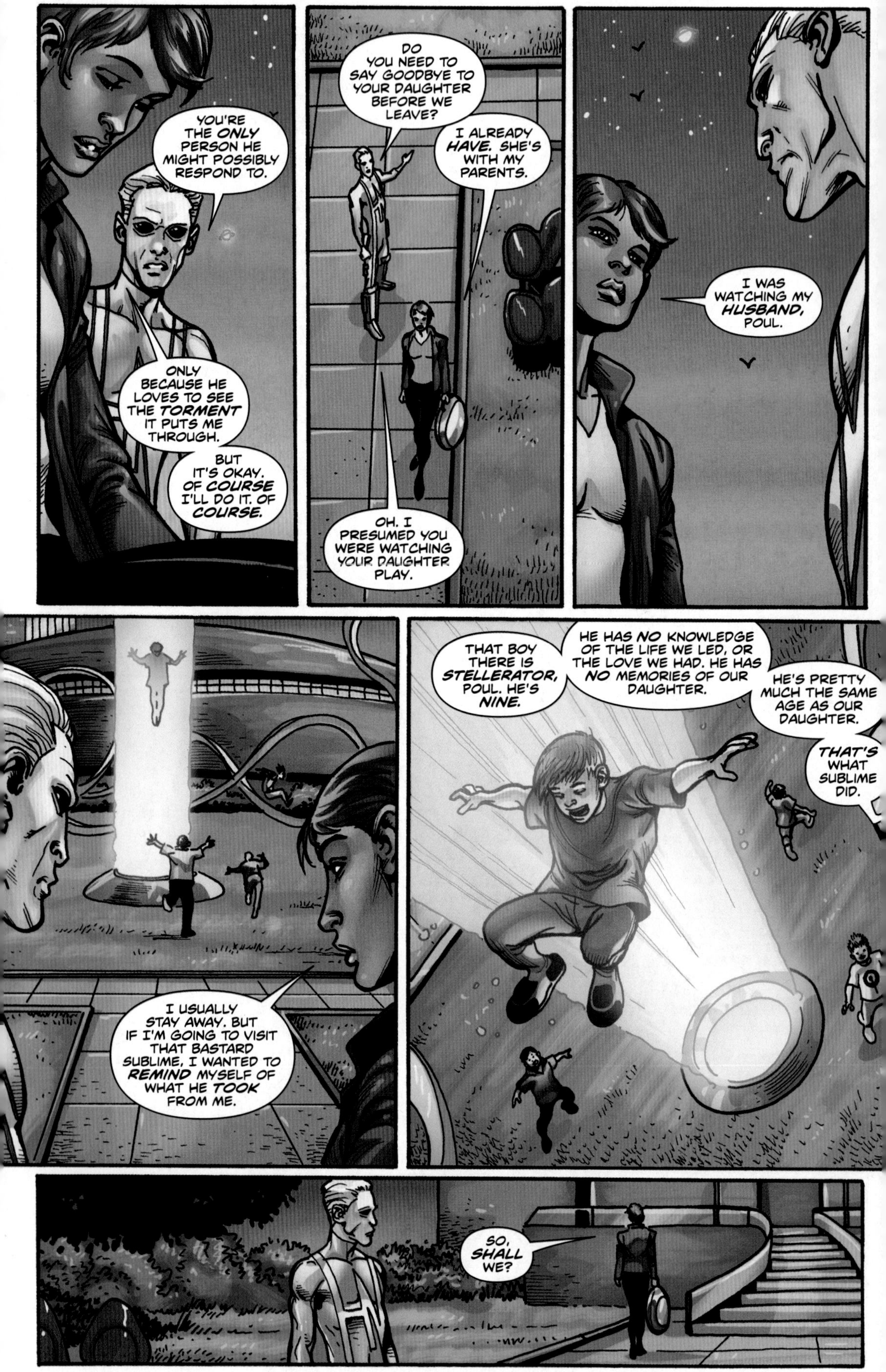
YOU'RE THE ONLY PERSON HE MIGHT POSSIBLY RESPOND TO.
ONLY BECAUSE HE LOVES TO SEE THE TORMENT IT PUTS ME THROUGH.
BUT IT'S OKAY. OF COURSE I'LL DO IT. OF COURSE.
DO YOU NEED TO SAY GOODBYE TO YOUR DAUGHTER BEFORE WE LEAVE?
I ALREADY HAVE. SHE'S WITH MY PARENTS.
OH. I PRESUMED YOU WERE WATCHING YOUR DAUGHTER PLAY.
I WAS WATCHING MY HUSBAND, POUL.
I USUALLY STAY AWAY. BUT IF I'M GOING TO VISIT THAT BASTARD SUBLIME, I WANTED TO REMIND MYSELF OF WHAT HE TOOK FROM ME.
THAT BOY THERE IS STELLERATOR, POUL. HE'S NINE.
HE HAS NO KNOWLEDGE OF THE LIFE WE LED, OR THE LOVE WE HAD. HE HAS NO MEMORIES OF OUR DAUGHTER.
HE'S PRETTY MUCH THE SAME AGE AS OUR DAUGHTER.
THAT'S WHAT SUBLIME DID.
SO, SHALL WE?

MAGNETAR - KOBALT BLUE - CLONE 46
ALFSHELL - MUSCLEWIRE - EGO/ID - ASTROMANCER

CENTENNIAL ITERATION
A CENTURY OF SERVICE

THINK WELL, CHOOSE WISELY

Poul Indersun, the Turing Professor of Cryptomathematics at Cambridge University, takes questions from Scientific Quantinuum's Crayse Jeffers.

Any questions.

Photographs by Charles Fife

SQ: You've often been described as the smartest man in the Quantinuum. Is that a title you have any time for?

PI: Not really. And it's not a question of modesty, merely accuracy. I have a Class 10 hyper-intellect further enhanced by Class 7 physical hyper-traits. I am extremely capable. But I am hardly the "smartest man." There are nineteen other known Class Ten intellects, plus an unconfirmed Class 11 in the Brantix System that representatives of the Hypernaturals Program are just now investigating. Then of course, there's Byrd.

SQ: You mean John Alvin Byrd?

PI: Yes, better known as Sublime. Sublime was a very grave threat to Quantinuum security. Seven years ago, he almost destroyed the very basis of our society and brought the Nanocene to a crashing end.

SQ: This is his attack on the Quantinuum Computer itself?

PI: That's correct. Byrd believed—still believes, I understand—in human determinism. When the Quantinuum Computer achieved singularity in 0 A.Q. and our modern age began, everyone considered this to be a liberation of humanity. With the Quantinuum AI watching over us and managing our culture, we were free to set our own destinies. The improbable became likely and the impossible became possible. Byrd disagreed. He felt that we had manufactured a god to decide our destiny for us. He felt we had shackled ourselves and removed personal determinism from our lives. He felt that science had finally removed the necessity for God, only to replace it with another, artificial god...Anyway, my point is that in order to become that level of threat, where the Quantinuum Core was actually under

a real and present threat, Byrd needed to be smart. Like me, his intellect is enhanced by physical hyper-gifts, or alterations, as he would see them. But the basic fact is that his intellect is his greatest weapon.

SQ: He is said to be Class 13.

PI: I've seen the spread of the testing data. He varies from Class 12 to Class 15 depending on the attribute and conditions.

SQ: You sound like you admire him.

PI: He is eminently admirable. I mourn the fact that an intellect of that magnitude chooses to work against the cultural good, but I cannot help admire it. Byrd is a brilliant man, but he is also psychotic, sociopathic and formidably dangerous.

SQ: You were on the team that stopped him.

PI: Yes.

SQ: Tell us about your service as a Hypernatural.

PI: I served the maximum three terms, between 85 A.Q. and 99 A.Q. I was privileged to be part of the so-called "Nineteenth Tour" that seems to have won a particular place in the public imagination. It was infinitely rewarding.

SQ: Would you have liked to continue? If not for the term-limit cap?

PI: No. I had done my service. My research work at Cambridge is where my real interest lies. And I was always a most unlikely "hero."

SQ: Unlikely?

PI: Unorthodox.

SQ: How do your physical hyper-traits function? The "ink"?

PI: It's an almost unfathomable mystery. A freak occurrence. As far as research is so far able to determine, the "ink" within me is a form of dark matter or dark energy that I can manipulate and shape, and through which I can extend and manifest my sentience and my intellect. It is a transcendent data-cognitive substance, a self-aware instrument for the transfer or interpretation of information.

SQ: So the one great mystery that your mind cannot fathom is yourself?

PI: [laughs] Yes, ironically. Actually, there are many mysteries in the cosmos I haven't figured out yet. But certainly, I am one of them.

SQ: Your hyper-power was certainly very popular with kids across the Quantinuum. Writing ink marks on the air, equations that then transformed reality. Like magic.

PI: I suppose so, according to Clarke's famous law. As I said, it's simply a way of expressing information or data in physical form.

SQ: What do you think of the team these days? The newly announced "Centennial Iteration"?

PI: I've not really been following it. I'm sure the directors of the Hypernaturals Program have made some excellent choices. I am rather lost in research, these days.

SQ: Forgive me, but editorial at Scientific Quantinuum is very keen to explore the limits of your mind. Would you be up for some random testing?

PI: [smiles] Why not?

SQ: Is Selinger's Postulation provable?

PI: Yes. People seem needlessly distracted by the fundamental integer series. I see no particular problem.

SQ: Can you calculate shift-light as a non-stable dynamic?

PI: For what?

SQ: Well...my notepad?

PI: 847.5 Kiloquants.

SQ: Is that...?

PI: Please check.

SQ: What about Burgman's Thesis? Does it—

PI: Burgman's Thesis is, I'm sorry to say, rubbish. It is entirely undone by his failure to rationalize the initial number code.

SQ: Is there a god?

PI: There has been one since 0 A.Q. Is there a Creator? That's a different question.

SQ: Frate Prady at IMT believes that the "Krole" language of 34 Giovanni can be turned into a sustainable form of low-impact biofuel.

PI: Your question?

SQ: Is he right?

PI: Yes, Frate is right. Except it's a human patois, not a language. You need to translate the language into quantum numerals, and it automatically recodes as an energy form.

SQ: How do you solve Antebilt's Last Theorum?

PI: First, you need to set aside the proxy numerics, then divide the remaining component...

[continued on page 65]

"...there are many mysteries in the cosmos I haven't figured out yet. But certainly, I am one of them."

CHAPTER THREE

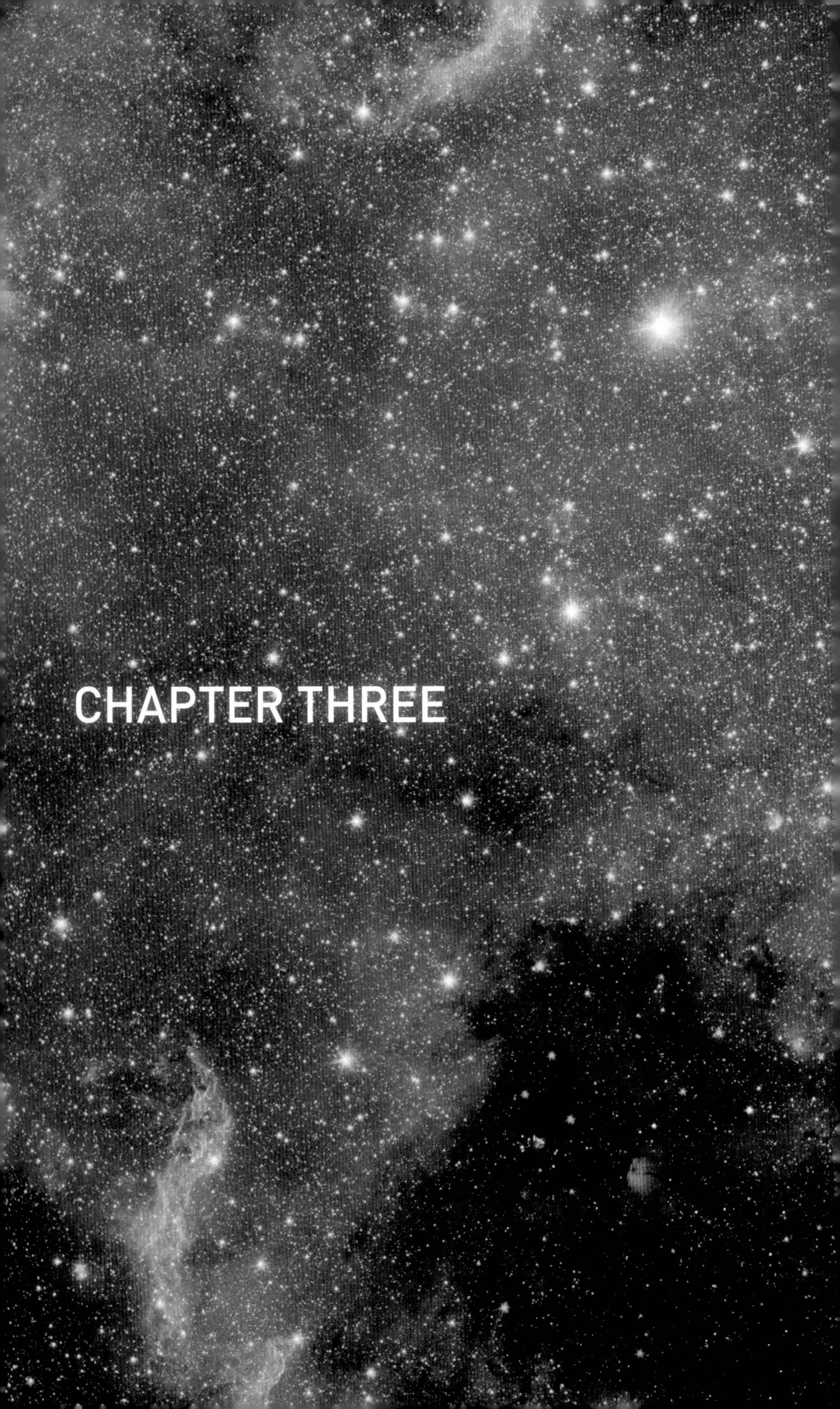

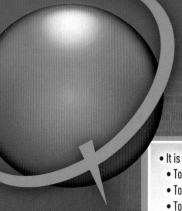

• You have selected Q-Data link.

• It is the 10th of January in the year 100 A.Q.
  • Touch here to select an alternative to the **Anno Quantinuum** calendar system.
  • Touch here to load local weather reports for your **current cosmic location**.
  • Touch here to access **Q-Data newsflows** from planets near your current cosmic location.
  • Touch here for latest **Quantum Trip** transit times.

• Q-Data entry: The Quantinuum

• The Quantinuum is the name for the human galactic culture, and also for the **artificial intelligence** that controls its function.

• The Quantinuum was created 100 years ago at the start of the **Nanocene Era**. The Nanocene began when the Quantinuum AI achieved Singularity and refashioned human galactic culture. Succeeding the **Holocene Era**, the Nanocene is the next progression of human evolution and...

(to read this entry in full, touch here)

• You have selected live feed newsflow.

• Cyclonic super-storm hits **22 Hassan**
• **Plent-Morgan-Fraber** recalls eight million vapor-bikes after accident ruling
• Vostok **All-Stars** go through to third round, **Berlin Bears** go out
• **AI Law** star Fed Cartney marries long-time life partner
• Concern remains high for fate of the Centennial Year Iteration of the **Hypernaturals Team**, apparently lost during an emergency response mission to 28 Kosov

• The Hypernaturals are the Quantinuum's foremost champions. Famous across the entirety of human galactic culture, the team members are selected on the basis of their hypernatural powers and their strength of character, and serve for five-year terms. In honor of the start of the twenty-first term, the line-up of the team's so-called "Centennial Year Iteration" has recently been announced amid huge publicity and--

...BREAKING NEWS... unconfirmed sources report the entire Hypernaturals Team has vanished on its inaugural mission to 28 Kosov... according to a spokesperson at Hypernaturals Central, San Diego, a special reserve formation of Hypernaturals, including now-retired team members Bewilder and Thinkwell from the classic "Nineteenth Tour" line-up, has investigated the site on 28 Kosov... rumors of a survivor have circulated...

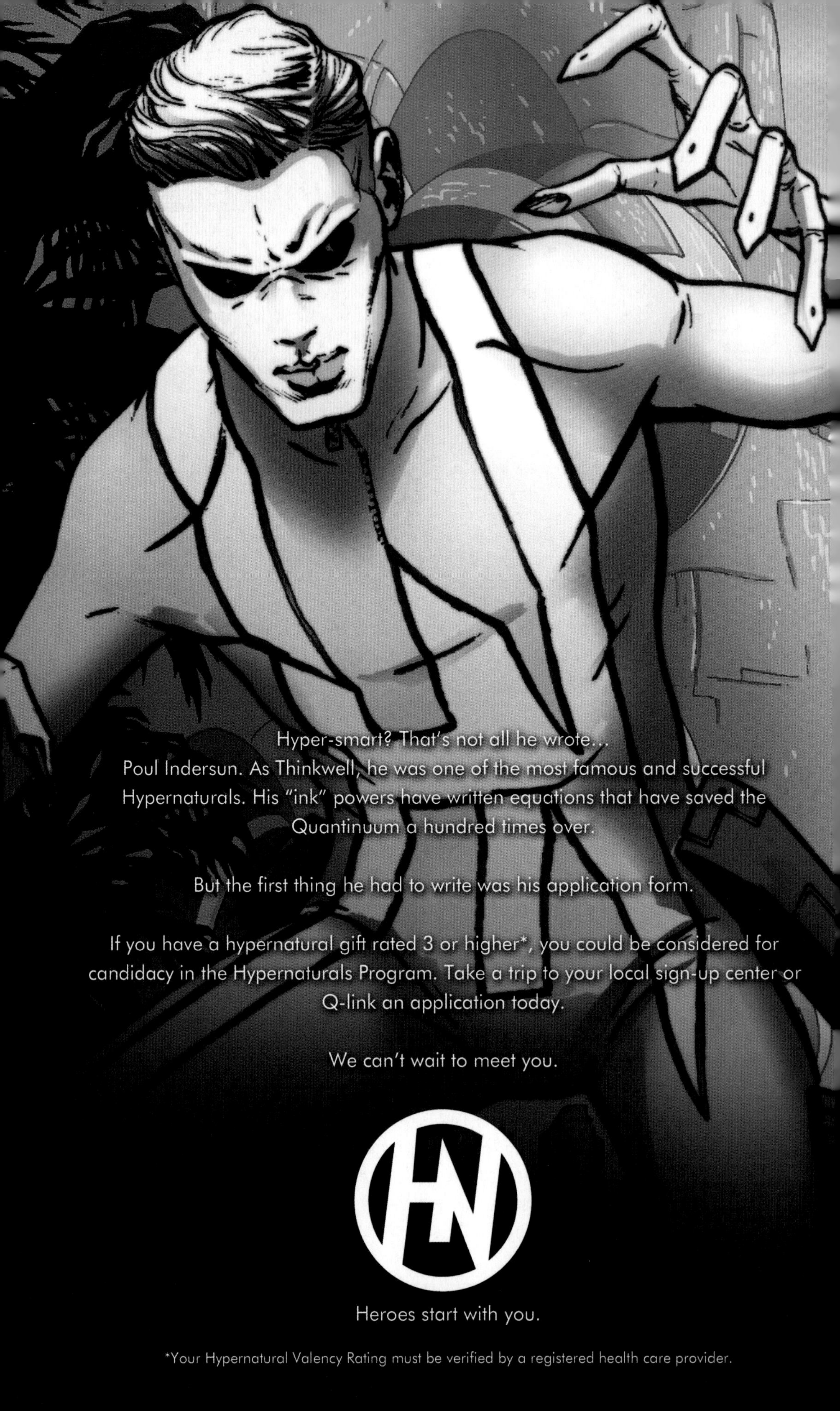
Hyper-smart? That's not all he wrote...
Poul Indersun. As Thinkwell, he was one of the most famous and successful Hypernaturals. His "ink" powers have written equations that have saved the Quantinuum a hundred times over.
But the first thing he had to write was his application form.
If you have a hypernatural gift rated 3 or higher*, you could be considered for candidacy in the Hypernaturals Program. Take a trip to your local sign-up center or Q-link an application today.
We can't wait to meet you.
HN
Heroes start with you.
*Your Hypernatural Valency Rating must be verified by a registered health care provider.

THE BAD TRIP
77 ZASTRUGI ICE WORLD,
93 A.Q. (SEVEN YEARS AGO)

--IN PURSUIT! I SAY AGAIN, I AM IN PURSUIT! SUBLIME'S TRYING TO MAKE A BREAK FOR IT! HE'S TRIPPING--

STELLERATOR? SAY AGAIN! REPEAT! WHAT IS YOUR LOCATION?

STELLERATOR TO ALL HYPERNATURALS. SUBLIME IS RUNNING! REPEAT, SUBLIME IS RUNNING!

HE'S HACKED INTO THE TRIP NETWORK. HE'S TRIPPING! I'VE LOCKED ONTO HIM WITH A MAGNETIC FIELD--

--ZASTRUGI! Q-DATA'S TELLING ME WE'VE JUST TRIPPED TO 77 ZASTRUGI!

EN ROUTE! STAND BY!

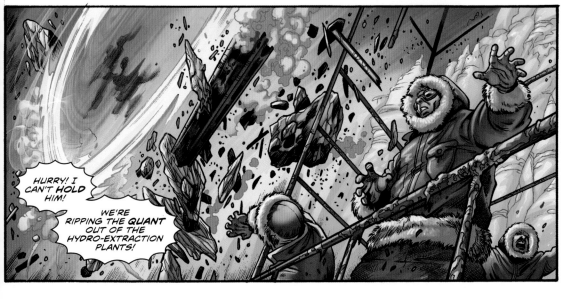

HURRY! I CAN'T HOLD HIM!

WE'RE RIPPING THE QUANT OUT OF THE HYDRO-EXTRACTION PLANTS!

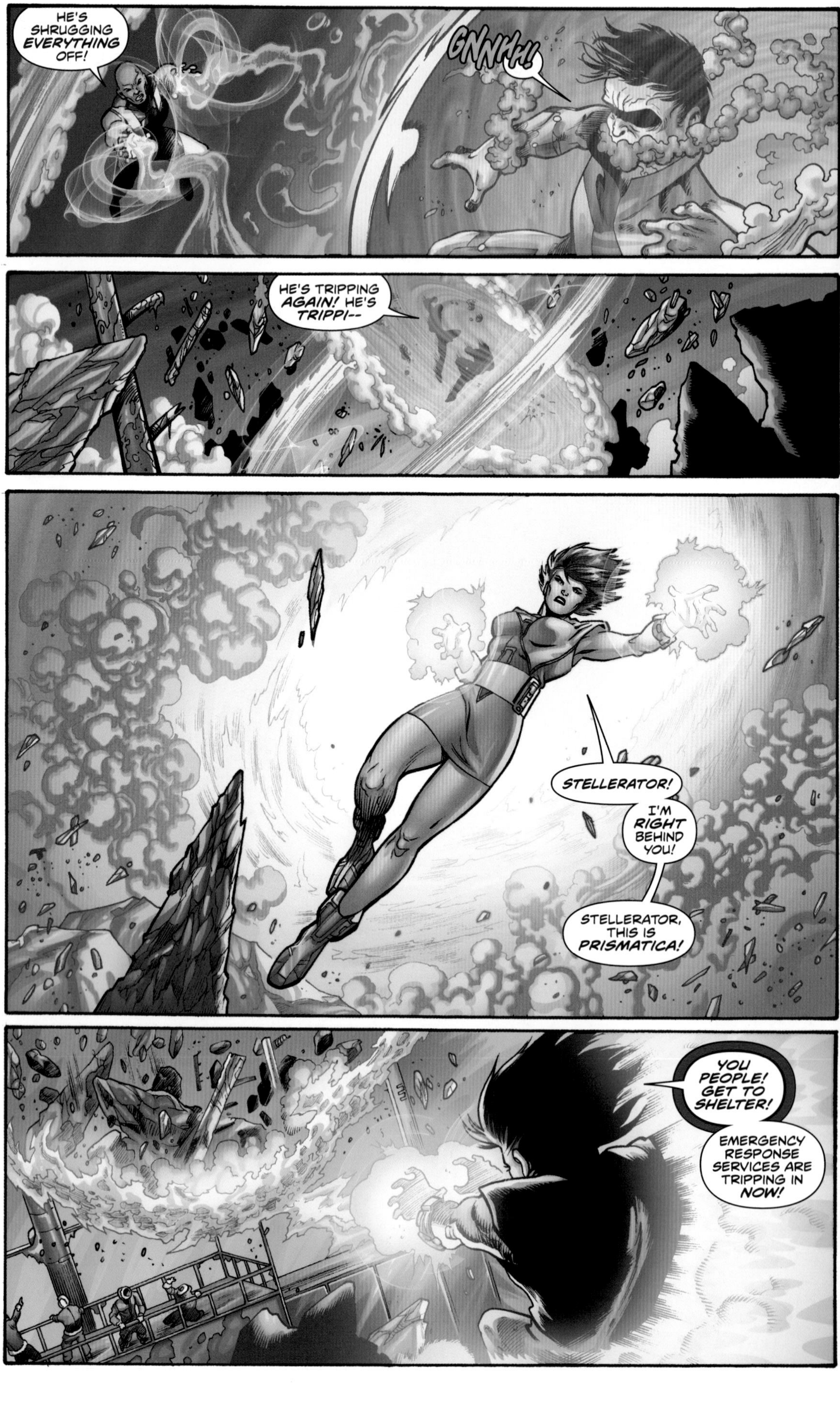
HE'S SHRUGGING EVERYTHING OFF!
GNHHH!!
HE'S TRIPPING AGAIN! HE'S TRIPPI--
STELLERATOR!
I'M RIGHT BEHIND YOU!
STELLERATOR, THIS IS PRISMATICA!
YOU PEOPLE! GET TO SHELTER!
EMERGENCY RESPONSE SERVICES ARE TRIPPING IN NOW!

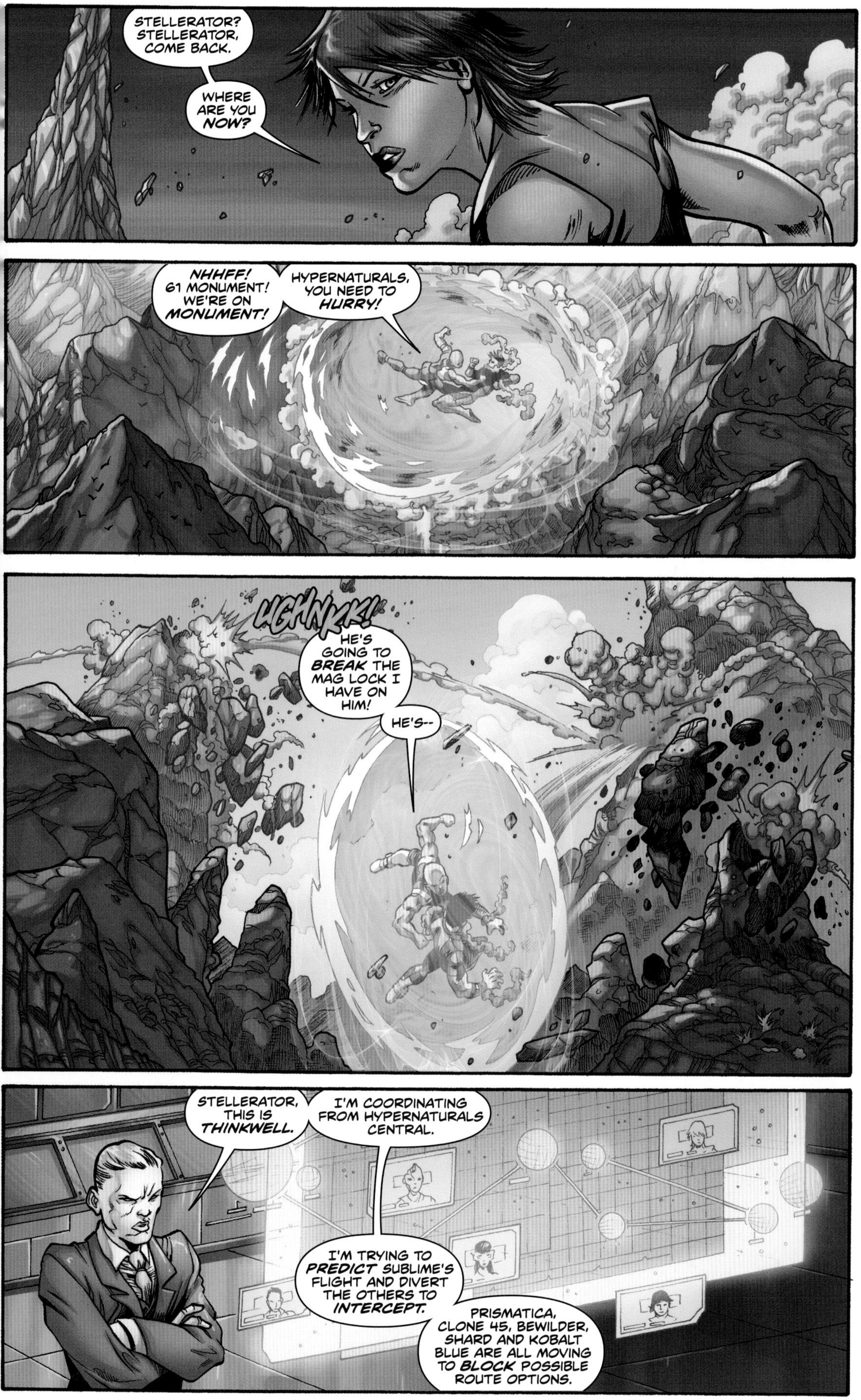
STELLERATOR? STELLERATOR, COME BACK.
WHERE ARE YOU NOW?
NHHFF! 61 MONUMENT! WE'RE ON MONUMENT!
HYPERNATURALS, YOU NEED TO HURRY!
UGHNKK!
HE'S GOING TO BREAK THE MAG LOCK I HAVE ON HIM!
HE'S--
STELLERATOR, THIS IS THINKWELL.
I'M COORDINATING FROM HYPERNATURALS CENTRAL.
I'M TRYING TO PREDICT SUBLIME'S FLIGHT AND DIVERT THE OTHERS TO INTERCEPT.
PRISMATICA, CLONE 45, BEWILDER, SHARD AND KOBALT BLUE ARE ALL MOVING TO BLOCK POSSIBLE ROUTE OPTIONS.

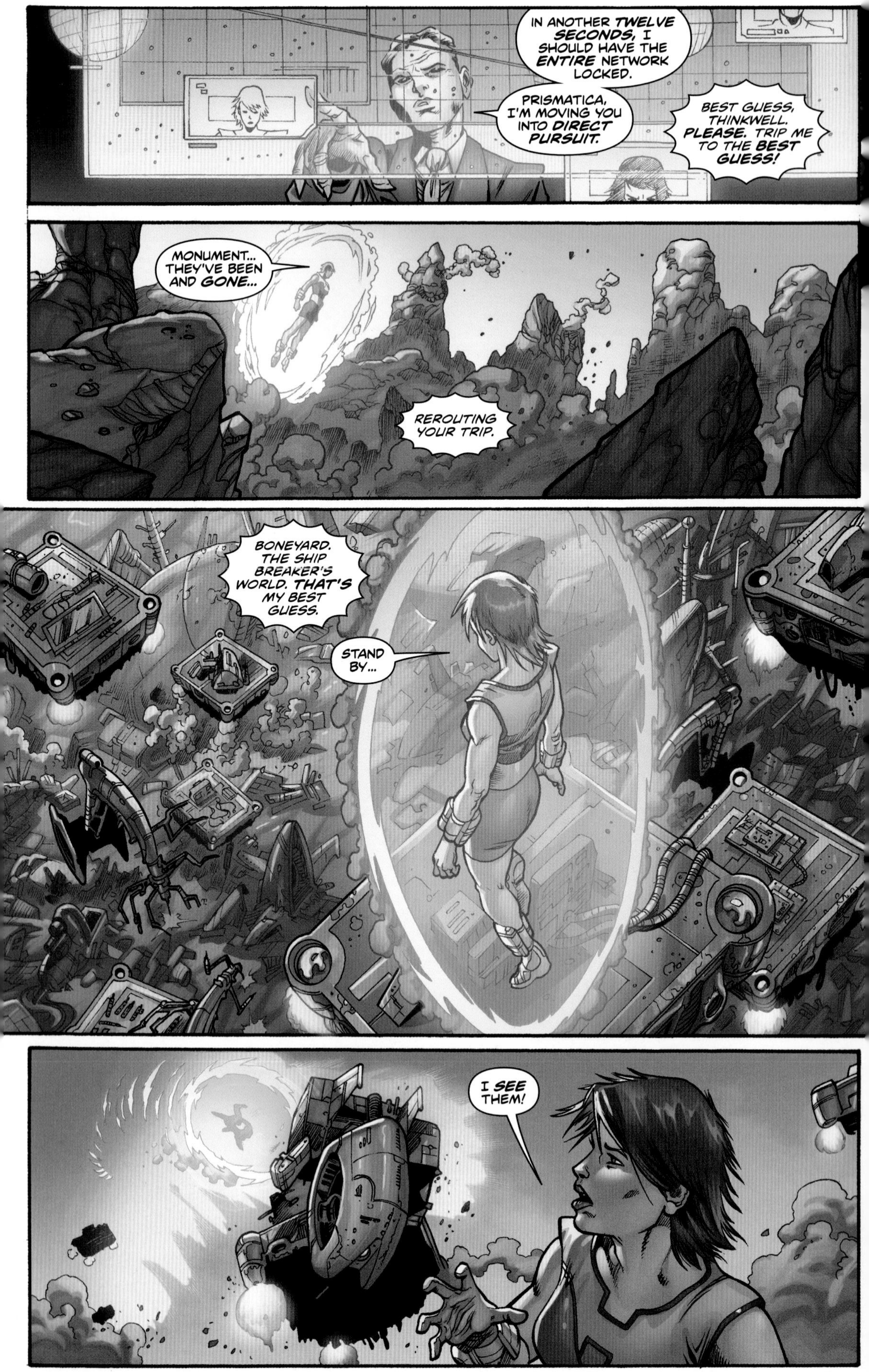

IN ANOTHER TWELVE SECONDS, I SHOULD HAVE THE ENTIRE NETWORK LOCKED.
PRISMATICA, I'M MOVING YOU INTO DIRECT PURSUIT.
BEST GUESS, THINKWELL. PLEASE. TRIP ME TO THE BEST GUESS!
MONUMENT... THEY'VE BEEN AND GONE...
REROUTING YOUR TRIP.
BONEYARD. THE SHIP BREAKER'S WORLD. THAT'S MY BEST GUESS.
STAND BY...
I SEE THEM!

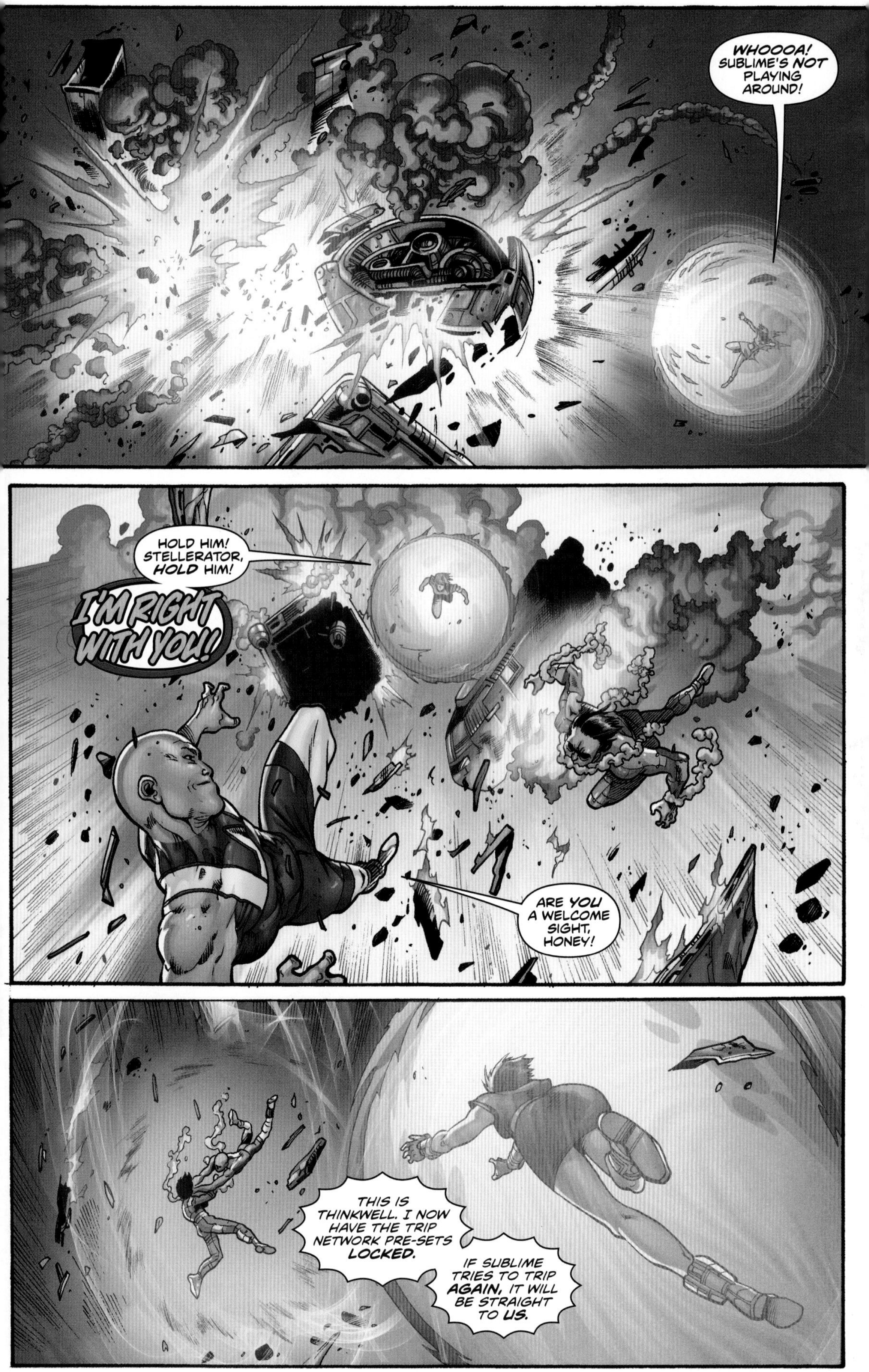

WHOOOA! SUBLIME'S NOT PLAYING AROUND!
HOLD HIM! STELLERATOR, HOLD HIM!
I'M RIGHT WITH YOU!
ARE YOU A WELCOME SIGHT, HONEY!
THIS IS THINKWELL. I NOW HAVE THE TRIP NETWORK PRE-SETS LOCKED.
IF SUBLIME TRIES TO TRIP AGAIN, IT WILL BE STRAIGHT TO US.

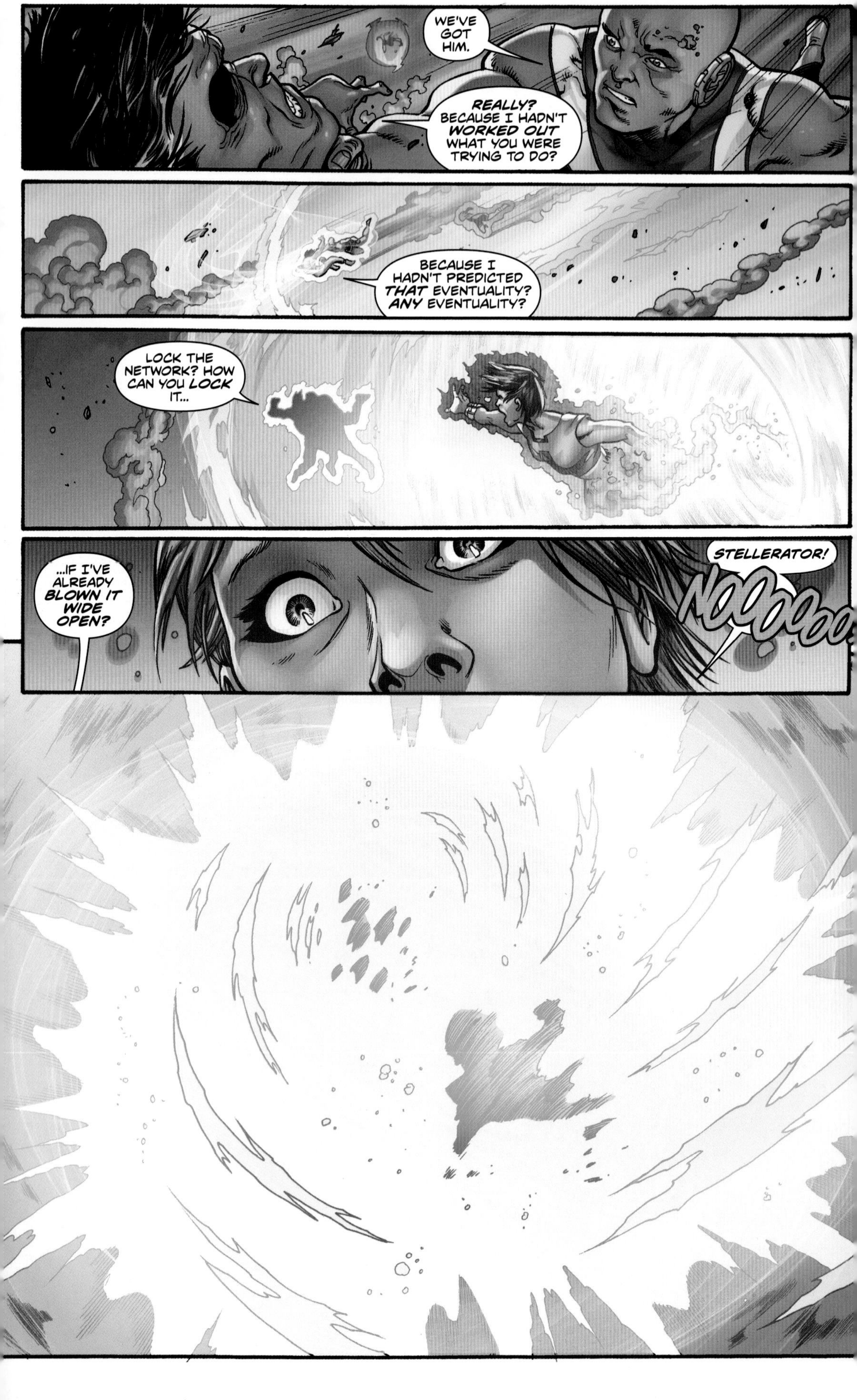
WE'VE GOT HIM.
REALLY? BECAUSE I HADN'T WORKED OUT WHAT YOU WERE TRYING TO DO?
BECAUSE I HADN'T PREDICTED THAT EVENTUALITY? ANY EVENTUALITY?
LOCK THE NETWORK? HOW CAN YOU LOCK IT...
...IF I'VE ALREADY BLOWN IT WIDE OPEN?
STELLERATOR!
NOOOOOOO

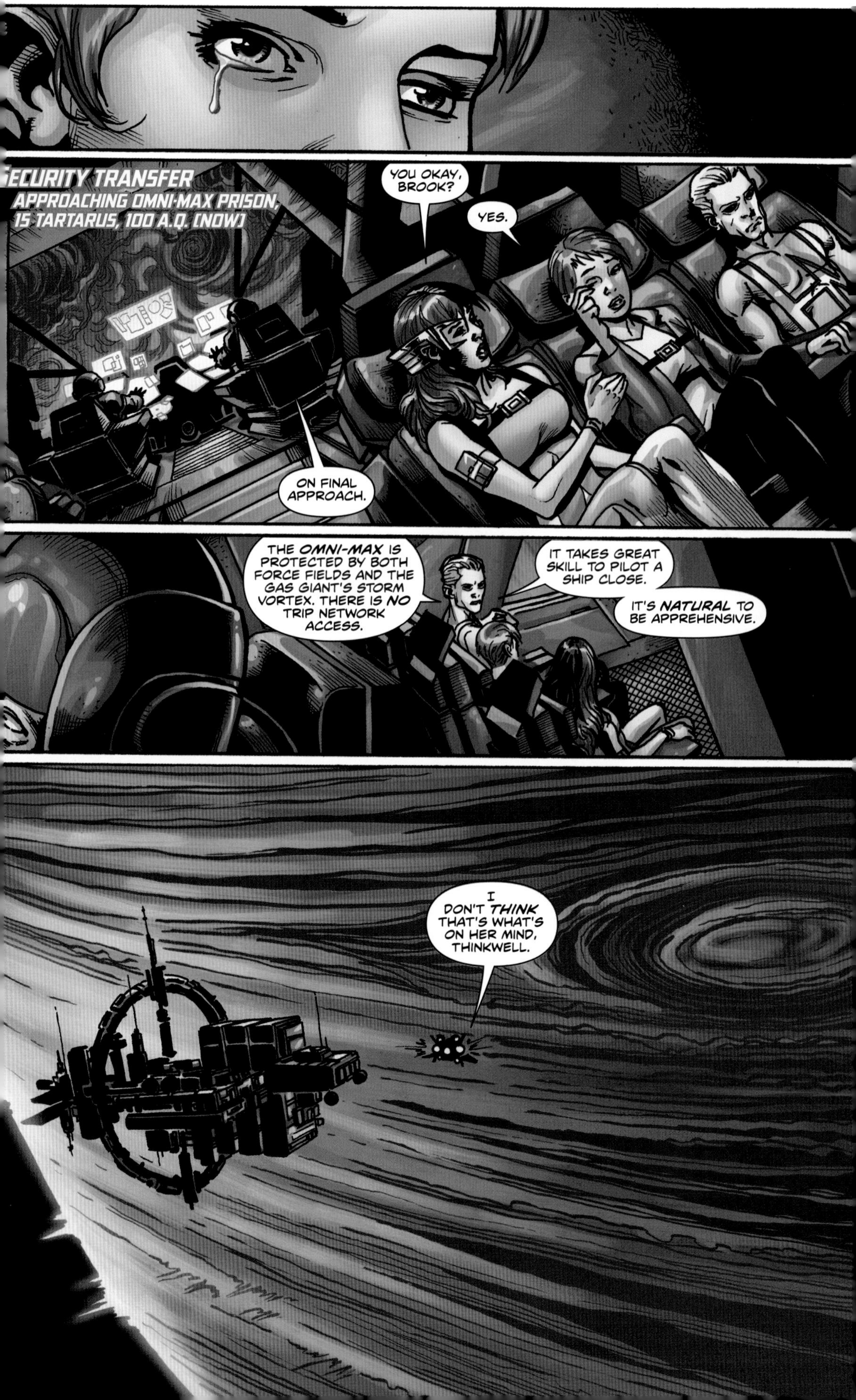
ECURITY TRANSFER
APPROACHING OMNI-MAX PRISON, 15 TARTARUS, 100 A.Q. [NOW]
YOU OKAY, BROOK?
YES.
ON FINAL APPROACH.
THE OMNI-MAX IS PROTECTED BY BOTH FORCE FIELDS AND THE GAS GIANT'S STORM VORTEX. THERE IS NO TRIP NETWORK ACCESS.
IT TAKES GREAT SKILL TO PILOT A SHIP CLOSE.
IT'S NATURAL TO BE APPREHENSIVE.
I DON'T THINK THAT'S WHAT'S ON HER MIND, THINKWELL.

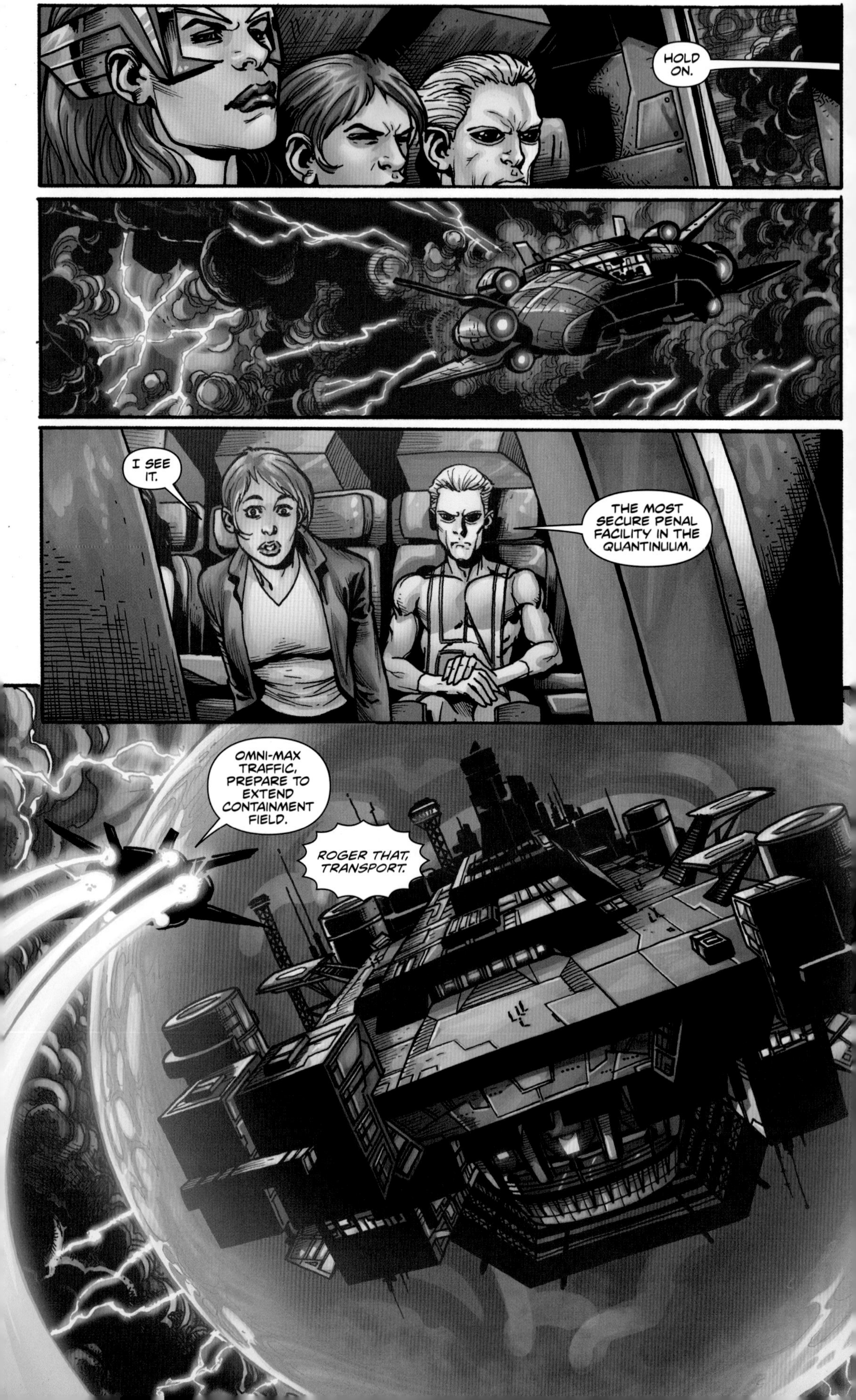
HOLD ON.
I SEE IT.
THE MOST SECURE PENAL FACILITY IN THE QUANTINUUM.
OMNI-MAX TRAFFIC, PREPARE TO EXTEND CONTAINMENT FIELD.
ROGER THAT, TRANSPORT.

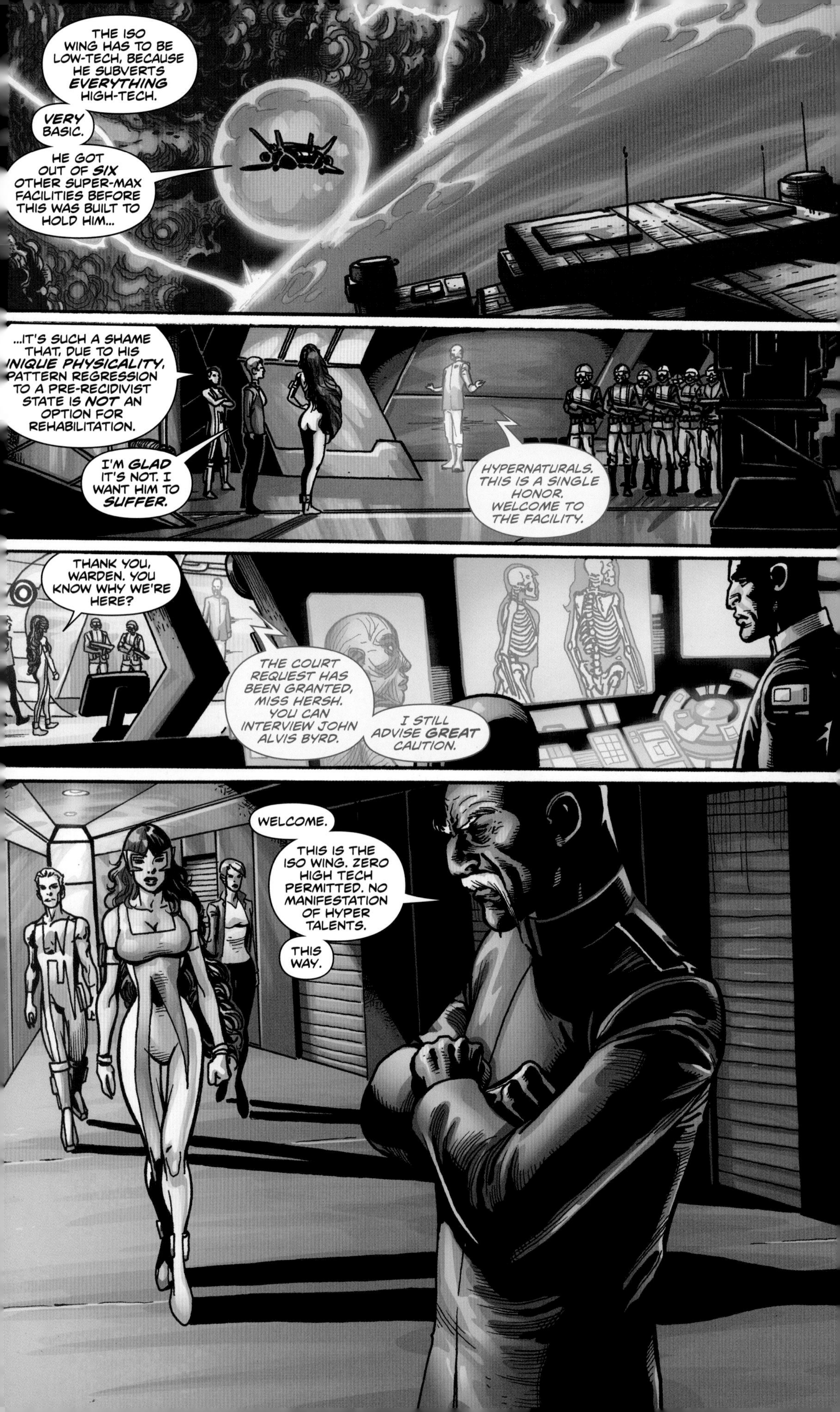
THE ISO WING HAS TO BE LOW-TECH, BECAUSE HE SUBVERTS EVERYTHING HIGH-TECH.
VERY BASIC.
HE GOT OUT OF SIX OTHER SUPER-MAX FACILITIES BEFORE THIS WAS BUILT TO HOLD HIM...
...IT'S SUCH A SHAME THAT, DUE TO HIS UNIQUE PHYSICALITY, PATTERN REGRESSION TO A PRE-RECIDIVIST STATE IS NOT AN OPTION FOR REHABILITATION.
I'M GLAD IT'S NOT. I WANT HIM TO SUFFER.
HYPERNATURALS. THIS IS A SINGLE HONOR. WELCOME TO THE FACILITY.
THANK YOU, WARDEN. YOU KNOW WHY WE'RE HERE?
THE COURT REQUEST HAS BEEN GRANTED, MISS HERSH. YOU CAN INTERVIEW JOHN ALVIS BYRD.
I STILL ADVISE GREAT CAUTION.
WELCOME.
THIS IS THE ISO WING. ZERO HIGH TECH PERMITTED. NO MANIFESTATION OF HYPER TALENTS.
THIS WAY.

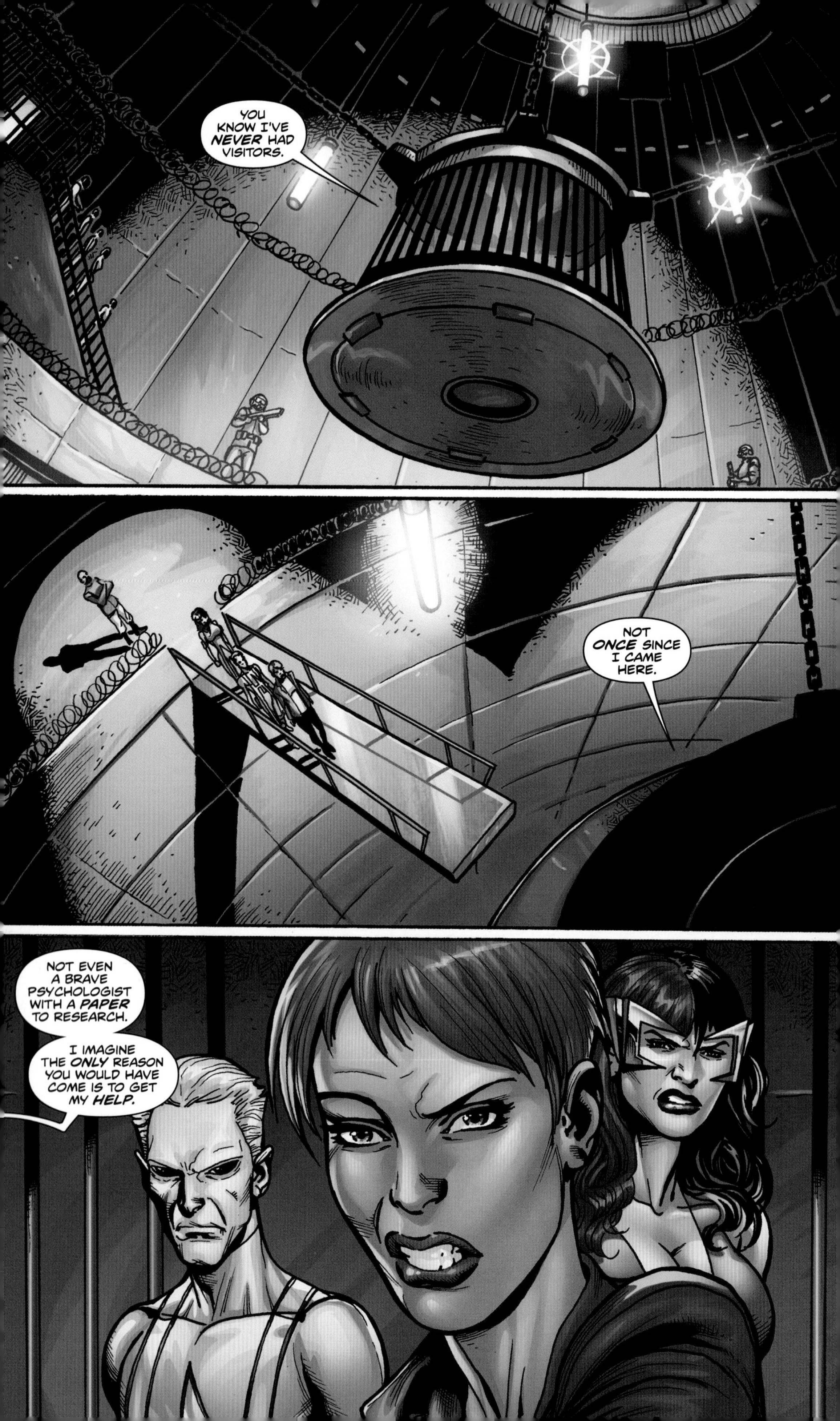
YOU KNOW I'VE NEVER HAD VISITORS.
NOT ONCE SINCE I CAME HERE.
NOT EVEN A BRAVE PSYCHOLOGIST WITH A PAPER TO RESEARCH.
I IMAGINE THE ONLY REASON YOU WOULD HAVE COME IS TO GET MY HELP.

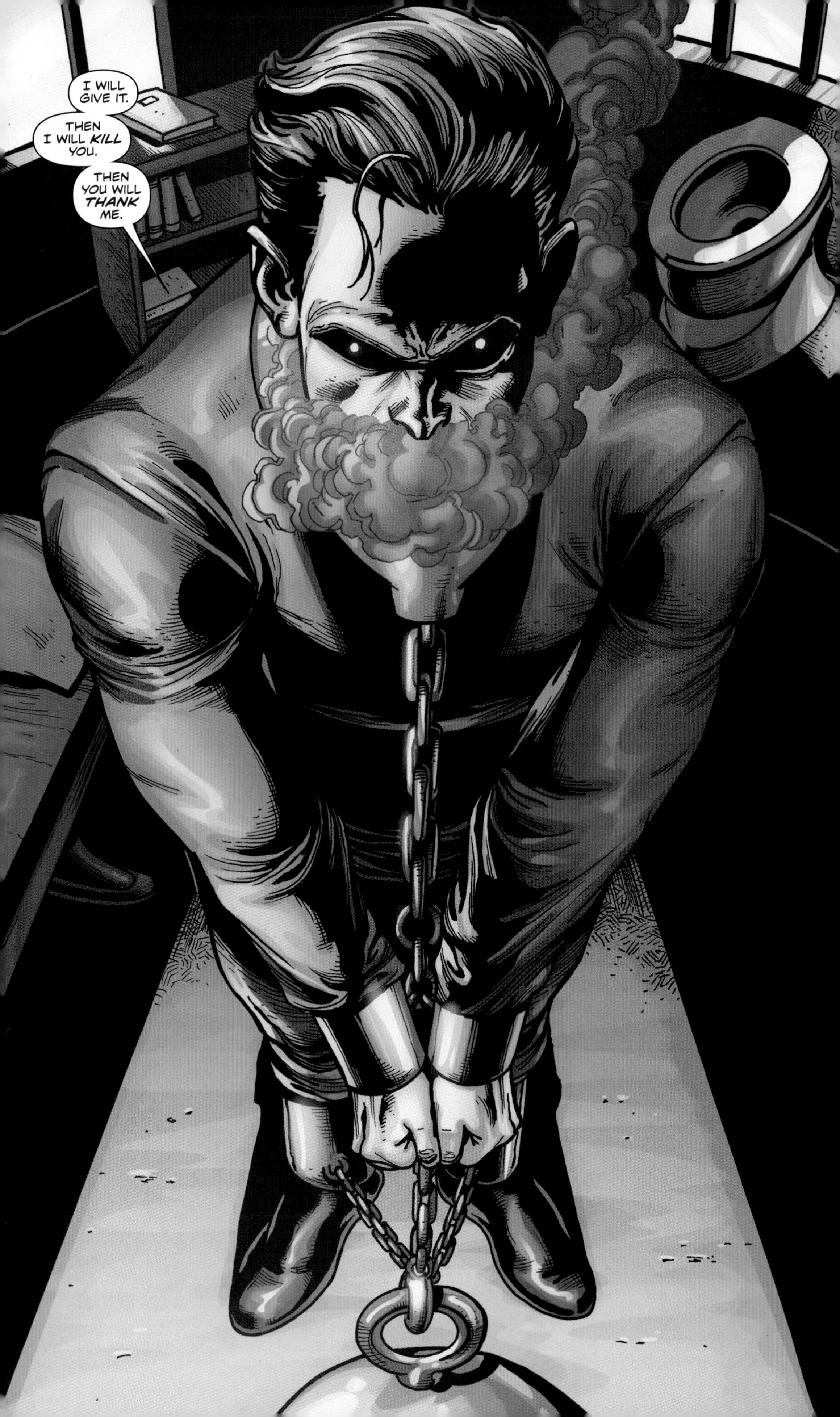
I WILL GIVE IT.
THEN I WILL KILL YOU.
THEN YOU WILL THANK ME.

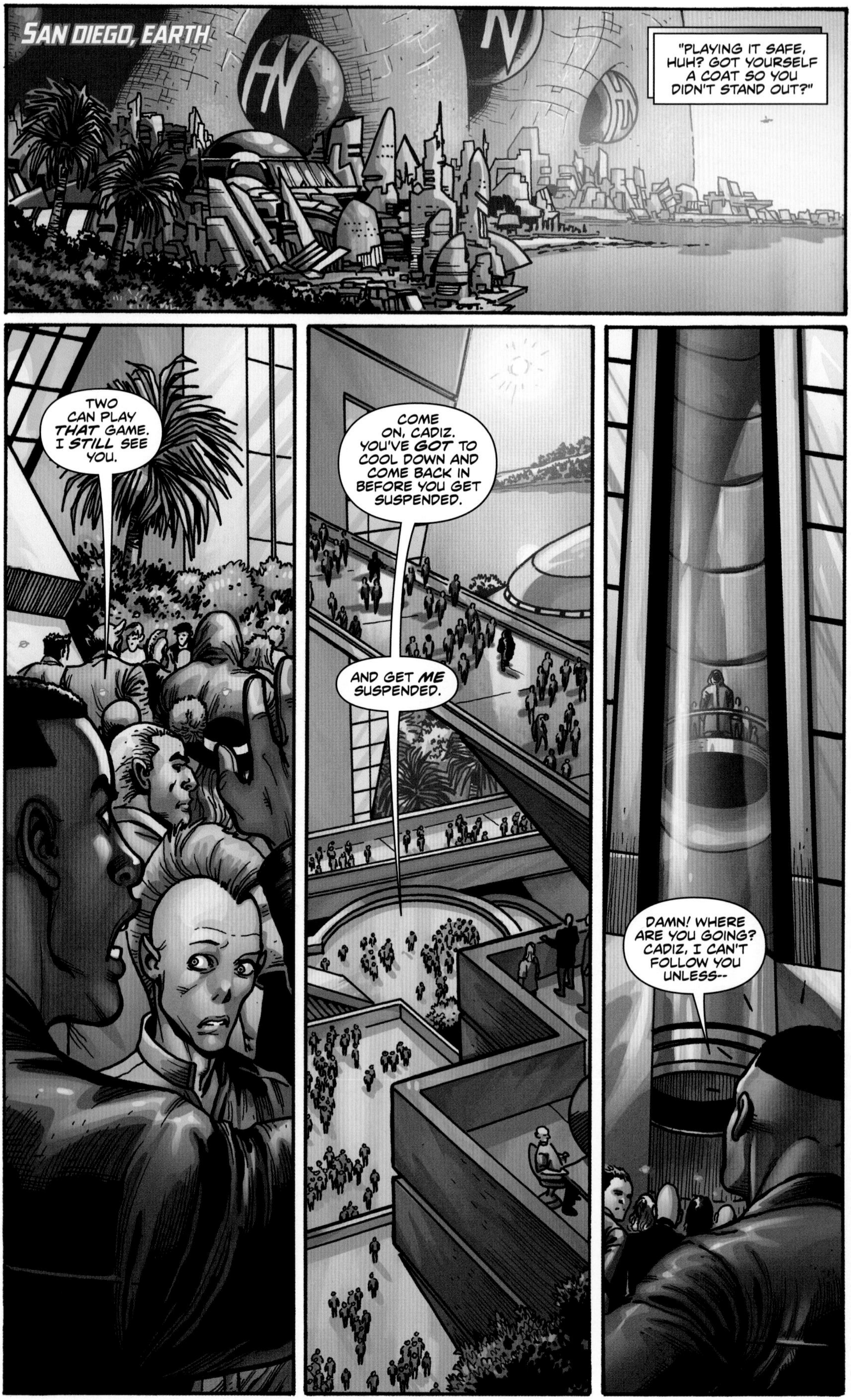
SAN DIEGO, EARTH
"PLAYING IT SAFE, HUH? GOT YOURSELF A COAT SO YOU DIDN'T STAND OUT?"
TWO CAN PLAY *THAT* GAME. I *STILL* SEE YOU.
COME ON, CADIZ. YOU'VE *GOT* TO COOL DOWN AND COME BACK IN BEFORE YOU GET SUSPENDED.
AND GET *ME* SUSPENDED.
DAMN! WHERE ARE YOU GOING? CADIZ, I CAN'T FOLLOW YOU UNLESS--

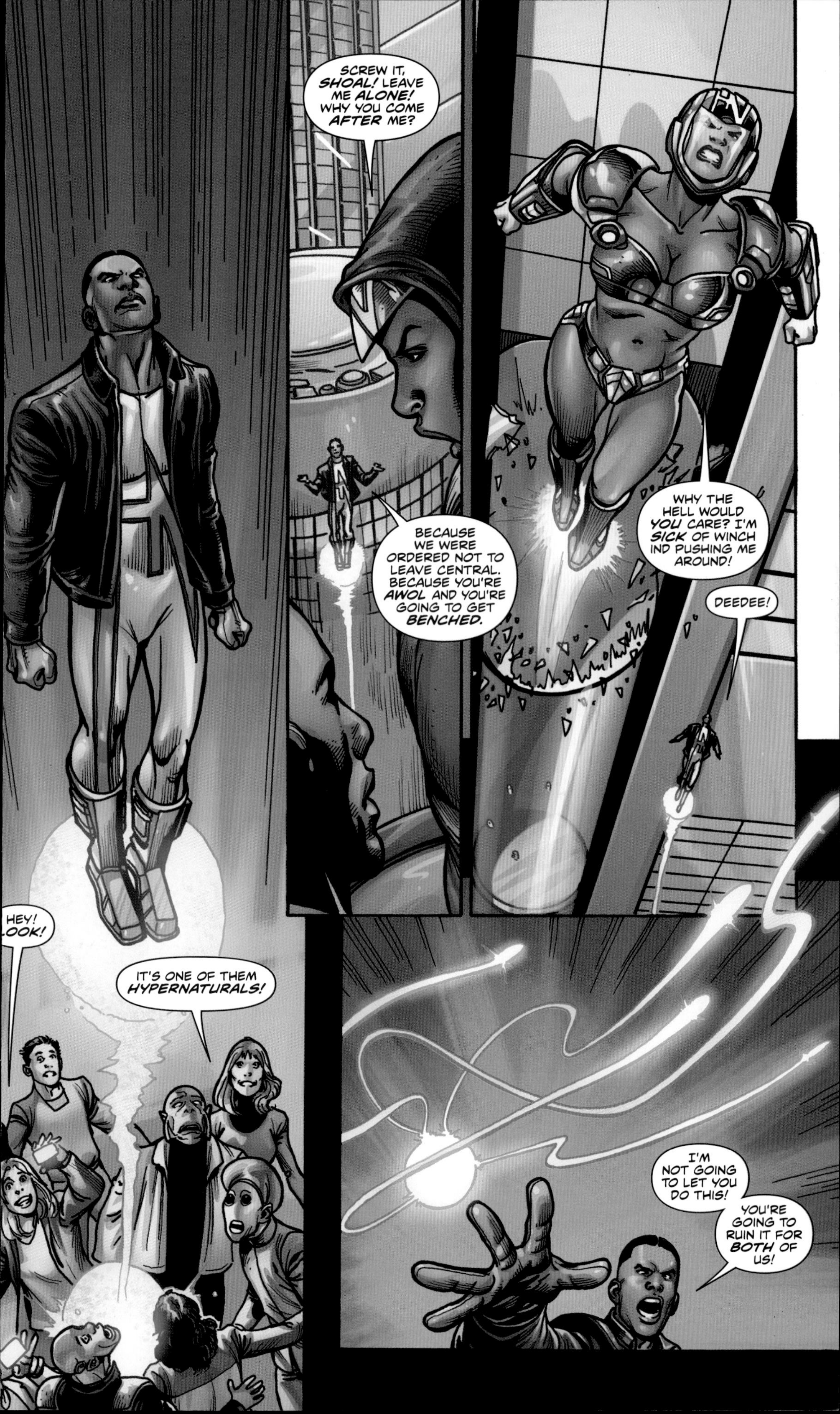
SCREW IT, SHOAL! LEAVE ME ALONE! WHY YOU COME AFTER ME?
BECAUSE WE WERE ORDERED NOT TO LEAVE CENTRAL. BECAUSE YOU'RE AWOL AND YOU'RE GOING TO GET BENCHED.
WHY THE HELL WOULD YOU CARE? I'M SICK OF WINCH IND PUSHING ME AROUND!
DEEDEE!
HEY! LOOK!
IT'S ONE OF THEM HYPERNATURALS!
I'M NOT GOING TO LET YOU DO THIS!
YOU'RE GOING TO RUIN IT FOR BOTH OF US!

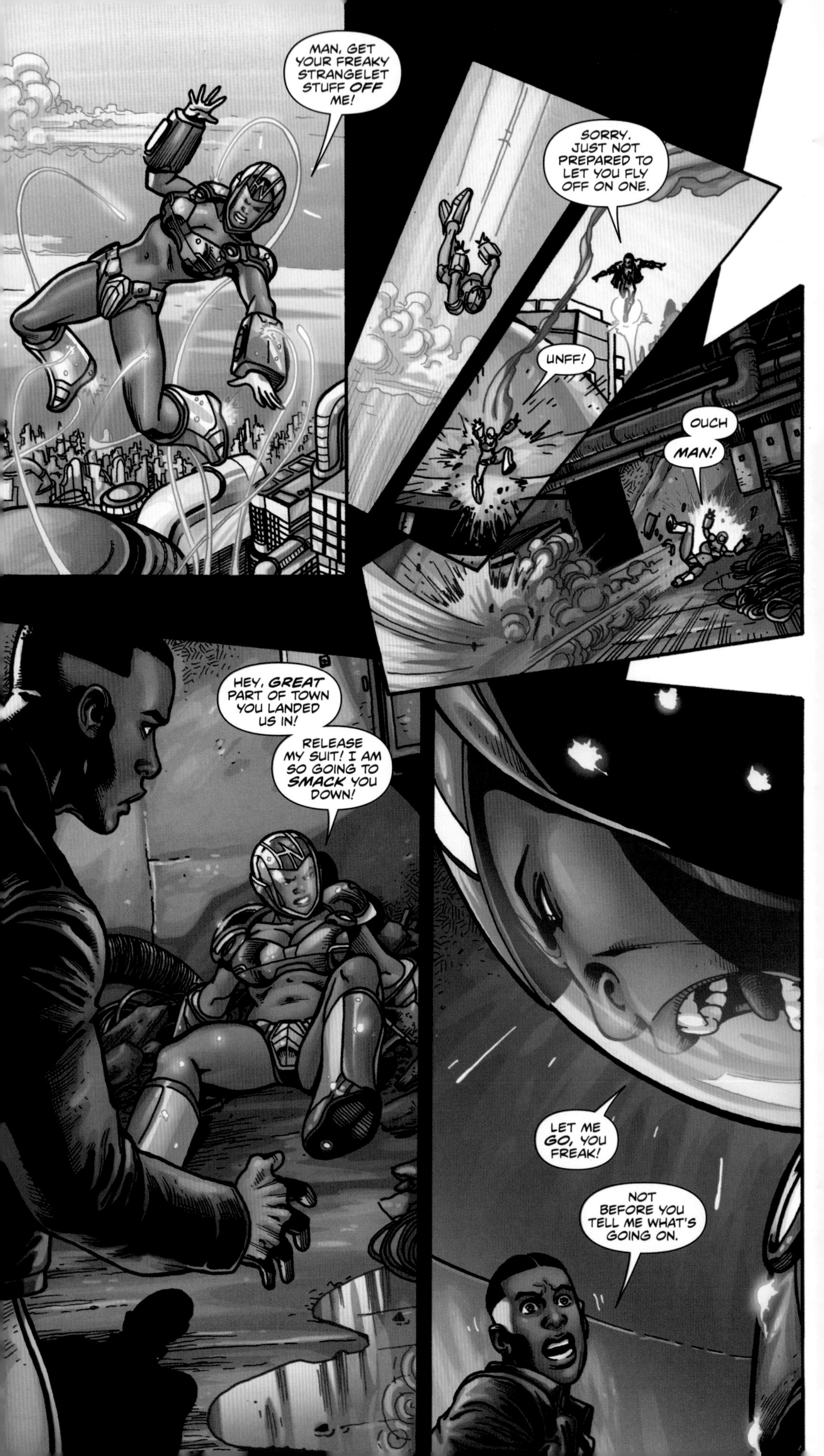
MAN, GET YOUR FREAKY STRANGELET STUFF OFF ME!
SORRY. JUST NOT PREPARED TO LET YOU FLY OFF ON ONE.
UNFF!
OUCH MAN!
HEY, GREAT PART OF TOWN YOU LANDED US IN!
RELEASE MY SUIT! I AM SO GOING TO SMACK YOU DOWN!
LET ME GO, YOU FREAK!
NOT BEFORE YOU TELL ME WHAT'S GOING ON.

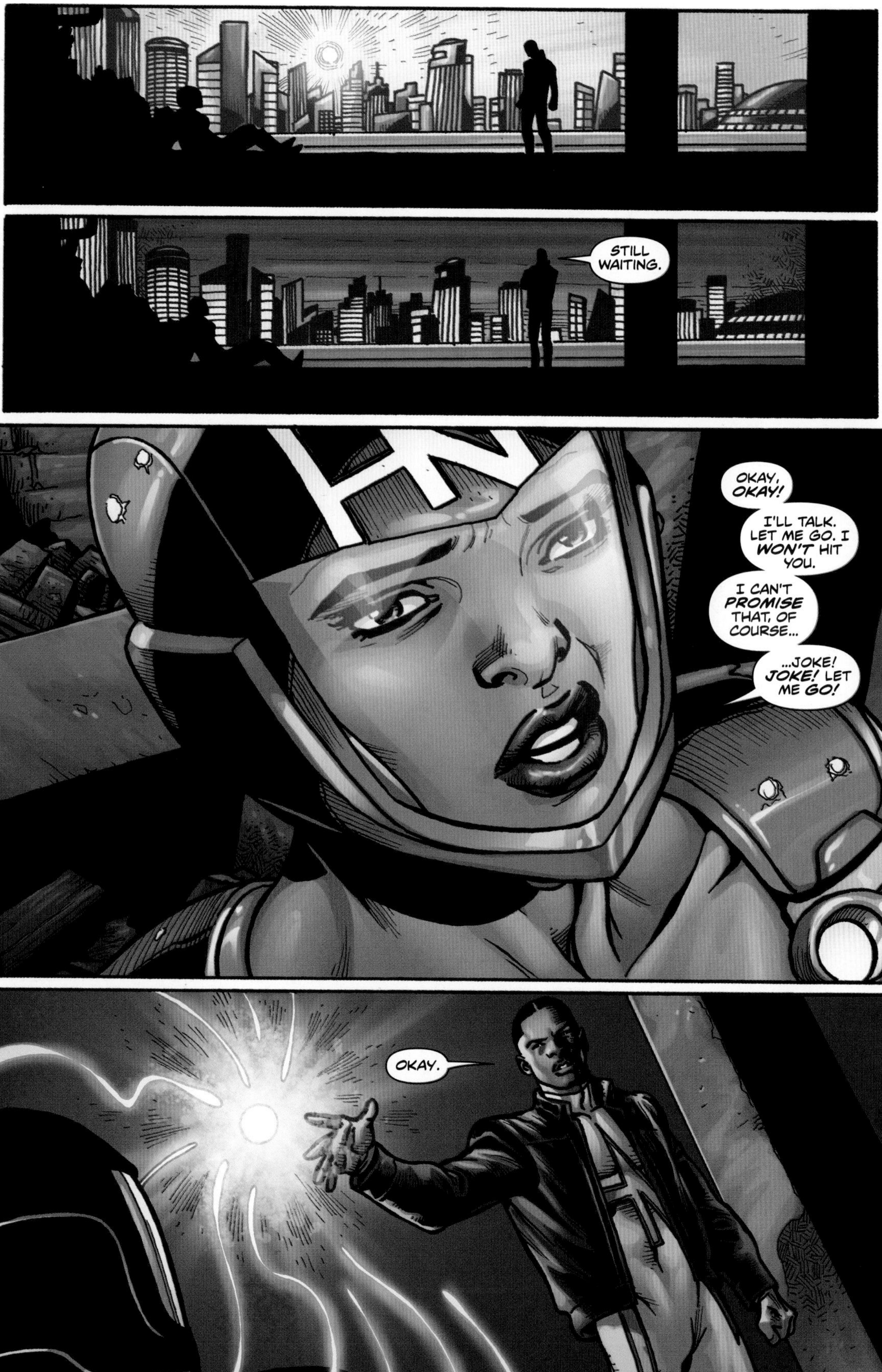

STILL WAITING.
OKAY, OKAY!
I'LL TALK. LET ME GO. I WON'T HIT YOU.
I CAN'T PROMISE THAT, OF COURSE...
...JOKE! JOKE! LET ME GO!
OKAY.

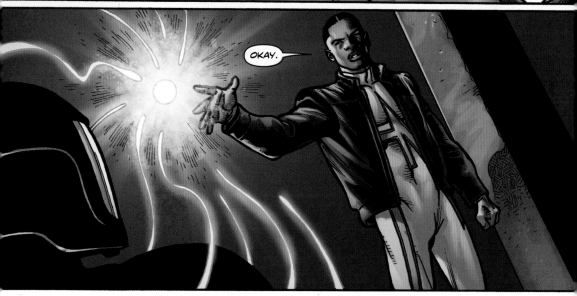

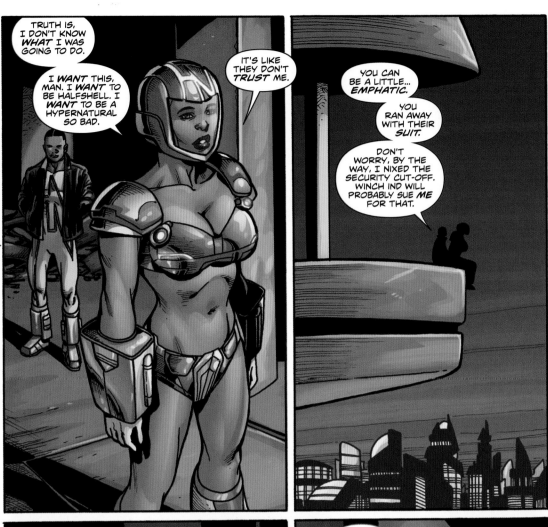

TRUTH IS, I DON'T KNOW *WHAT* I WAS GOING TO DO.

I *WANT* THIS, MAN. I *WANT* TO BE HALFSHELL. I *WANT* TO BE A HYPERNATURAL SO BAD.

IT'S LIKE THEY DON'T *TRUST* ME.

YOU CAN BE A LITTLE... *EMPHATIC.*

YOU RAN AWAY WITH THEIR *SUIT.*

DON'T WORRY, BY THE WAY, I NIXED THE SECURITY CUT-OFF. WINCH IND WILL PROBABLY SUE *ME* FOR THAT.

IF YOU JUST RELAXED, JUST A *LITTLE.* IF YOU DIDN'T ACT SO HARD TO LIKE...

...I THINK YOU'D BE *FINE.*

YOU *THINK,* HUH?

HEY-HEY. LOOK WHAT WE GOT.

UP-SIDERS WITH FAT POCKETS.

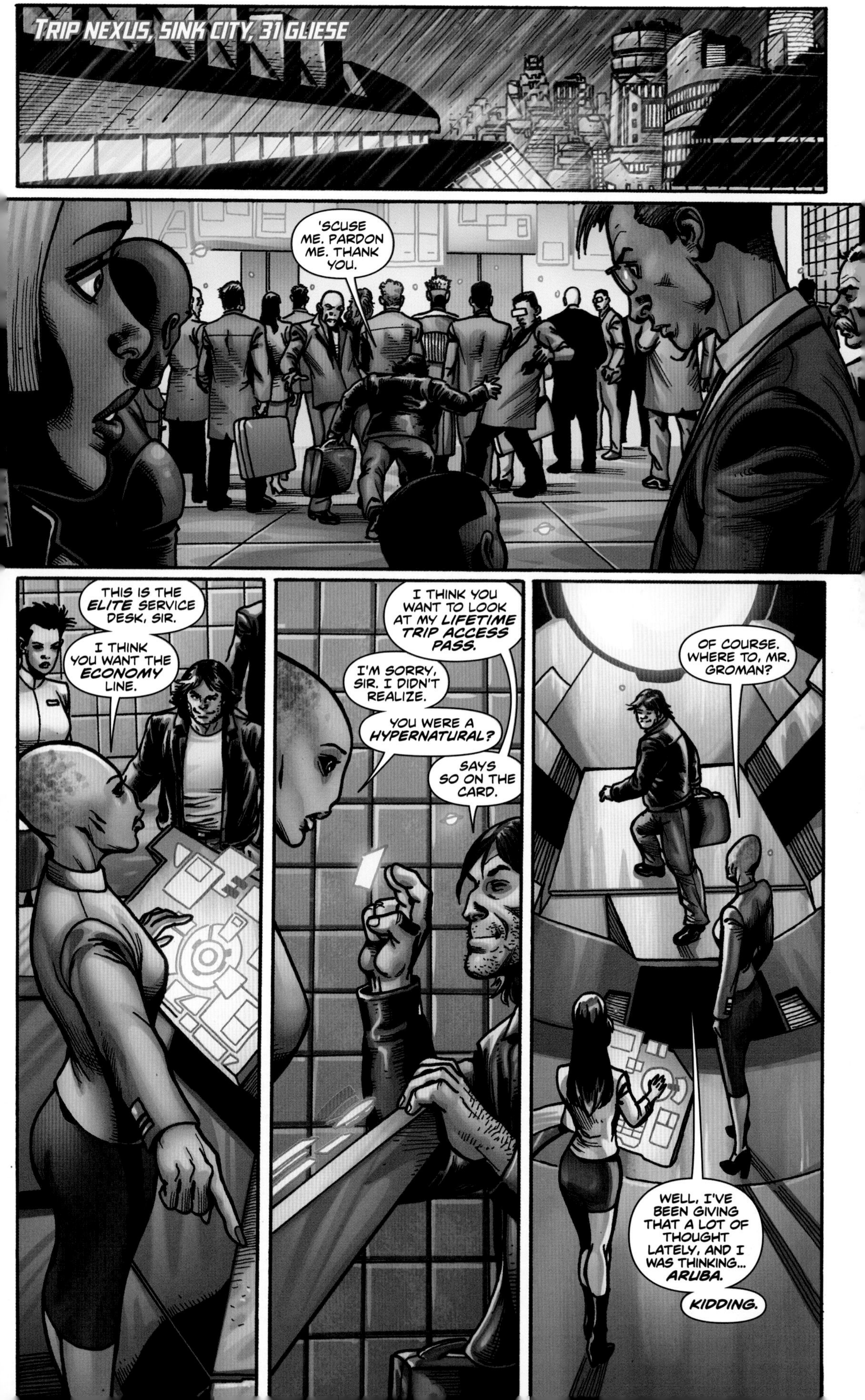
TRIP NEXUS, SINK CITY, 31 GLIESE
'SCUSE ME. PARDON ME. THANK YOU.
THIS IS THE ELITE SERVICE DESK, SIR.
I THINK YOU WANT THE ECONOMY LINE.
I THINK YOU WANT TO LOOK AT MY LIFETIME TRIP ACCESS PASS.
I'M SORRY, SIR. I DIDN'T REALIZE.
YOU WERE A HYPERNATURAL?
SAYS SO ON THE CARD.
OF COURSE. WHERE TO, MR. GROMAN?
WELL, I'VE BEEN GIVING THAT A LOT OF THOUGHT LATELY, AND I WAS THINKING... ARUBA.
KIDDING.

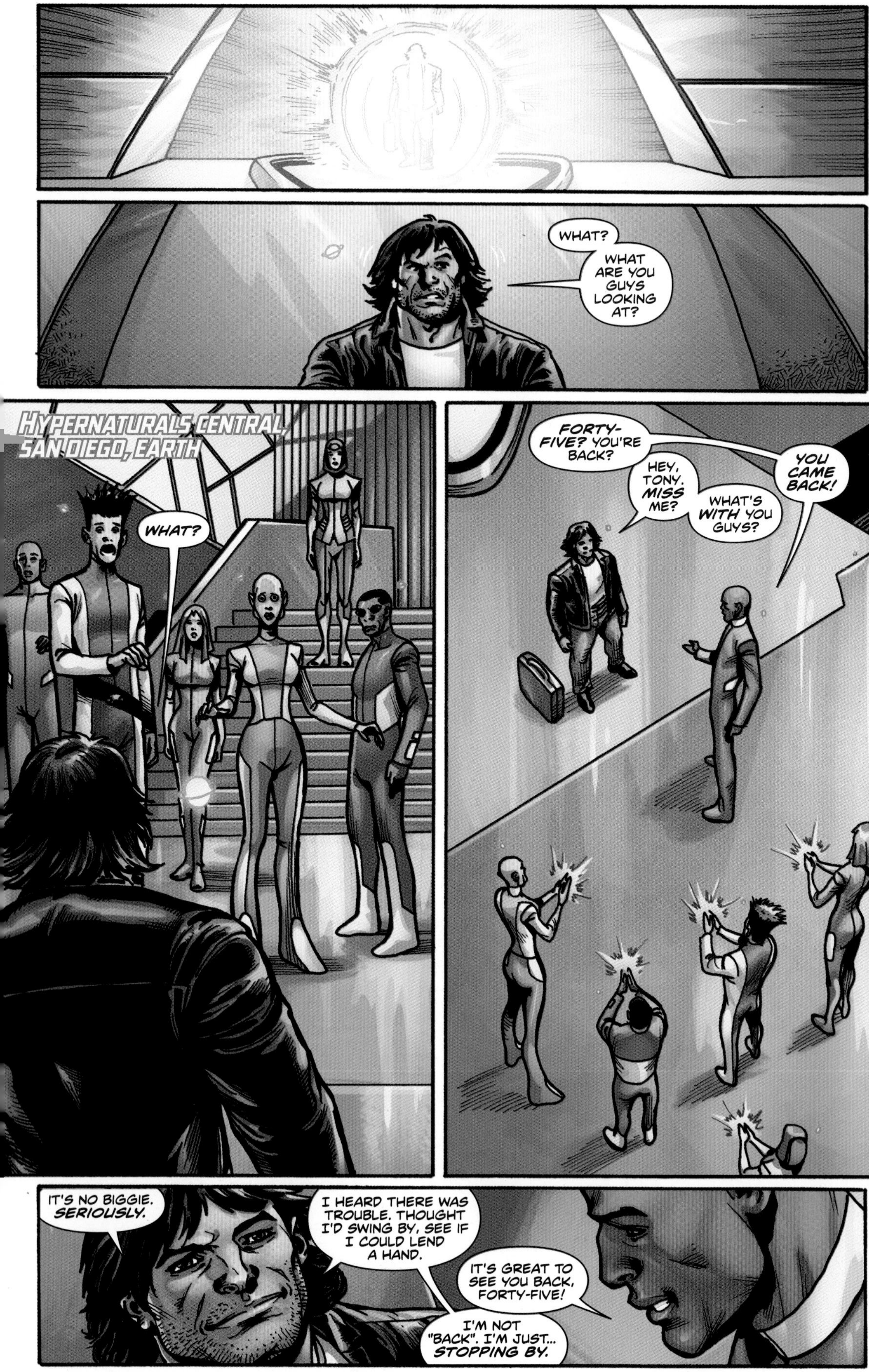
WHAT?
WHAT ARE YOU GUYS LOOKING AT?
HYPERNATURALS CENTRAL, SAN DIEGO, EARTH
WHAT?
FORTY-FIVE? YOU'RE BACK?
HEY, TONY. MISS ME?
WHAT'S WITH YOU GUYS?
YOU CAME BACK!
IT'S NO BIGGIE. SERIOUSLY.
I HEARD THERE WAS TROUBLE. THOUGHT I'D SWING BY, SEE IF I COULD LEND A HAND.
IT'S GREAT TO SEE YOU BACK, FORTY-FIVE!
I'M NOT "BACK". I'M JUST... STOPPING BY.

TALK TO US ABOUT 28 KOSOV.
NEVER BEEN THERE.
YOU KNOW WHAT I'M TALKING ABOUT.
HOW'S YOUR *HUSBAND*, PRISMATICA?
WALKING AND TALKING YET?
SON OF A--
NO HYPERS! NO POWER-UPS!

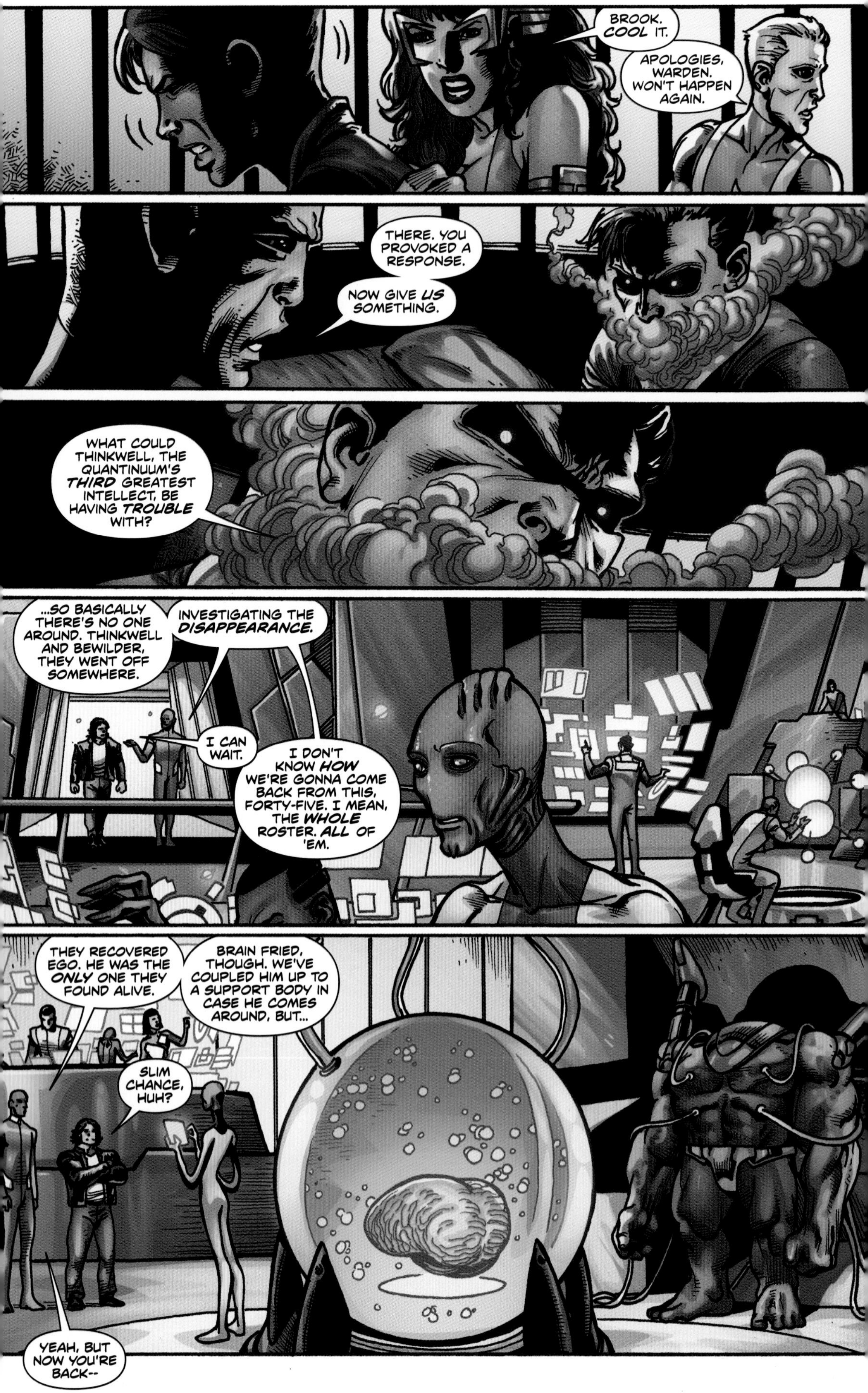
BROOK. COOL IT.
APOLOGIES, WARDEN. WON'T HAPPEN AGAIN.
THERE. YOU PROVOKED A RESPONSE.
NOW GIVE US SOMETHING.
WHAT COULD THINKWELL, THE QUANTINUUM'S THIRD GREATEST INTELLECT, BE HAVING TROUBLE WITH?
...SO BASICALLY THERE'S NO ONE AROUND. THINKWELL AND BEWILDER, THEY WENT OFF SOMEWHERE.
INVESTIGATING THE DISAPPEARANCE.
I CAN WAIT.
I DON'T KNOW HOW WE'RE GONNA COME BACK FROM THIS, FORTY-FIVE. I MEAN, THE WHOLE ROSTER. ALL OF 'EM.
THEY RECOVERED EGO. HE WAS THE ONLY ONE THEY FOUND ALIVE.
BRAIN FRIED, THOUGH. WE'VE COUPLED HIM UP TO A SUPPORT BODY IN CASE HE COMES AROUND, BUT...
SLIM CHANCE, HUH?
YEAH, BUT NOW YOU'RE BACK--

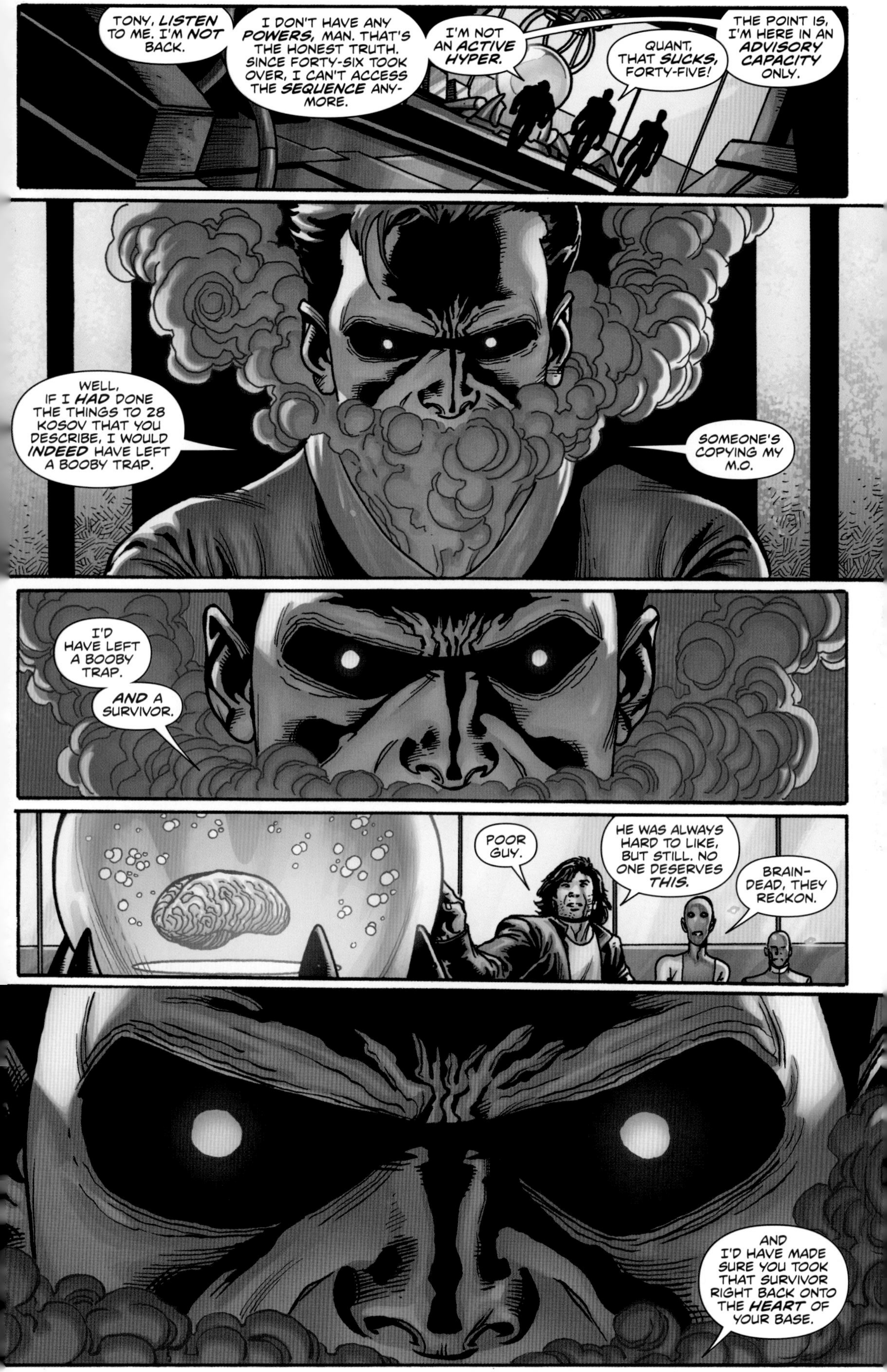

TONY, LISTEN TO ME. I'M NOT BACK.
I DON'T HAVE ANY POWERS, MAN. THAT'S THE HONEST TRUTH. SINCE FORTY-SIX TOOK OVER, I CAN'T ACCESS THE SEQUENCE ANYMORE.
I'M NOT AN ACTIVE HYPER.
QUANT, THAT SUCKS, FORTY-FIVE!
THE POINT IS, I'M HERE IN AN ADVISORY CAPACITY ONLY.
WELL, IF I HAD DONE THE THINGS TO 28 KOSOV THAT YOU DESCRIBE, I WOULD INDEED HAVE LEFT A BOOBY TRAP.
SOMEONE'S COPYING MY M.O.
I'D HAVE LEFT A BOOBY TRAP.
AND A SURVIVOR.
POOR GUY.
HE WAS ALWAYS HARD TO LIKE, BUT STILL. NO ONE DESERVES THIS.
BRAIN-DEAD, THEY RECKON.
AND I'D HAVE MADE SURE YOU TOOK THAT SURVIVOR RIGHT BACK ONTO THE HEART OF YOUR BASE.

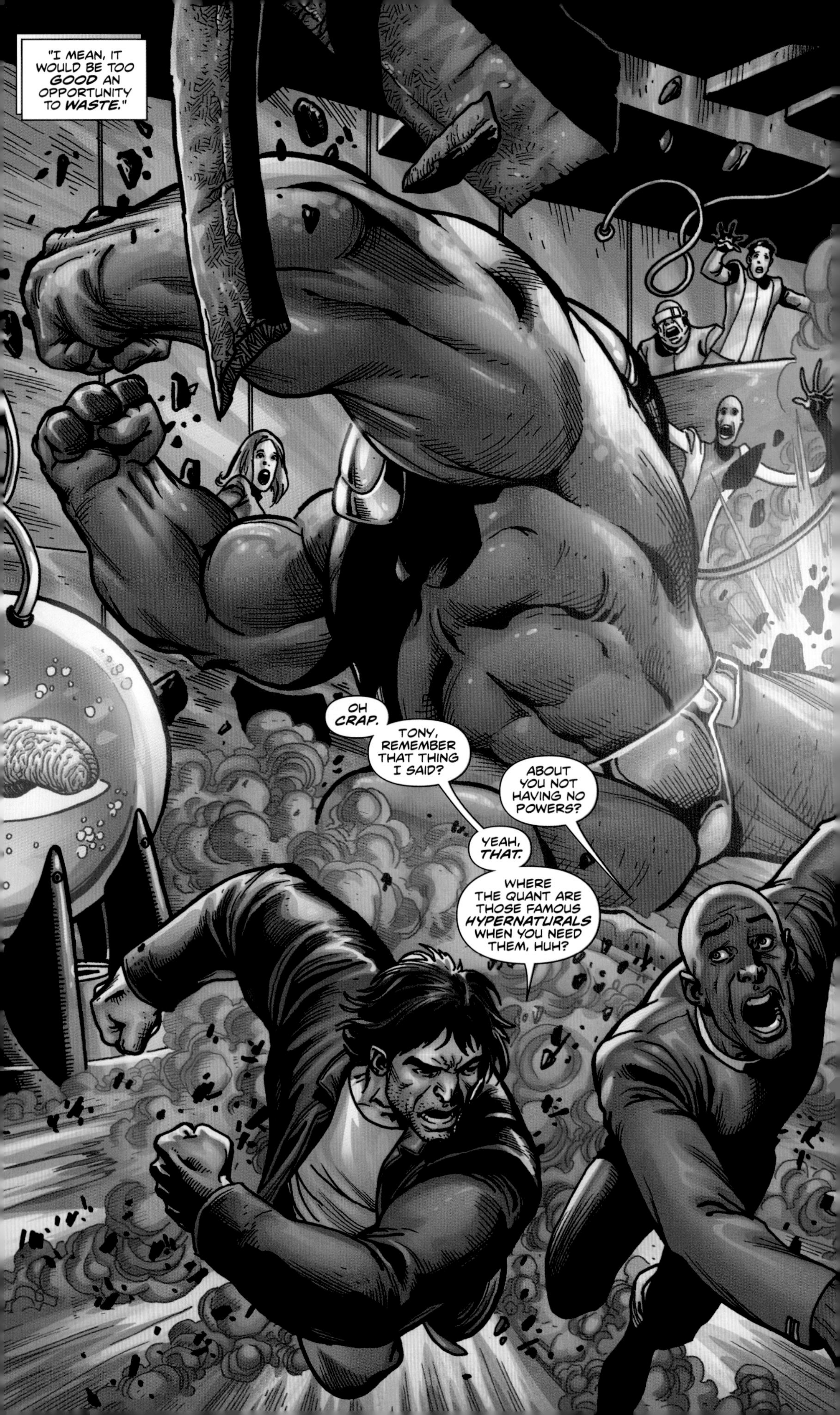
"I MEAN, IT WOULD BE TOO GOOD AN OPPORTUNITY TO WASTE."
OH CRAP.
TONY, REMEMBER THAT THING I SAID?
ABOUT YOU NOT HAVING NO POWERS?
YEAH, THAT.
WHERE THE QUANT ARE THOSE FAMOUS HYPERNATURALS WHEN YOU NEED THEM, HUH?

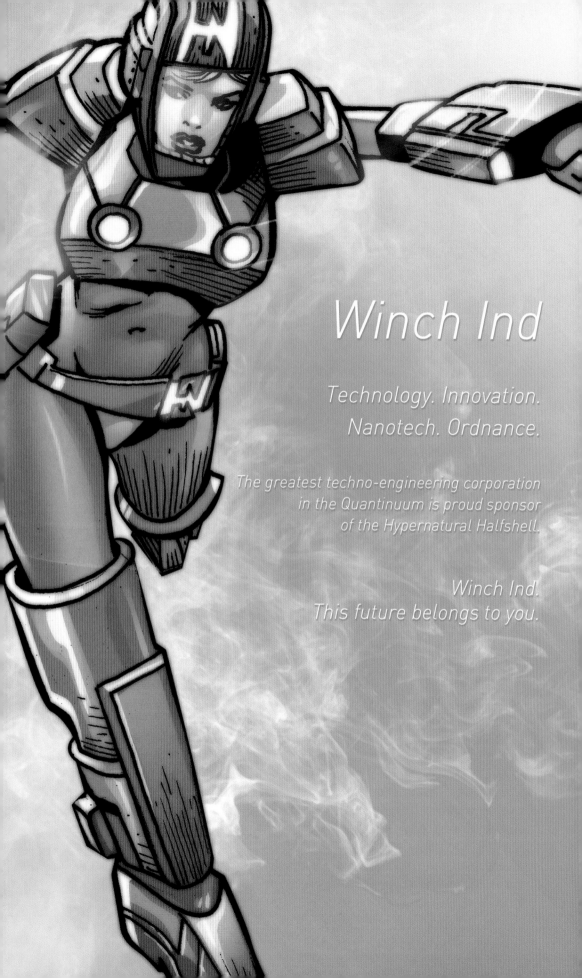

Winch Ind

Technology. Innovation.
Nanotech. Ordnance.

The greatest techno-engineering corporation
in the Quantinuum is proud sponsor
of the Hypernatural Halfshell.

Winch Ind.
This future belongs to you.

3rd October 94 A.Q.

THE TARTARUS SOLUTION

AN OVERSIGHT COMMITTEE DOCUMENT

QUANTINUUM COUNCIL FOR PENAL CORRECTION

prepared 3rd October 94 A.Q.

APPROVED

RATIFIED BY COUNCIL

With reference to the special subject John Alvis Byrd, aka "Sublime" (biographical details [redacted]), the committee posits the following solution to the problems of his continued incarceration, having rejected the working party's recommendation that the death penalty be re-introduced on this special case basis.

Byrd (correction number 373837383738373) represents a threat beyond any we have previously been required to contain. As previous attempt to hold him in super-max facilities have proven, he is extremely resistant, and capable of radically subverting any technology he is allowed interface with to his own ends. In essence, he turns prisons into his means of escape.

In the committee's opinion, the most viable way forward is to purpose-build a facility that can be used to contain Byrd, and tailor it to match and neutralize his specific abilities. The proposal is for an "Omni-Max" prison facility that will, in time, be capable of holding other extreme recidivists too.

The proposal is to construct an "omni-max" facility in the atmospheric storm zone of the gas giant Orcus in the 15 Tartarus System. Like Jupiter, Orcus has a "red spot", a permanent raging storm vortex. The facility will be surrounded by heavy duty force field and gravity webs which will hold it in position and protect it from the violent storms which can strip unshielded spaceships. The only access will be by armored drop ship. There will be no Quantum Trip transfer capability.

Isolated by the severe storms, Tartarus will be pure functionality. All technology will be pre-Nanocene level, with a significant reliance on old style mechanical and "wired devices", and virtually no electronic or higher grade nanoquantum processes. The facility's gravimetric containment sphere will protect it from the ferocious environment. The prison will have a compliment of 55 guards and support personnel that work in 3 month shifts/tours of duty.

To address one of the working party's key problems, it must be remembered that simple pattern regression is not an option in the case of Byrd. Though pattern regression is the rehabilitation method of choice in the Quantinuum, taking a criminal back to an earlier saved version of themself using Quantum Trip pattern buffering is very straightforward, it is not an adequate solution in this case. Pattern regression works by taking the subject back to an earlier version of themself, and thus prevents them from making the choices that led them to commit their crimes. It is the 'second chance' scenario. But ~~Byrd's super~~natural gifts make him impossible to regress. He was born with them.

Sublime is so dangerous and so clever he can eventually manipulate any advanced technology to his advantage and escape. The only option open is to revert to totally low-tech: ie lock and key, bars and bolts. The iso wing will be a circular cell block lined with razor wire and viewing portals set high in the walls where guards can man a 24 hour watch. A walkway will extend from the foot of the stairs bridging the 'moat' to the cell in the centre of the chamber. The cell will be a free-standing cage, a cube of reinforced glass with bars suspended by massive chains over the circular shaft. The 'moat' is capable of dropping away into the red spot vortex thousands of feet below if the cell is breached

COVER GALLERY

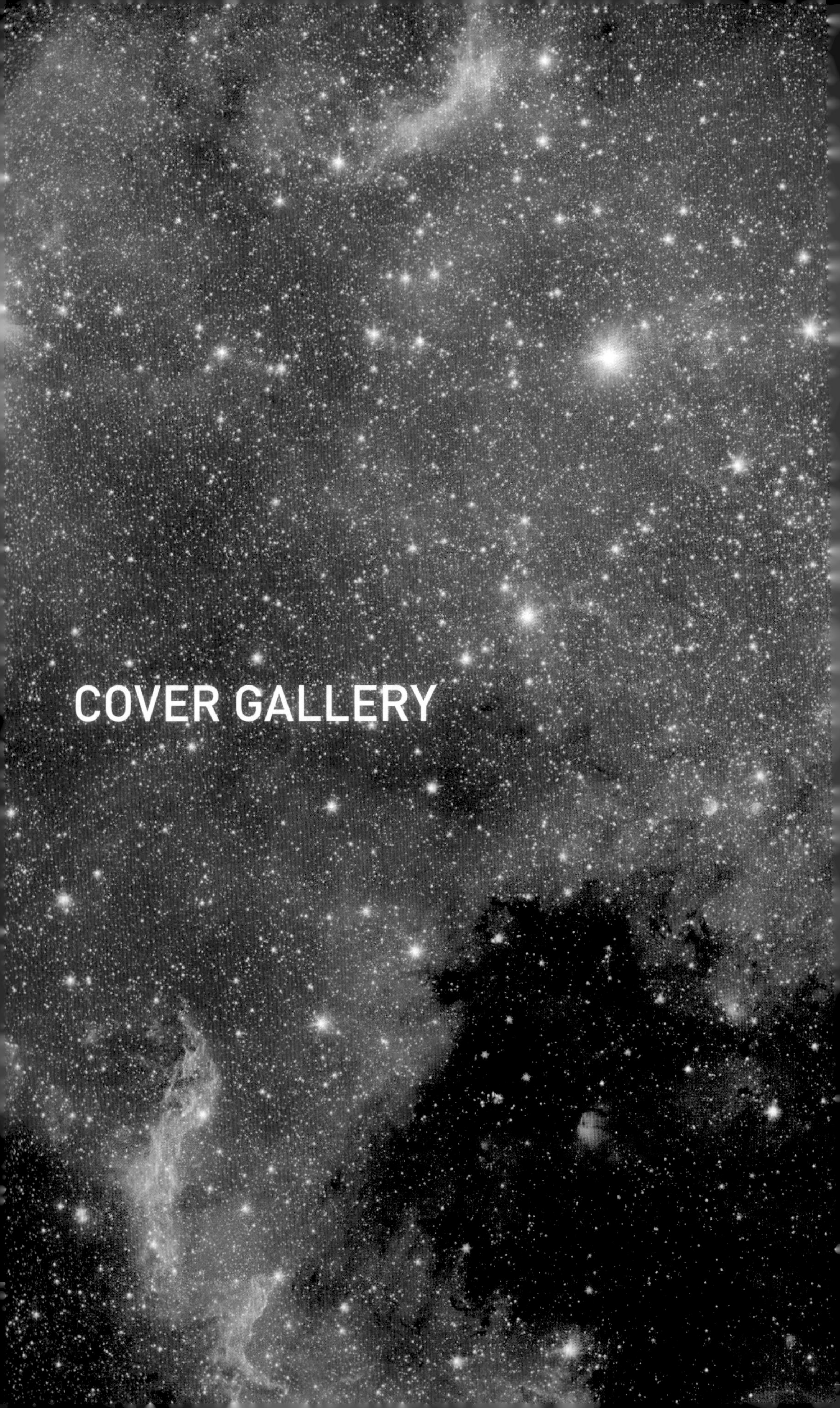

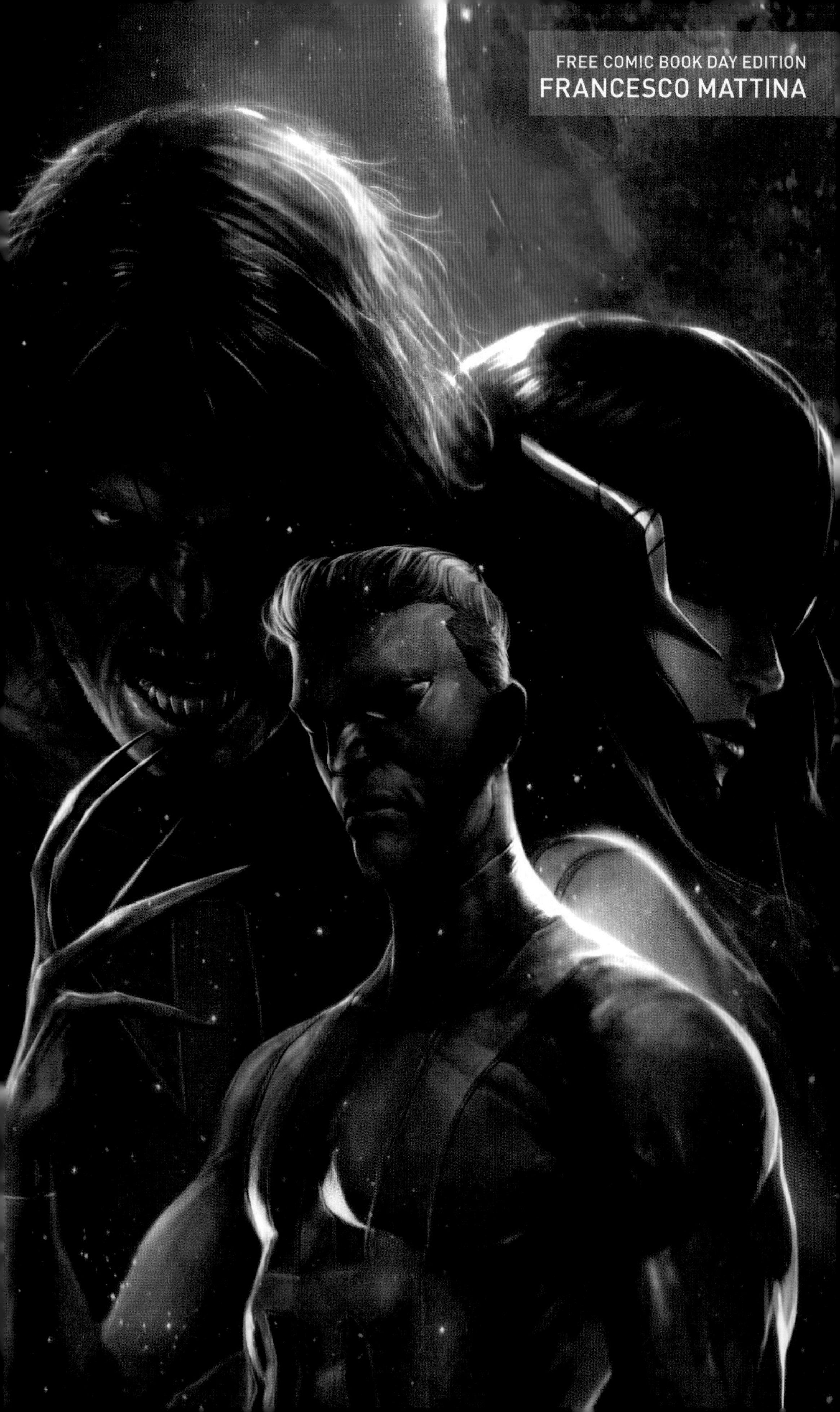
FREE COMIC BOOK DAY EDITION
FRANCESCO MATTINA

ISSUE ONE
FRANCESCO MATTINA

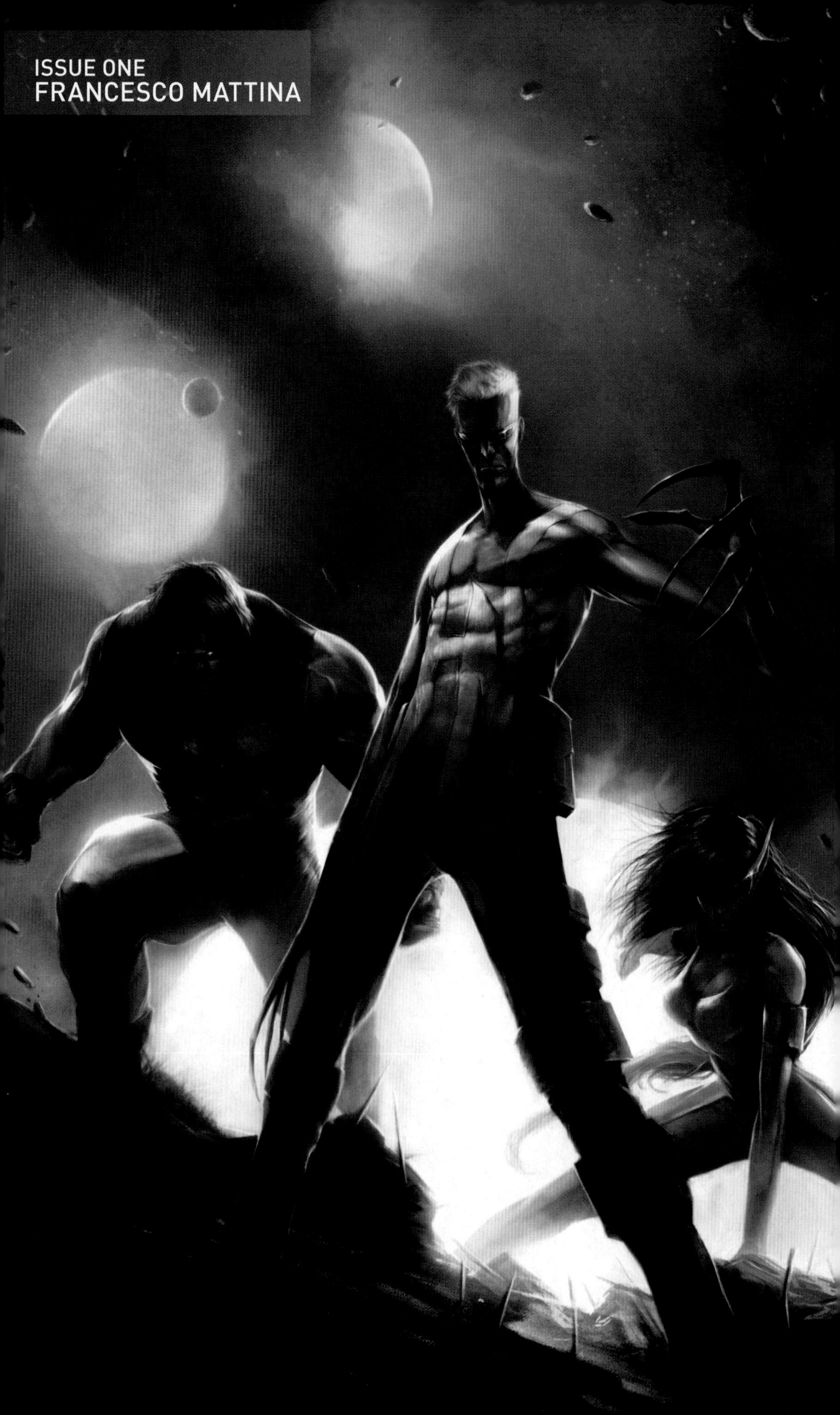

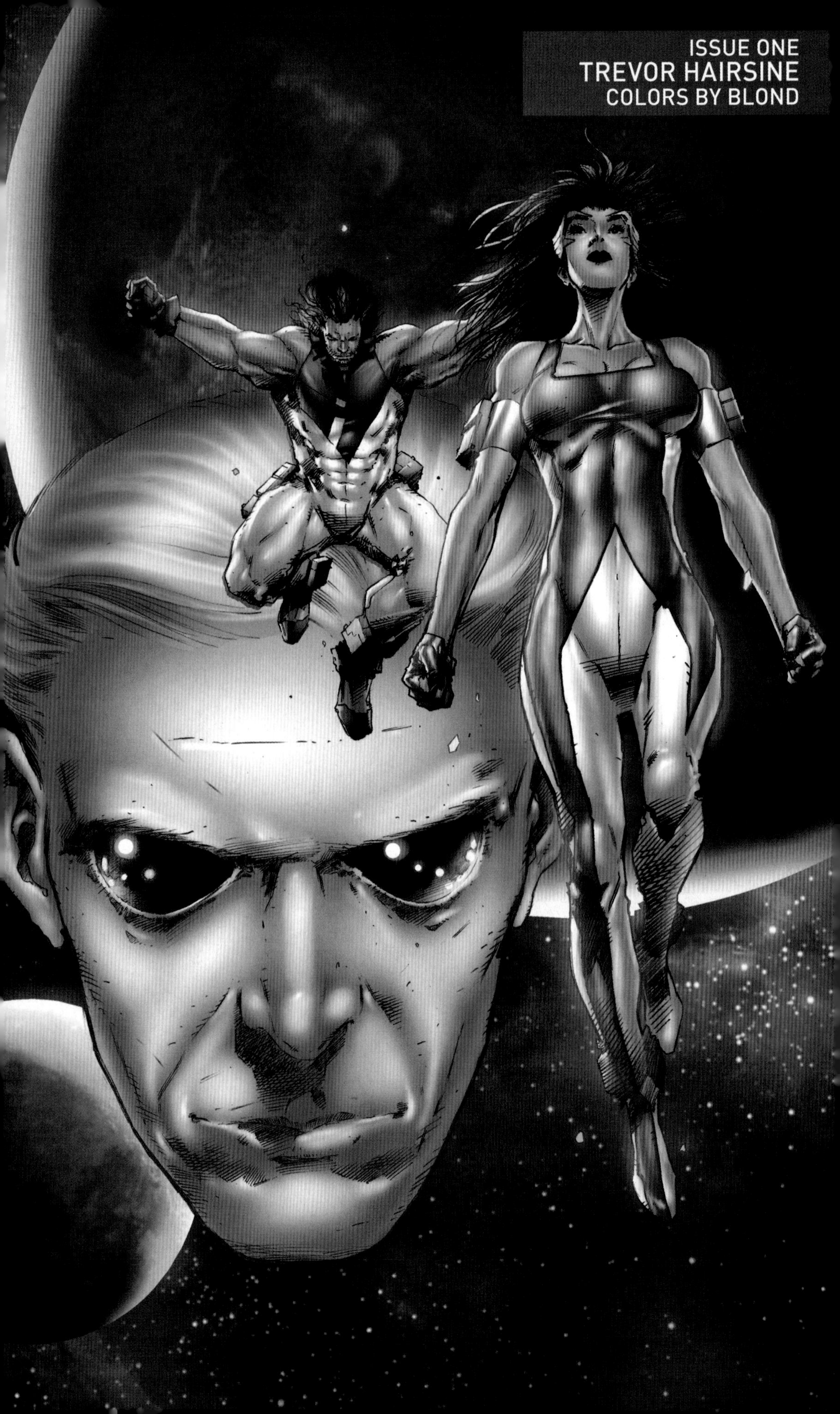

ISSUE ONE
TREVOR HAIRSINE
COLORS BY BLOND

ISSUE ONE
PHIL NOTO

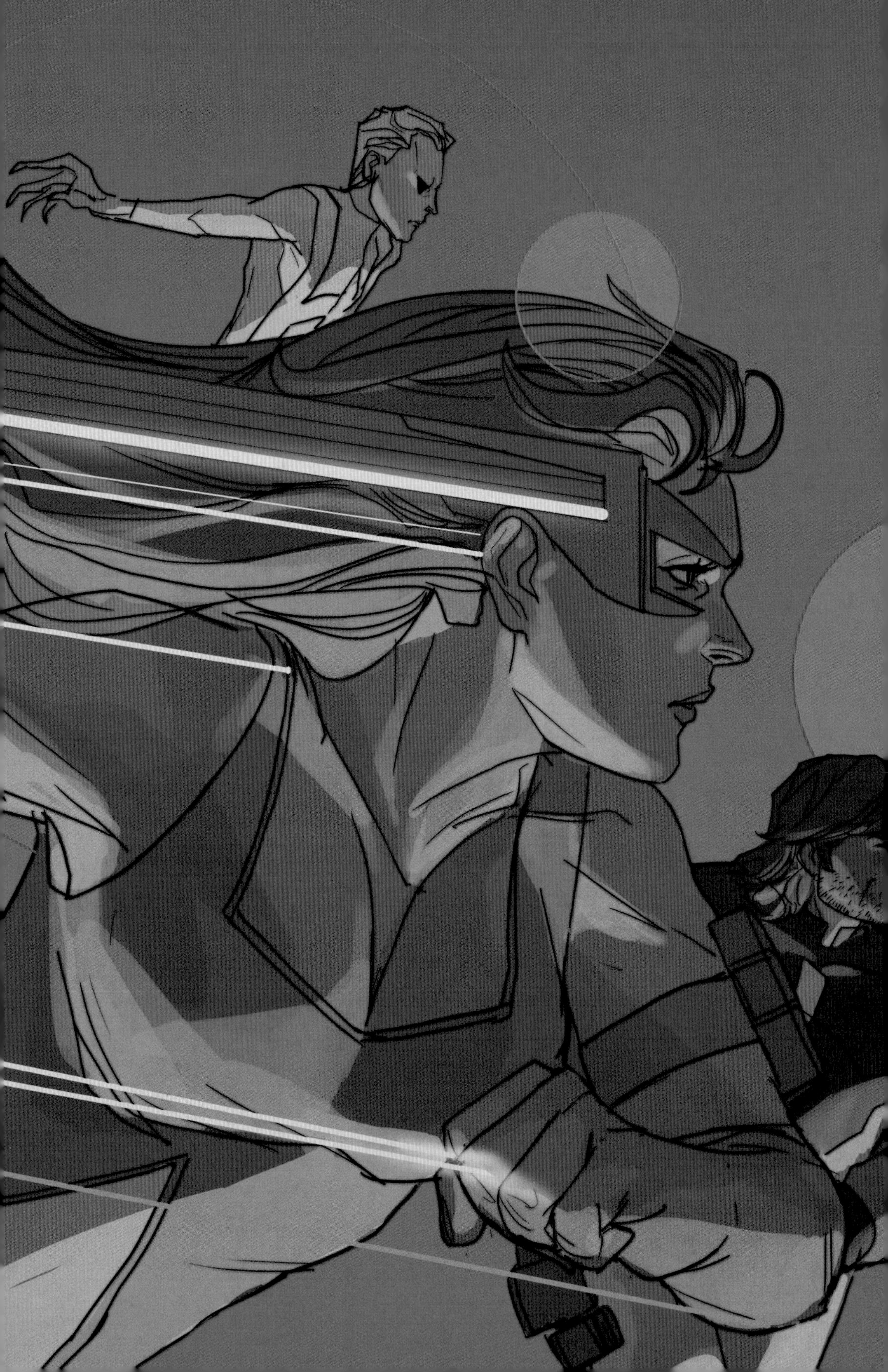

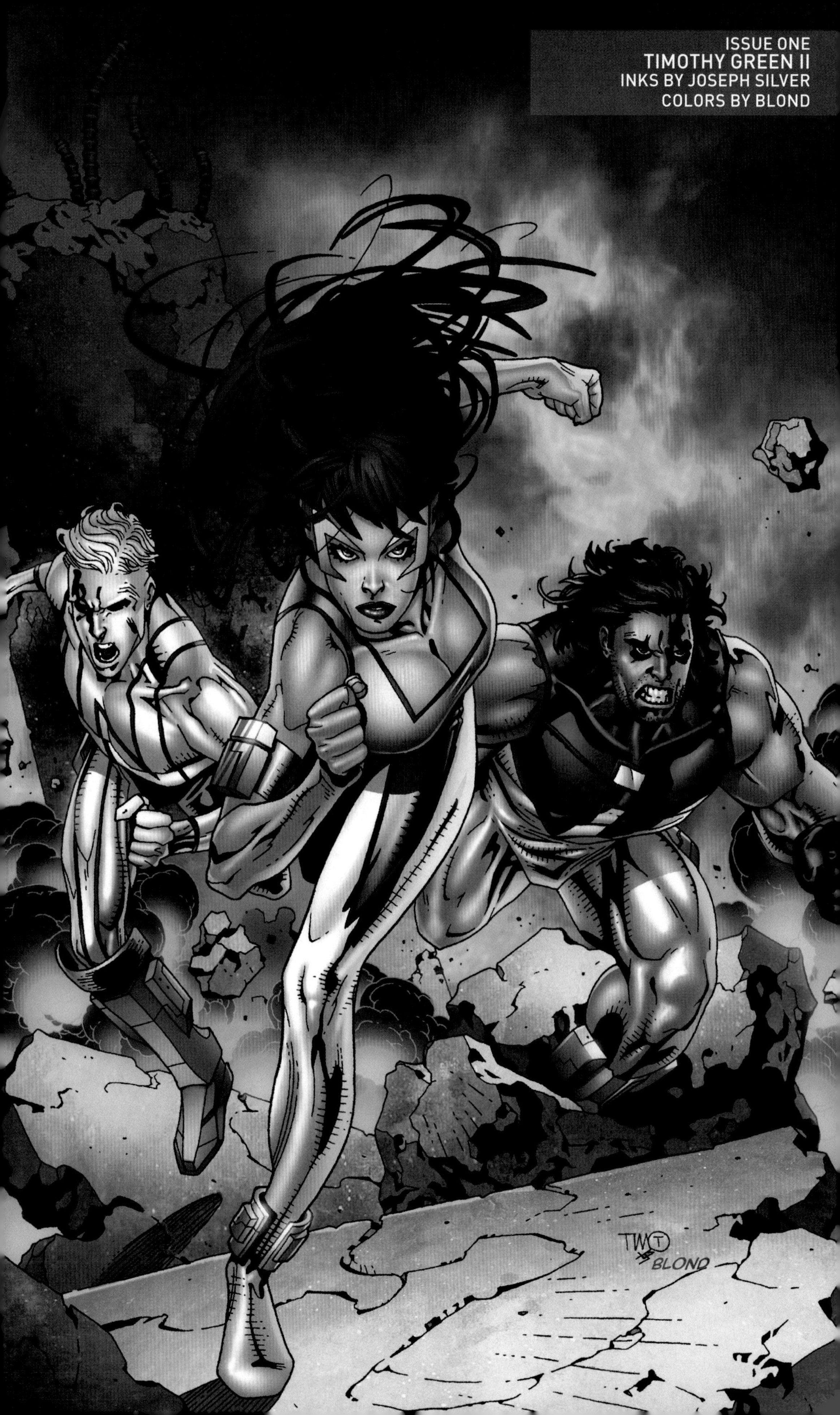

ISSUE ONE
TIMOTHY GREEN II
INKS BY JOSEPH SILVER
COLORS BY BLOND

ISSUE ONE
STEPHANIE GONZAGA

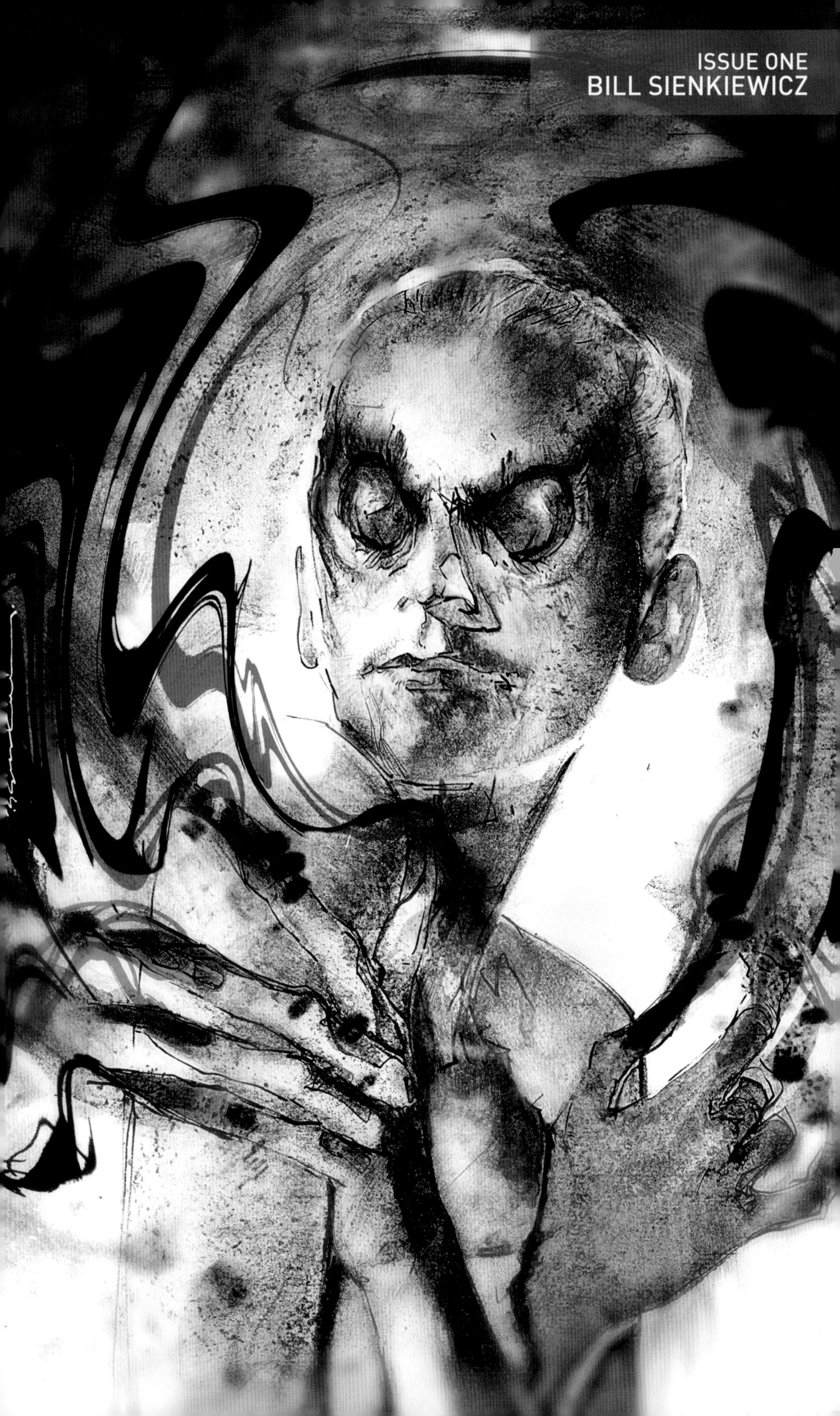
ISSUE ONE
BILL SIENKIEWICZ

ISSUE ONE
MITCH BREITWEISER

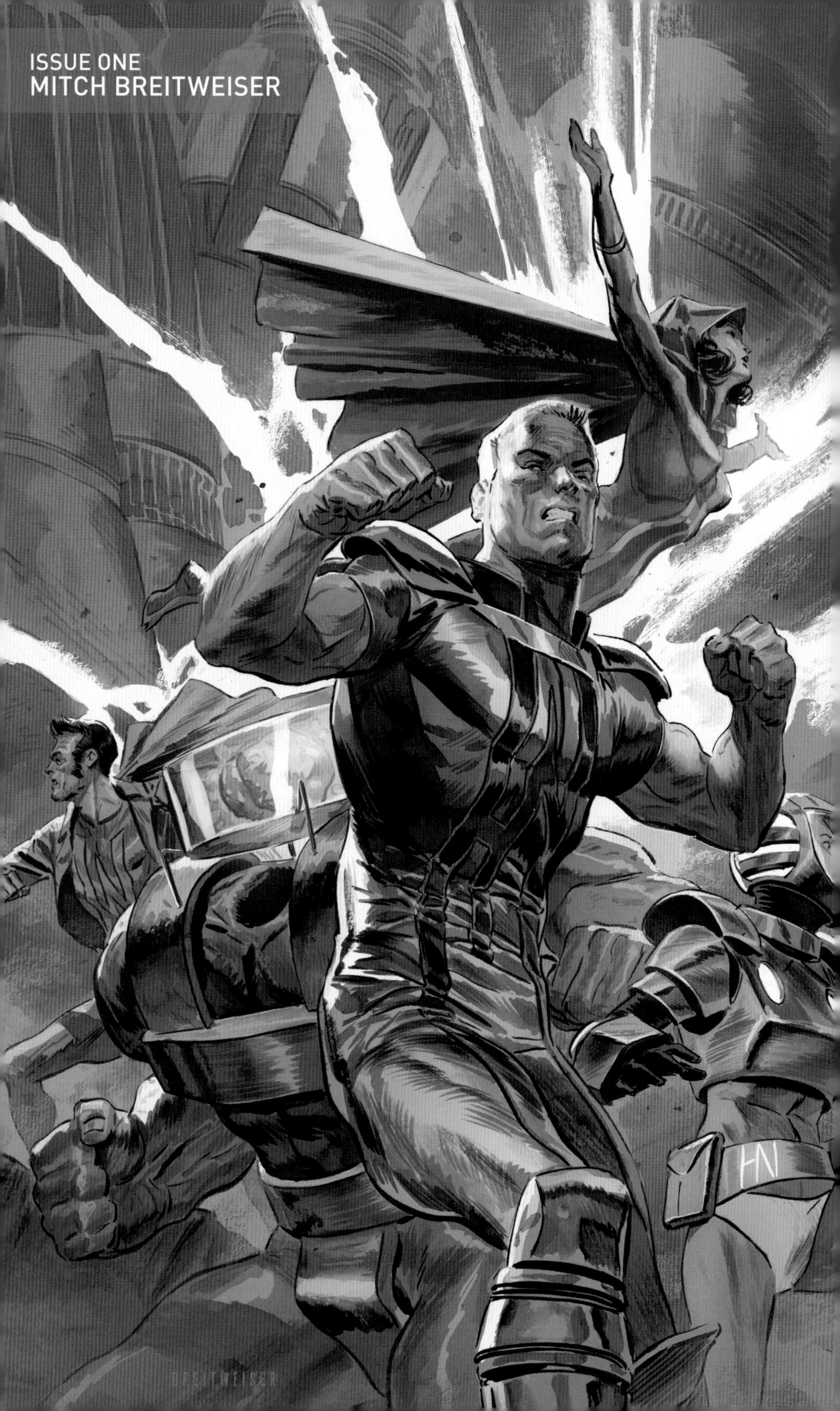

BREITWEISER

ISSUE ONE
DAVID YARDIN

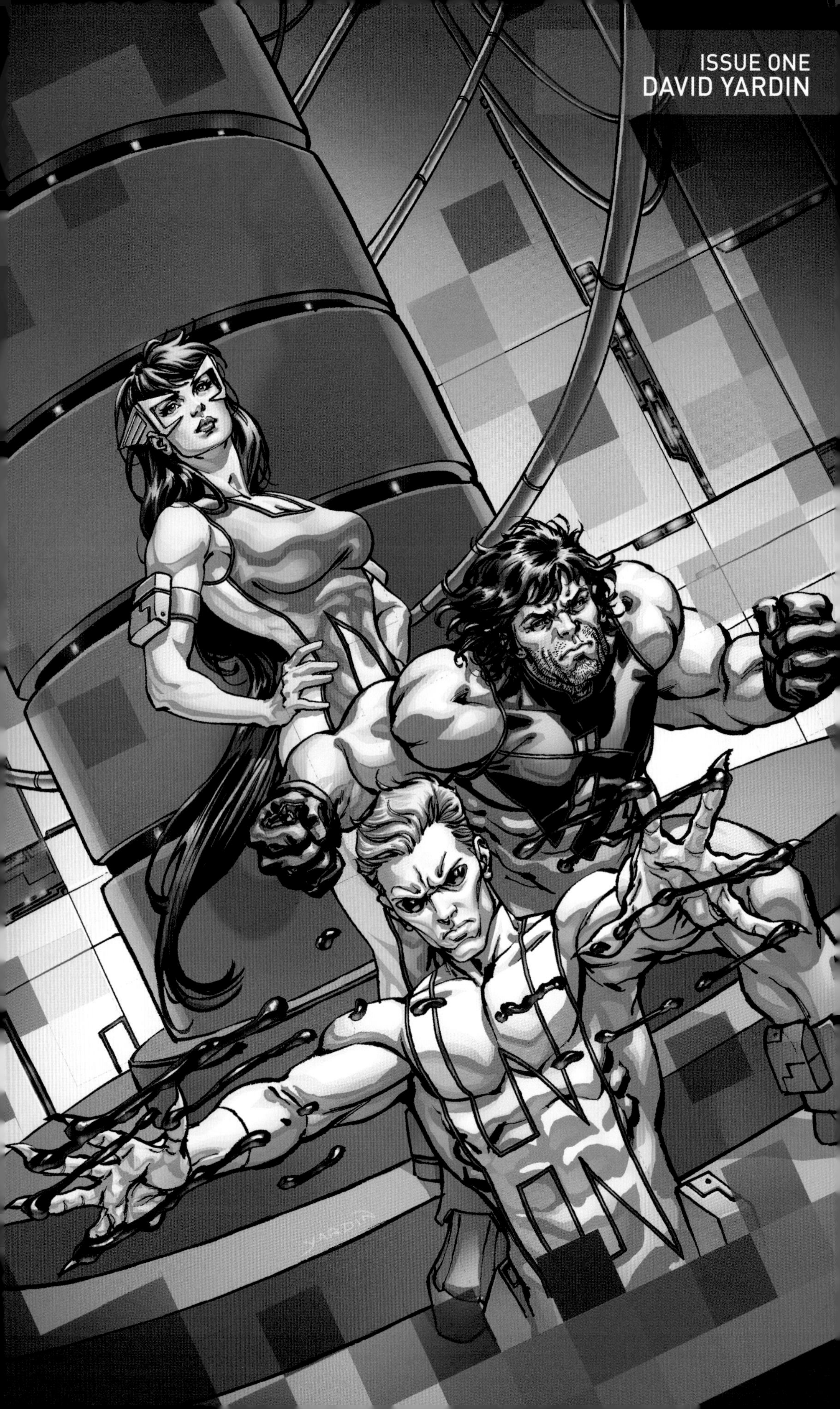
YARDIN

ISSUE TWO
FRANCESCO MATTINA

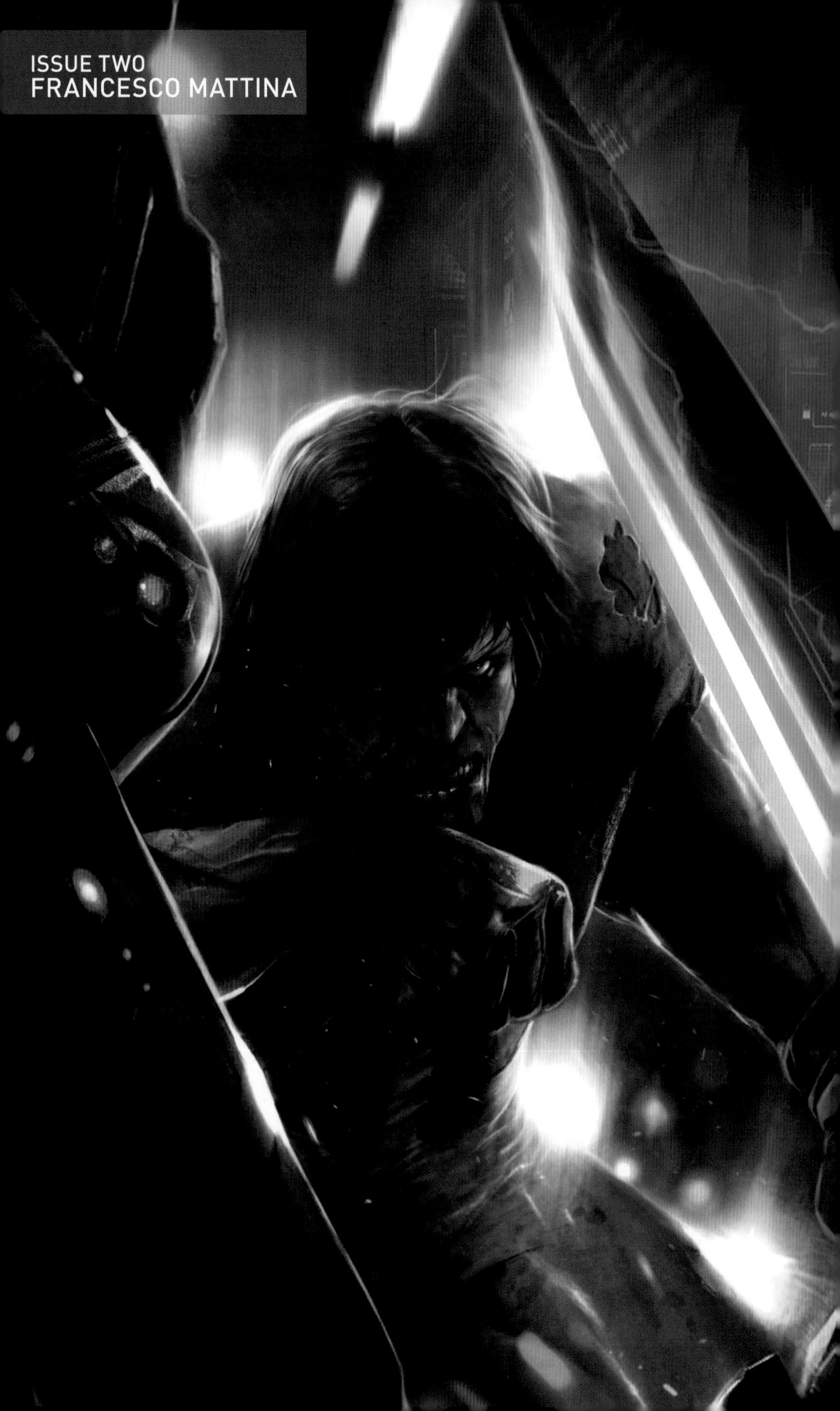

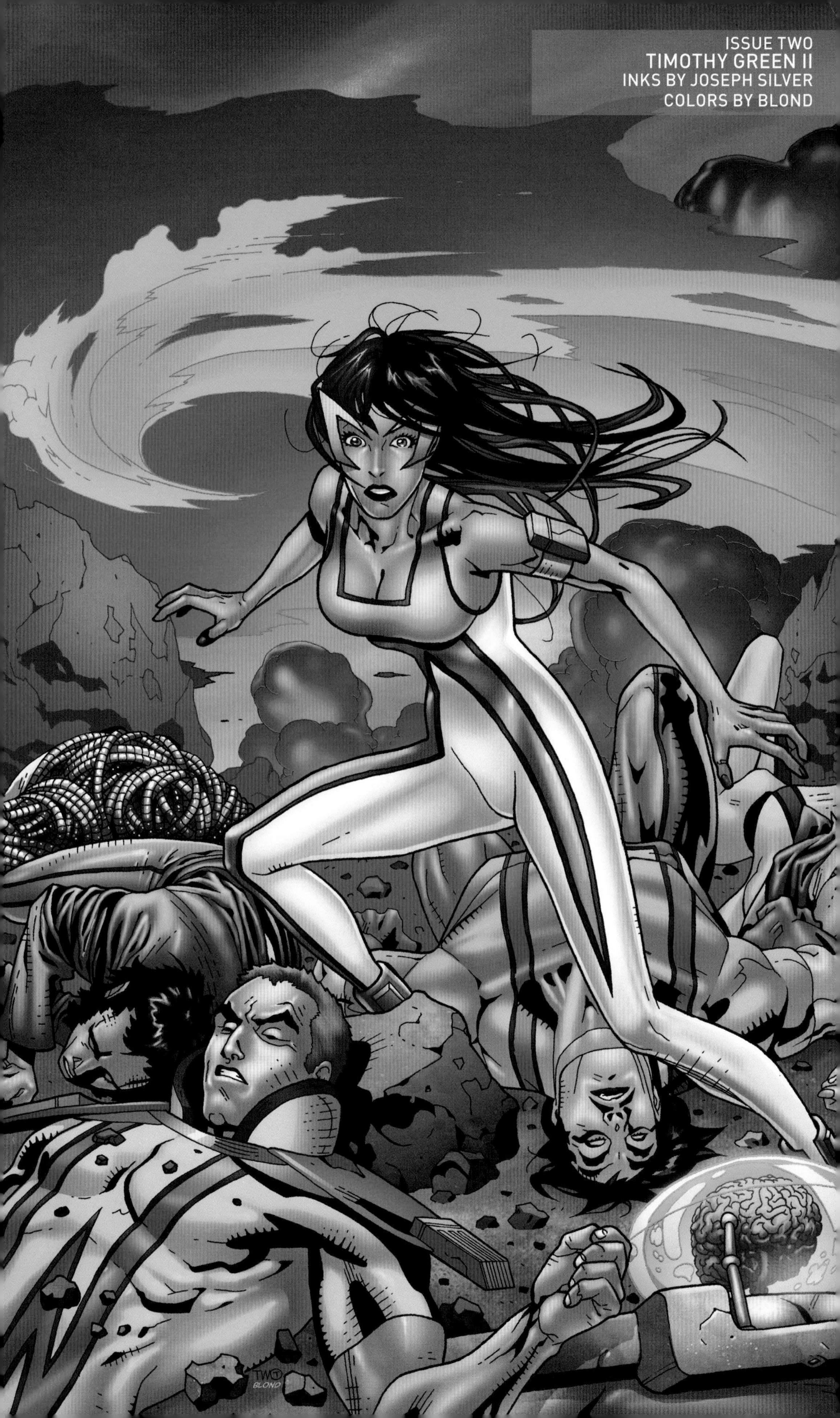

ISSUE TWO
TIMOTHY GREEN II
INKS BY JOSEPH SILVER
COLORS BY BLOND

ISSUE TWO
TREVOR HAIRSINE
INKS BY ANDY LANNING
COLORS BY BLOND

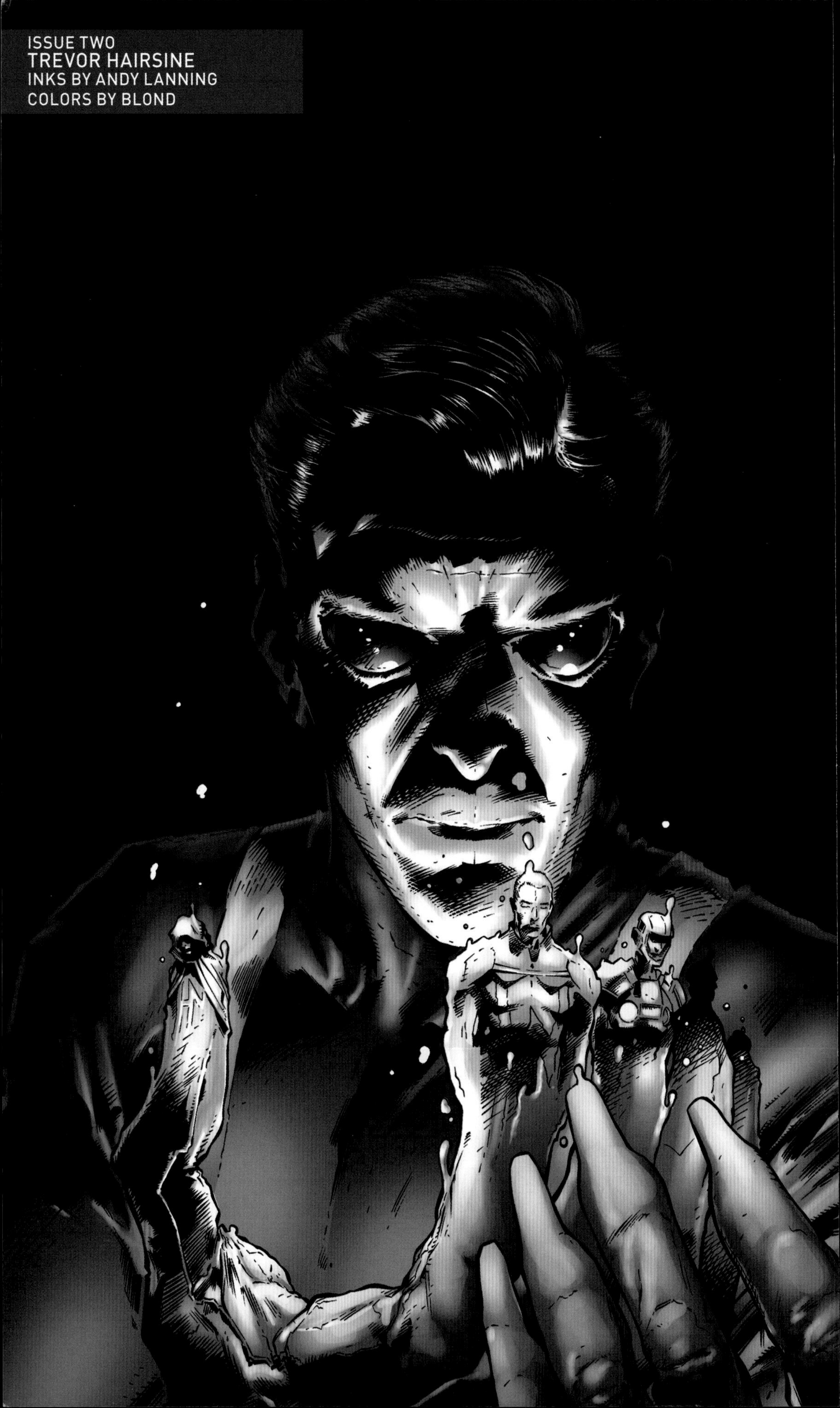

ISSUE TWO
BILL SIENKIEWICZ

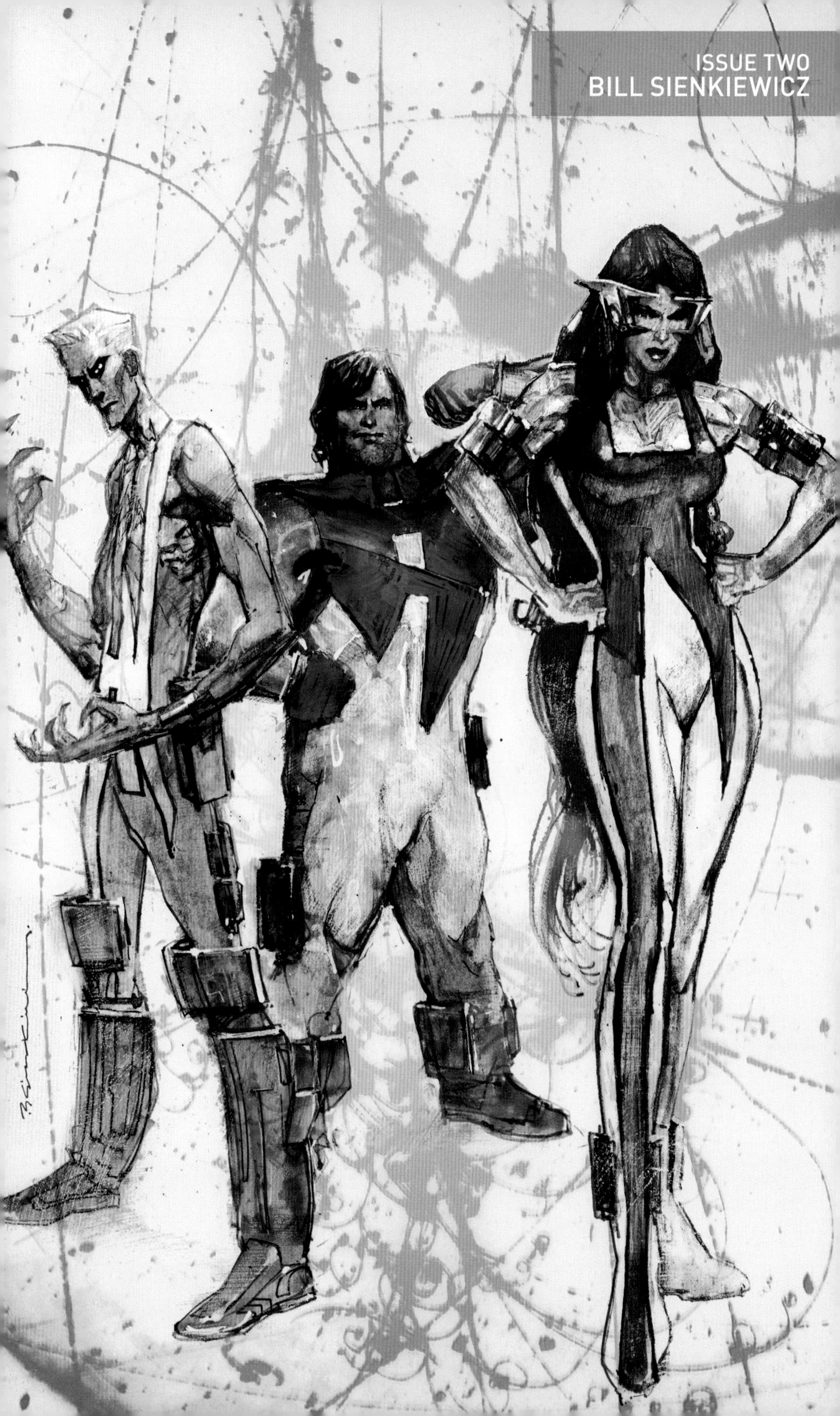

ISSUE TWO
KRIS ANKA

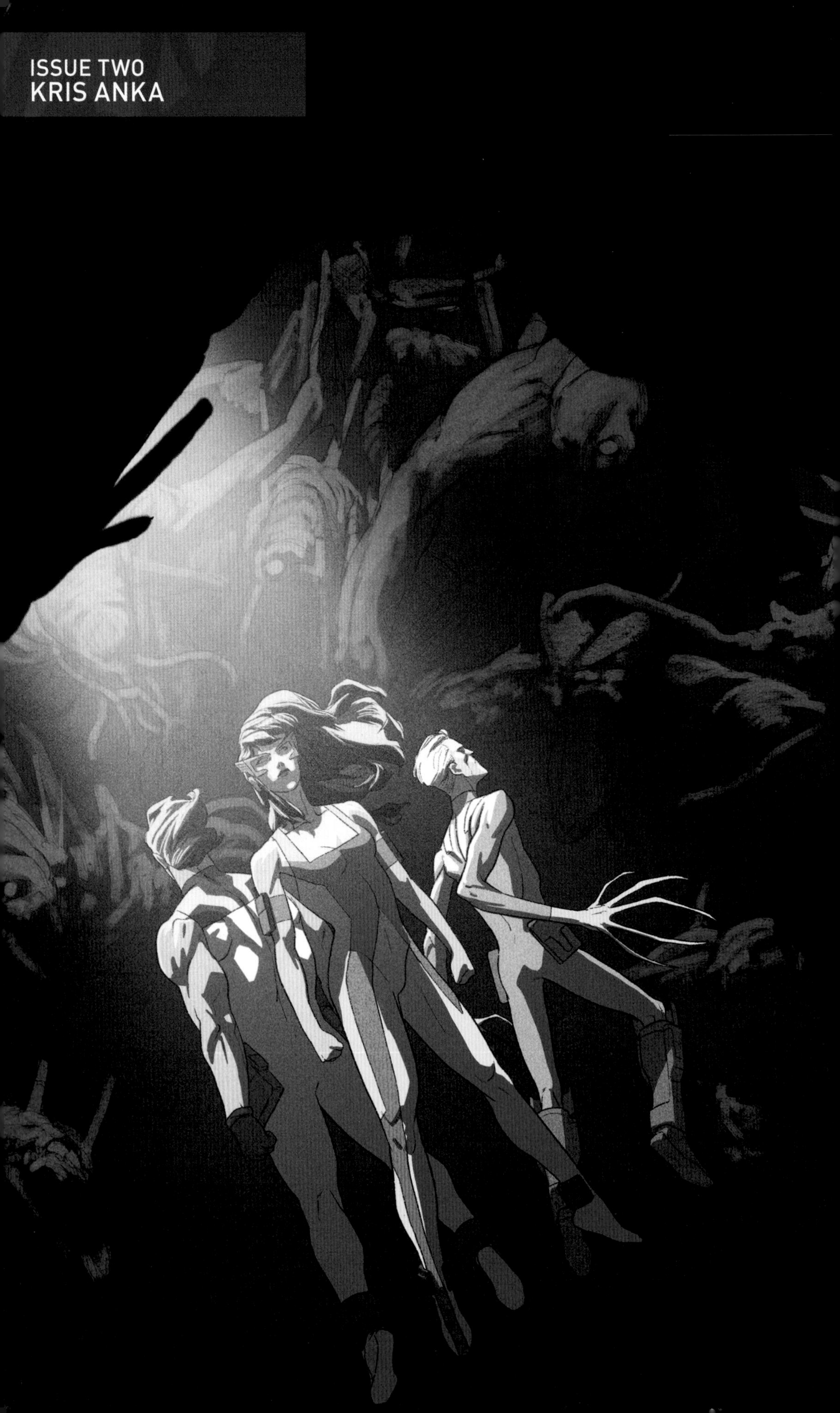

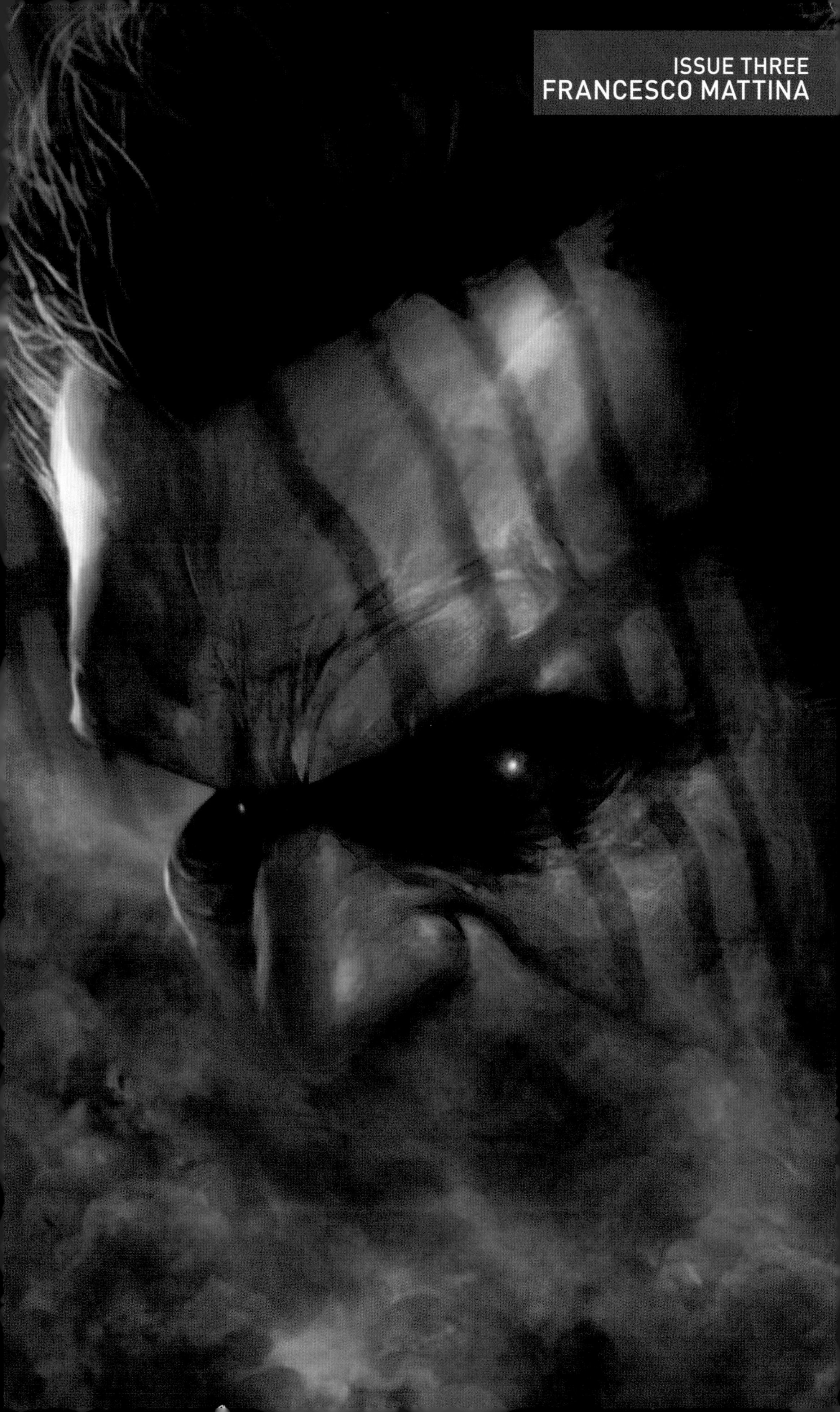
ISSUE THREE
FRANCESCO MATTINA

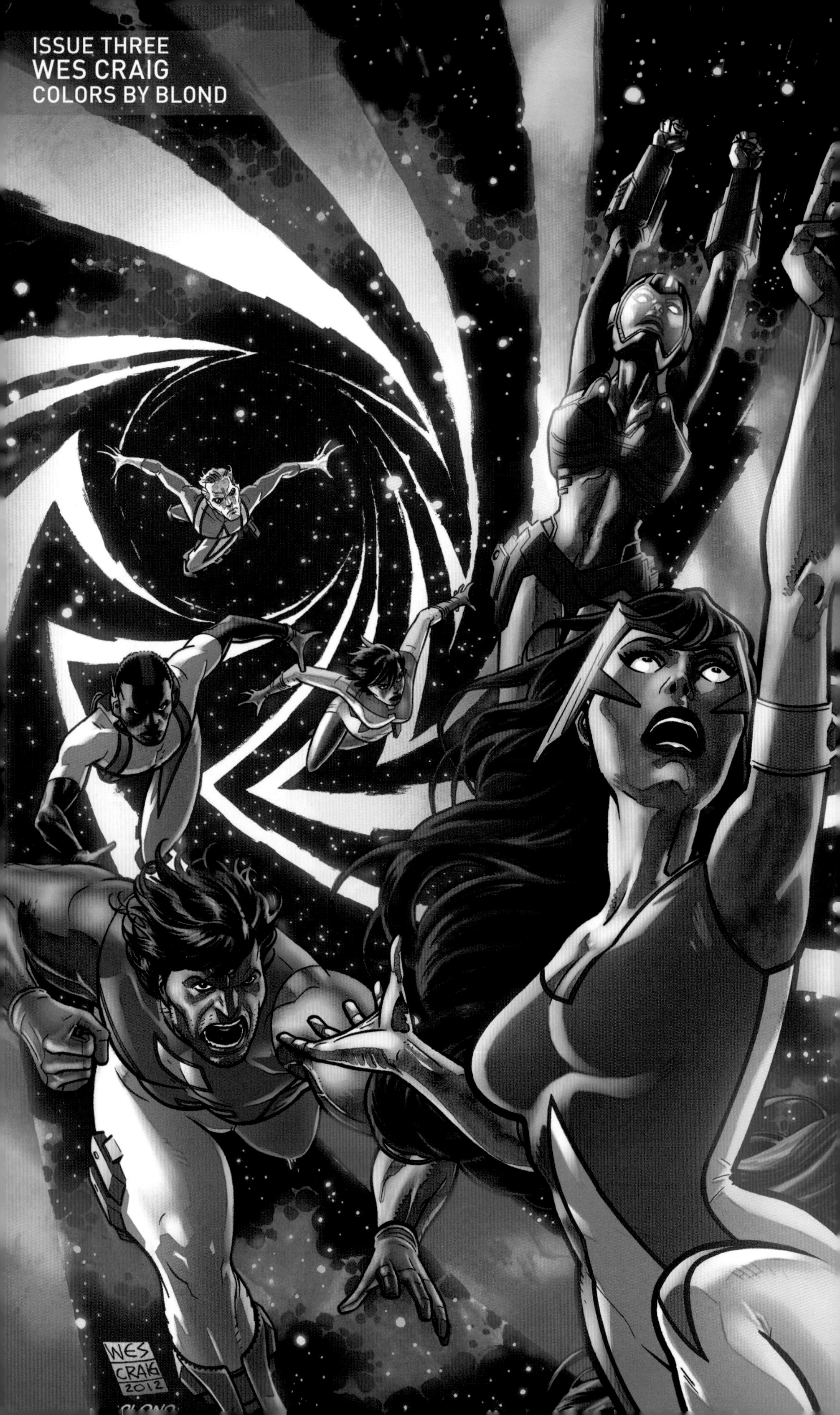
ISSUE THREE
WES CRAIG
COLORS BY BLOND
WES CRAIG 2012

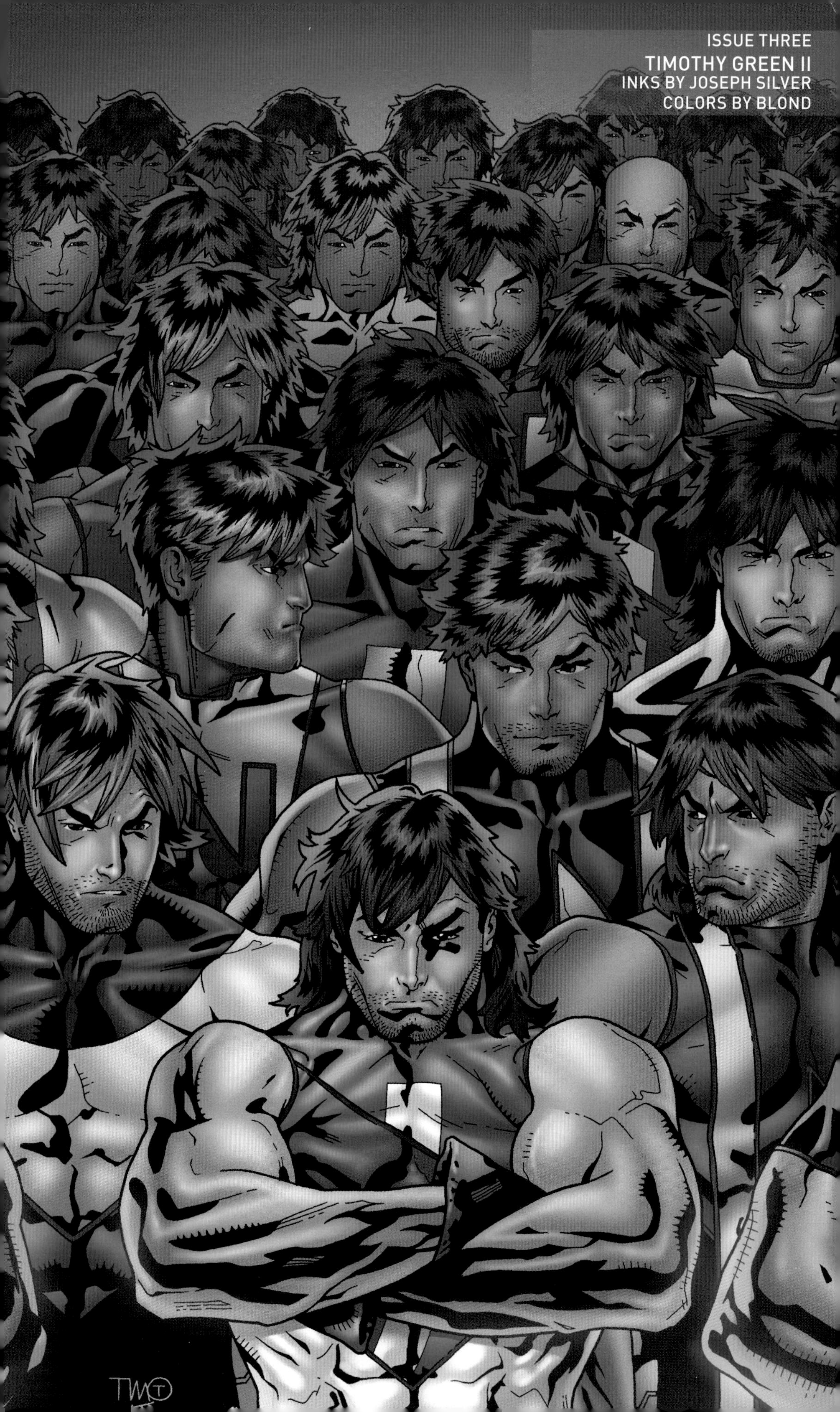
ISSUE THREE
TIMOTHY GREEN II
INKS BY JOSEPH SILVER
COLORS BY BLOND

ISSUE THREE
BILL SIENKIEWICZ

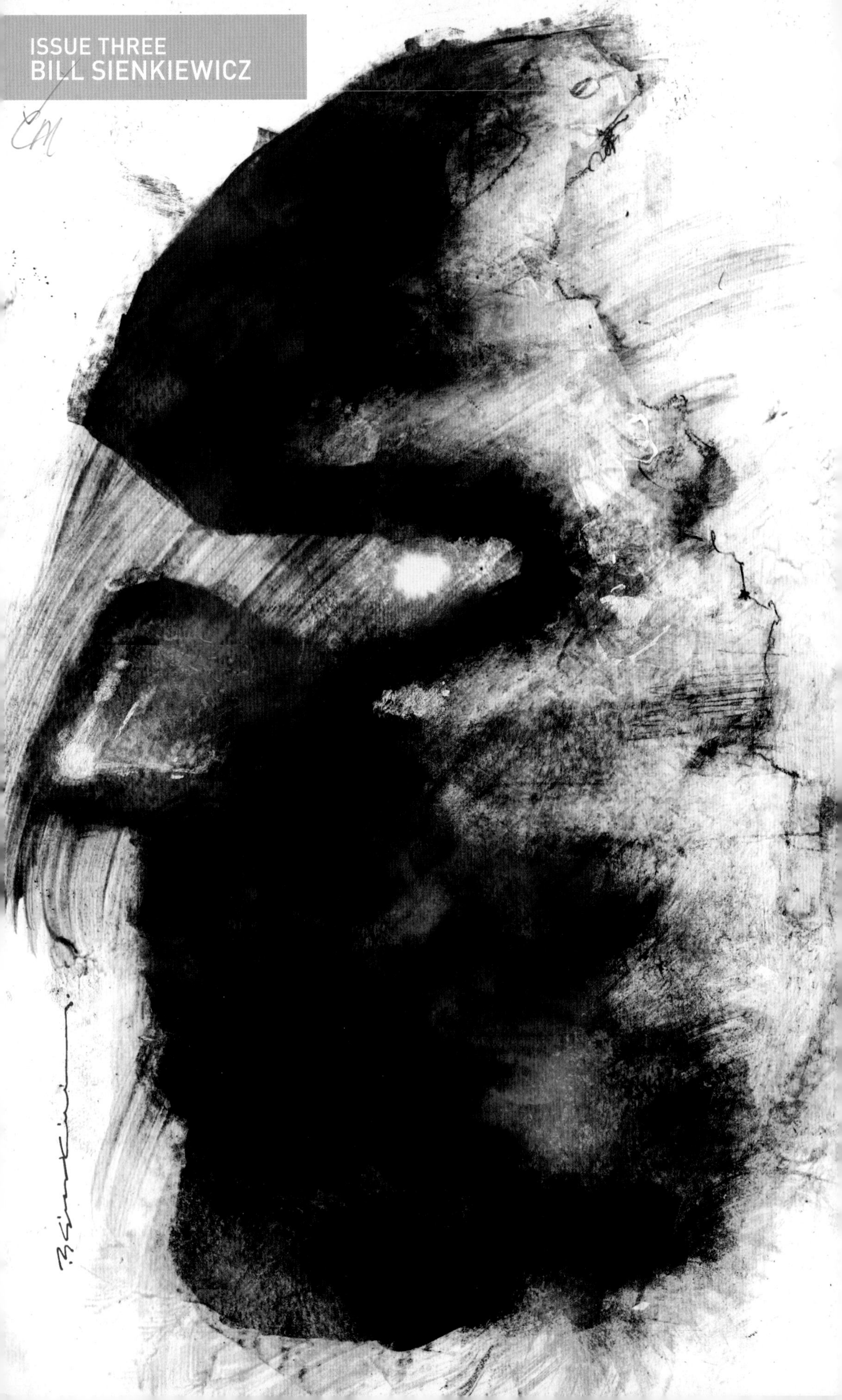